Puerto Ricans in the United States

A Contemporary Portrait

Edna Acosta-Belén
Carlos E. Santiago

LYNNE
RIENNER
PUBLISHERS

BOULDER
LONDON

Published in the United States of America in 2006 by
Lynne Rienner Publishers, Inc.
1800 30th Street, Boulder, Colorado 80301
www.rienner.com

and in the United Kingdom by
Lynne Rienner Publishers, Inc.
3 Henrietta Street, Covent Garden, London WC2E 8LU

Library of Congress Cataloging-in-Publication Data
Acosta-Belén, Edna.
    Puerto Ricans in the United States : a contemporary portrait / Edna Acosta-Belén, Carlos E. Santiago.
        p. cm.
    Includes bibliographical references and index.
    ISBN 978-1-58826-399-5 (hardcover : alk. paper)
    ISBN 978-1-58826-400-8 (pbk. : alk. paper)
    1. Puerto Ricans—United States—History.   2. Puerto Ricans—Emigration and immigration—History.   3. Puerto Rico—History.   I. Santiago, Carlos Enrique.   II. Title.
E184.P85A23 2006
973'.04687295

                                                2006002396

British Cataloguing in Publication Data
A Cataloguing in Publication record for this book
is available from the British Library.

Printed and bound in the United States of America

To the memory of our loving mothers,
Marcolina Belén Vega
and
Irma Luisa Pedrosa

Contents

Figures

Illustrations

Acknowledgments

This book responds to the need for a comprehensive source on the history of Puerto Ricans in the United States that also offers a portrait of the contemporary demographic and socioeconomic conditions faced by this population. In various ways, the book summarizes many of the ideas and issues introduced in our previous individual research, adding new information and insights that we hope will inspire others to continue documenting different aspects of the Puerto Rican migrant experience. For us, this is a challenging, stimulating, and never-ending endeavor. This study is more than the product of intellectual labor; it also represents a labor of love and commitment to our community. Thus, we are hopeful that the book's virtues and usefulness outweigh any shortcomings it may have. We recognize that there is still a great deal of work to be done to fully document the Puerto Rican experience in the United States, and new generations of Puerto Rican Studies scholars will undoubtedly rise to the challenge.

Whenever a book is completed, there are many people to thank who made things easier along the way. First, we need to acknowledge each other for being able to combine our respective scholarly interests with our enduring enthusiasm to work together, which we have been doing for almost two decades as department colleagues and friends. Next, we must express our gratitude to several individuals who greatly facilitated our archival research and compilation of statistical data. These include Alba I. Castillo Blancovich, a now retired librarian at the University of Puerto Rico; archivists Nélida Pérez and Pedro Juan Hernández, and Christopher R. Medina, staff member of the Centro de Estudios Puertorriqueños Library and Archives. They all provided invaluable help in locating documents and photographs that enhanced our work. At the University of Wisconsin–Milwaukee, data and statistical support were provided by Virginia Carlson of the Department of Urban Planning and Terence Johnson and Peter Maier of the Center for Urban Initiatives and Research. Ruby Wang of the Center for Social and Demographic Analysis at the University at Albany, SUNY, was also instrumental in providing census data and information. Our thanks go as well to Gabriel Aquino for his assistance with the design of some of the tables and figures, to Carmen Caamaño and Patricia McCarthy for their help with the References section, and to Librada Pimentel for lending a hand in many different ways throughout the process of completing the manuscript. A special mention to the Juan Antonio Corretjer Puerto Rican Cultural Center (PRCC) in Chicago; José E. López, its executive director; and Alejandro Luis Molina, secretary of its board of directors, for their generosity in giving us permission to use a photograph of the mural *Sea of Flags* by artists Gamaliel Ramírez and Eren Star Padilla on the paperback cover and in Chapter 7. Appreciation also goes to Juan Sánchez for his permission to include his artwork *Conditions that Exist* and *A Puerto Rican Prisoner of War and Much More* in Chapter 7; to Barbara R. Sjostrom for her insightful content and editorial suggestions; and to Susan Liberis-Hill for her valuable assistance with the English translations of some of the cited material.

This book is part of Lynne Rienner Publishers' new series Latinos: Exploring Diversity and Change. We are very pleased that this prominent Latin American and Caribbean Studies publisher is now promoting scholarly endeavors in the growing field of Latino Studies. Our gratitude to Lynne Rienner, Leanne Anderson, and Alan McClare for supporting our manuscript and for their helpful suggestions during the different stages of the publication process.

Last but not least, we want to thank our respective families for their steady encouragement and patience during the time-consuming and occasionally trying process of finishing the manuscript. Christine E. Bose and Azara Santiago-Rivera, especially, understand this process much too well, since they have experienced it so many times in their own research and writing. They also understand that the best creative sanctuary is found at home, surrounded by the people you love. Their many invaluable comments and suggestions made the book better.

—*Edna Acosta-Belén*
and Carlos E. Santiago

Puerto Ricans
in the
United States

1

Introduction: Portrait of a Commuter Nation

The US Puerto Rican population has reached 3.4 million, according to the 2000 census, a figure rapidly approaching that of the island of Puerto Rico's 3.8 million inhabitants. Thus it is not unreasonable to predict that before 2010 the number of Puerto Ricans living in the United States will surpass the total island population (see Chapter 4). In fact, some of the most recent population estimates are being used to support the claim that this has already happened (see Falcón 2004). Although more than half (58 percent) of the Puerto Rican diaspora was born in the continental United States, this fact does not change the reality that a large portion of this population remains strongly connected to the island of Puerto Rico. Consequently, the lives of Puerto Ricans from both shores seem to be inexorably intertwined; and more than ever before, the Boricuas *"de la banda acá"* and *"de la banda allá"* (Puerto Ricans from this shore here and that shore there) described in a popular *plena* (a type of folk music),[1] are experiencing the diverse effects of reciprocal cultural and socioeconomic exchanges between the island and the US metropolis. They also experience those stemming from over one hundred years of a colonial relationship that lingers without any signs of a prompt resolution.

Puerto Rican migration to the North American continent grew out of specific political and socioeconomic conditions, whether it happened under Spanish colonial rule or under the US regime. After the US invasion of Puerto Rico, a result of the Spanish-Cuban-American War of 1898,[2] contract labor to Hawaii, New York, and other US localities, as well as to the Dominican Republic and Cuba, became a colonial government strategy for dealing with the island's high rates of poverty and unemployment, and for satisfying the expanding North American industrial and agricultural sector's need for low-wage labor. Nonetheless, to this day, migration has never been acknowledged as part of any official policy either by US or Puerto Rican government officials.

The current association between the United States and Puerto Rico is the result of a set of economic and political circumstances that developed throughout the nineteenth century, intensified during the twentieth, and still shape the present lives and conditions faced by the Puerto Rican people in both settings (see Chapters 2 and 3). This colonial relationship has brought forth both positive and negative consequences and changes for Puerto Ricans that continue to limit their possibilities of envisioning a future that responds to their national needs and self-interests rather than to those of the North American nation. In this sense, the situation of Puerto Ricans offers a compelling example of US government policies and actions in pursuit of its hegemonic ambition in the hemisphere that continue to influence the present. An obvious aftereffect of these policies and actions is the uninterrupted and overwhelming influx of Puerto Ricans and other Latino populations to the United States.

Latinos, with a population in the United States that had reached 41.3 million in 2005, are now the largest and fastest-growing minority group in US society. Puerto Ricans represent over 9 percent of the total Latino population, and more than double that percentage, if one combines the US-based Puerto Rican population with that of the island of Puerto Rico.[3] The dramatic growth in the number of US Latinos, which is projected to continue throughout the twenty-first century, is transforming the lives of almost every Latin American and Caribbean nationality—Puerto Ricans included—both in the United States and in their respective countries of origin. The Caribbeanization and Latinization of many major cities and localities are adding a new vitality to US society while challenging the melting pot or Anglo-conformity assimilation model, as new (im)migrant groups, most noticeably Latinos, are now more inclined than before to preserve their respective cultural and linguistic heritage, and are quite comfortable functioning in two cultures and languages. This pattern is common in many European countries, but was not so in the United States until the latter part of the twentieth century.

When describing Puerto Rican migration, scholars have often referred to "a commuter nation" (Rivera-Batiz and Santiago 1994; Torre, Vecchini, and Burgos 1994) or characterized it as a "revolving door" or "circular" migration (Tienda and Díaz 1987; Meléndez 1993b). All these characterizations share the basic notion not only that Puerto Rican migration is a continuous occurrence but also that there is a great deal of back-and-forth movement of Puerto Ricans between the island and the US metropolis. These descriptions also imply that some Puerto Ricans migrate to the United States but do not necessarily stay there permanently and eventually return to the island. The reality is that although migration might have been originally envisioned by government officials as a one-way movement of people settling in the United States that would alleviate Puerto Rico's severe unemployment and surplus labor problems, some workers saw this move as a temporary measure for economic survival. Many migrated to the United States to try their lot before deciding to uproot their families. Some returned to Puerto Rico, but a large number of those first-generation migrants established permanent residence in the United States.

There were those who kept alive the idea of sooner or later returning to the island, and some did and still do. But the research on return-migration patterns is not adequate to determine the magnitude of this incidence, and that research is already dated (Hernández Alvarez [1967] 1976; Meléndez 1993c). The studies that have shown that about two-thirds of Puerto Ricans who emigrate to the United States have lived there before and those returning to Puerto Rico also have lived there at some point have confirmed the presence of a circular migration pattern and of transnational processes than continue to fortify the connection between the island and the diaspora (Meléndez 1993c). Year after year, Puerto Rican workers in the blue-collar, professional, and business sectors, students, politicians, and others continue to move with relative ease between Puerto Rico and the United States in pursuit of their respective endeavors. It can be thoroughly documented that the great majority of Puerto Ricans who migrate settle and carry on productive lives in the United States, eventually producing new generations of US-born Puerto Ricans that develop or maintain different kinds of connections to Puerto Rico (see Chapters 4 and 5).

Migration, which is not by any means a fortuitous process, and the unique status of Puerto Ricans as colonial migrants contribute to the demographic conditions described above, which are projected to continue in the decades ahead. The current *"guagua aérea"* (air or flying bus)—a metaphor invented by renowned Puerto Rican writer Luis Rafael Sánchez to characterize the back and forth migratory movement between the island and the United States—is making it unavoidable for Puerto Ricans from both shores to ignore each other anymore.[4] Mass migration from Puerto Rico is closely linked to the advent of air travel (see Chapter 3). Therefore, the image of a commuter nation or a "nation on the move" (Duany 2002) is now more solidified, and this transnational migration pattern is influencing Puerto Rican lives in ways that make it no longer possible to ignore or downplay. Its socioeconomic, political, and cultural ramifications are ever present and are shaping discussions and decisions on major issues influencing the well-being and future of all Puerto Ricans. It is now quite common for US Puerto Ricans and Latinos serving in Congress to be sought out or lobbied by island politicians on issues related to federal funding for Puerto Rico's social programs, or to rally them to exert pressure on political issues that have a bearing on some aspect of island life. A case in point occurred when island Puerto Ricans were trying to get the US Navy to cease its bombing-training practices in Puerto Rico's island municipality of Vieques (see Chapter 8). Conversely, US Puerto Ricans have been making it clear that they want to be included in any future congressional discussions or decisions related to the process of seeking new alternatives to end the island's current colonial status.

Whether one refers to the "crossroads," "dilemmas," or "paradoxes" facing Puerto Ricans, these characterizations indicate that after more than a century of US domination, Puerto Rico remains "an unincorporated territory" of the North American nation; neither a state of the federal union nor a sovereign nation. It is a remnant of colonialism, a nation still wedged in an ambivalent political condition that keeps it a considerable source of profits for US corporate capital. Puerto Rico, although not so much as in the past, is a major strategic military site for US armed forces. At the same time, the island maintains a large degree of economic dependence and reaps the benefits of its association with the most powerful country in the world. Among those benefits is US citizenship, which Puerto Ricans have held since 1917 as a result of the Jones Act, a congressional decree that, paradoxically, also gave island Puerto Ricans a larger degree of self-government (see Chapter 3). The fact that Puerto Ricans do not enjoy the same equal treatment or benefits held by other US citizens living in the fifty states of the union is negligible to some island residents, although many, especially those who oppose the current Commonwealth status, still regard their US citizenship as "second class." These feelings stem from the fact that island Puerto Ricans lack any representation in the US Congress besides the presence of a nonvoting "resident commissioner."[5] They do not vote in presidential or congressional elections, nor do they pay federal income taxes.[6] However, Puerto Rico receives more than $13 billion annually in federal transfers from the US Congress to support its social programs and infrastructure. Programs such as Social Security, Medicare, Medicaid, unemployment compensation, and a few others are extended to the island as if it were another state of the union. Concomitantly, US corporations make incalculable profits and receive substantial federal tax benefits from their investments in Puerto Rico, and they exert an overwhelming control over the island's economy, which in reality is totally integrated into the US economy and thus, subject to its cyclical fluctuations and flows. All in all, Puerto Ricans frequently find themselves in the odd position of being treated by the US Congress—site of the ultimate decisionmaking power regarding island affairs—as an entity that is "foreign to the United States in a domestic sense."[7] What this paradoxical and ambiguous statement really means is that island Puerto Ricans are often treated like colonial subjects who happen to be the holders of US citizenship and who should be grateful for all the benevolence bestowed upon their nation by the United States but who are, in the end, culturally different foreigners and thus not considered "real" Americans.

Underlying these contradictions is a deep-rooted reluctance on the part of the US Congress to contemplate either future statehood for Puerto Rico—an idea that often seems as insurmountable or unpalatable to some North American government officials as the idea of independence—or, for that matter, any of the other possible alternatives for removing some of the colonial limitations and enhancing the current Commonwealth. This political status is officially known in Spanish as the Estado Libre Asociado (Associated Free State) (see Chapter 3), a clear misnomer when one considers that Puerto Rico is neither a free nor a sovereign nation, and Puerto Rican citizenship is not legally recognized in an international context. The harsh reality is that resolving Puerto Rico's colonial "association" with the United States is an issue that has a long history of being rejected or tabled by the US Congress almost every time it comes up for discussion.[8] In addition, these same officials continue to pay lip service to the notion that "Puerto Ricans must make up their minds" about their future political status, and they do not miss an opportunity to boast about the nation's generosity toward Puerto Rico or decry the island's ceaseless dependence on federal funds. They also manage to downplay the fact that the US Congress, the only body empowered to change Puerto Rico's present condition, has historically shown little interest in doing so. Perhaps the only certainties about what is often described as Puerto Rico's "colonial dilemma" (Meléndez and Meléndez 1993) is that Puerto Ricans across the political spectrum have not been able to envision a future for their country without some kind of close relationship to the United States and that they continue to reaffirm passionately the integrity of their distinctive Caribbean/Latin American cultural connections and the Spanish language. Nor has the US government shown any compelling desire to support substantial changes in the island's current status. In the meantime, the influx of Puerto Rican migrants into the United States continues unabated, maintaining a commuter or circular migration pattern between the island and the colonial metropolis. This transnational flow daily brings large numbers of Puerto Rican workers to the United States searching for better economic and professional opportunities and simultaneously allows the generations of Puerto Ricans born or raised in the United States to keep up their connections with the country of their ancestors.

It is within the context outlined above that we approach this interdisciplinary portrait of Puerto Ricans in the United States as a commuter nation. This brief introduction is followed in Chapter 2 by an overview of the historical and cultural roots of the Puerto Rican people, with special emphasis on their colonial experience under both Spanish and US rule. A framework is provided for analyzing migration in terms of the dynamics of colonialism and capitalist development in Puerto Rico. Control of the island's economy by US capitalist interests intensified after the 1898 takeover, making the Puerto Rican worker part of a flexible and movable labor reserve to satisfy the needs of North American companies both in the island and the metropolis. Early on, migration became an official tool or "safety valve" to deal with Puerto Rico's widespread poverty and unemployment. Migration continued to grow throughout the twentieth century, especially after World War II, unleashing a process that is still a vital aspect of Puerto Rican life.

The bulk of Chapters 3 and 4 is dedicated to a discussion of the factors that contributed to the various Puerto Rican migratory waves to the United States, including a comparative analysis of different phases and patterns of migration. Chapter 3 deals with the early settlements, or *colonias,* established in New York City and other US localities during the second half of the nineteenth century and first three decades of the twentieth, and Chapter 4 focuses on the postwar "Great Migration" of the 1940s and 1950s and the migratory patterns that have developed since then.

A demographic portrait of Puerto Ricans in the United States is provided in Chapter 5; census data from the year 2000 and other subsequent population reports are used to assess their current collective status. Relying on the most recent data, we analyze the changes that have occurred in the overall status of US Puerto Ricans, emphasizing population increases and geographic dispersion, labor force participation, income, as well as other socioeconomic and educational indicators. We also discuss some major differences in the demographic profile of US and island Puerto Ricans.

In Chapter 6 we provide a detailed account of the diaspora's social, political, and educational struggles during the civil rights era, inserting Puerto Ricans into a movement that is still largely identified with the African American population. We provide a profile of the most vital community organizations and of their different activities. Chapter 7 focuses on the diaspora's creativity in literature, music, and the arts, emphasizing Puerto Rican efforts to build a distinctive cultural tradition within the United States. The voices and images of writers and artists represent another dimension of the contemporary portrait of US Puerto Rican life that we provide in this book. Chapter 8 features concluding observations that highlight the uniqueness of the Puerto Rican migrant experience and the present dilemmas and future challenges still confronting Puerto Ricans on the island and within the diaspora.

The underlying thread of this book is twofold. First, in order to provide a contemporary portrait of Puerto Ricans in the United States, we document and analyze the historical, socioeconomic, and political factors that propel Puerto Ricans to migrate in large numbers. Second, we examine how Puerto Ricans adapt and forge their lives in the metropolis and the socioeconomic conditions and challenges they currently face. Due attention is given to the creative ways in which migrants adjust to a new environment, how they carry out their lives and create new communities, and how they contribute to US society, struggle for their rights, claim their cultural spaces, and negotiate their exposure to two different cultures and languages. Of special interest to the authors is the Puerto Rico–US back and forth transnational connection and how it shapes the construction of Puerto Rican identities and creates an enduring sense of cultural affirmation and resistance within the diaspora. US Puerto Rican writers and artists have found their own creative ways of asserting their differences from island Puerto Ricans by embracing new labels to identify themselves, such as Nuyoricans, Neoricans, or Diasporicans.[9] Others have just adopted the term "Boricua," which is a form of identification traditionally used by island Puerto Ricans. But unlike the popular term "Chicano," adopted in the 1960s by a large portion of the population of Mexican descent in the United States to differentiate itself from Mexico's population and from more recent immigrants from that country, there is no adequate single term that has yet captured the imagination of most US Puerto Ricans in a similar way. Thus they continue to identify themselves primarily as Puerto Ricans, whether they are living on the island or in the metropolis.

The authors have attempted to address and carefully document the information and issues included in the various chapters. Nevertheless, there is a great deal of research that still needs to be done in order to achieve a more complete picture of the collective lives and endeavors of Puerto Rican migrants in the numerous US localities where they have settled and in new emerging communities.

In the early 1970s, Frank Bonilla, founder of the Centro de Estudios Puertorriqueños in New York City, in his essay "Beyond Survival: *Por qué seguiremos siendo puertorriqueños*" (Why We Will Continue Being Puerto Rican, 1974), deplored the negative portrayals of Puerto Ricans perpetuated in most of the social science literature. He argued then for the need to break away from the barrage of recurrent and confining negative images and from the internalized inferiority complex that dominated the discourses about the Puerto Rican people, and which were by-products of their subordinate colonial experience. Bonilla also stressed the urgency for "an unprecedented job of psychological and cultural reconstitution and construction" in order for Puerto Ricans "to grow affirmatively as a culturally integrated and distinctive collectivity" (363–364). This process would make it possible for them to move beyond the mere notion of survival as a community and engage in developing "a collective vision that reaches out to Puerto Ricans everywhere" (370).

Bonilla was responding to basic shortcomings in the available scholarship on US Puerto Ricans, which was often shortsighted, misinformed, or full of problem-oriented or despairing representations. Little had been done to document the full history of Puerto Rican migration to the United States, and with few exceptions, the majority of the studies about the diaspora were markedly skewed or recycled prevalent myths or stereotypes. But, above all, there was the recognition that a great divide existed between island and migrant communities, and that those Puerto Ricans living on the island were largely indifferent to or ignorant about the lives and struggles faced by their compatriots in the United States. These statements stand out even more if one considers that migration continues to be part of the normal course of life and an acceptable condition for the Puerto Rican people. Despite these assertions, there is no question that for a long time the separation between island and US communities was palpable, and islanders tended to perceive of the Puerto Rican migrant as poverty ridden, welfare dependent, and culturally deprived.

A great deal has changed since the 1970s thanks largely to the initiative and commitment of many US-based Puerto Rican Studies scholars and activists who, like Frank Bonilla, challenged old assumptions, rectified omissions, and produced new scholarship that depicts more accurately the wide range of experiences and contributions of a primarily working-class Puerto Rican diaspora. Now a legitimate and fairly institutionalized academic endeavor, the field of Puerto Rican Studies was first conceptualized in the United States and was shaped by the experiences and struggles of Puerto Ricans as a marginalized ethnoracial minority within US society.[10] Part of the wider ethnic studies movement, and made possible by the advocacy and vision of intellectuals, students, and community activists, Puerto Rican Studies and other nontraditional fields made important strides in generating new scholarship and pedagogy that not only drew attention to the multiracial and multiethnic character of US society but also exposed some of the ethnocentric, racist, and sexist biases and normative assumptions of the traditional disciplines in their depictions of subaltern groups.

Thus, since the early 1970s, both US-based and island researchers have been developing a more nuanced understanding of the historical roots, power relations, and colonial dynamics that explain Puerto Rican migration, including an analysis of the transnational links that exist between island and US communities. In this book we explore many different aspects of this transnational circuit.

For many years, most studies of the Puerto Rican diaspora limited their scope to the larger and more established New York City community. But since the 1990s, geographic dispersion has become an important characteristic of Puerto Rican migration, and the New York population now represents about one-fourth of the total Puerto Rican population currently residing in the United States (see Chapter 4). This new reality is forcing scholars to pay more attention to the history and evolution of other communities, particularly the Puerto Rican presence in cities like Chicago (Padilla 1985), Hartford (Cruz 1998), Philadelphia (Whalen 2001), and the Hawaiian islands (Camacho Souza 1982, 1986; Rosario Natal 1983). Other growing communities, such as those in Orlando and Kissimmee, Florida (Duany and Matos-Rodríguez 2005), and several cities in Massachusetts and California are increasingly drawing the attention of researchers. We made an effort to synthesize some of the available research but also relied on primary sources of information, especially community newspapers and the records of several grassroots organizations largely overlooked in previous studies, as well as the most current US census data. At the same time, we hope that this study brings other researchers and readers new insights into the unfinished quest to advance knowledge about the realities, struggles, and enduring legacies of those Puerto Ricans who under a variety of circumstances made their lives away from their native island. These migrants are producing new generations that seek a more accurate understanding of their roots, the history of their respective communities, and their collective place in US society.

Notes

1, The expression "Boricuas de la banda allá, Boricuas de la banda acá" comes from the lyrics of the *plena* "A los boricuas ausentes" (To the Boricuas Who Left) popularized by César Concepción and his Orchestra. "Boricua," a word of Taino indigenous origin, was used during the Spanish colonial period to refer to the native inhabitants of Puerto Rico and is now a synonym for Puerto Rican.

2. Generally known as the Spanish-American War, some scholars have argued that when the United States invaded Cuba in 1898, there was a war going on between the Spanish and the Cubans that had started in 1895, thus making the name Spanish-Cuban-American War more appropriate. The United States declared war against Spain in retaliation for the explosion of the *Maine* at the port of Havana. The declaration of war was followed by the invasion of, first, Cuba and, a few months later, Puerto Rico. US intervention in the Spanish-Cuban War was magnified by the North American press's mythification of the role of Teddy Roosevelt and the Rough Riders in defeating the Spanish and liberating Cuba. Thus the role of the Cuban rebel army was undermined in US official accounts of the war. We are in agreement with those scholars who argue that the name Spanish-Cuban-American War reflects more accurately the historical reality behind this conflict. This conflict is also often referred to as the War of 1898. See Philip Foner, *The Spanish-Cuban-American War and the Birth of U.S. Imperialism* (New York: Monthly Review Press, 1972); and Louis A. Pérez, *The War of 1898: The United States and Cuba in History and Historiography* (Chapel Hill: University of North Carolina Press, 1998).

3. The US census official definition of the Hispanic (Latino) population includes only the twenty nationalities from the Spanish-speaking countries of Latin America, the Caribbean, and Spain, but excludes the Puerto Rican population residing in Puerto Rico. In other words, Puerto Ricans are not counted as part of the Hispanic population unless they reside in one of the fifty states.

4. See Luis Rafael Sánchez, *La guagua aérea* (San Juan: Editorial Cultural, 1994).

5. A nonvoting "resident commissioner," elected by the voting residents of Puerto Rico, has represented Puerto Rico in the US Congress since 1900. Between 1993 and 1995, under the Democratic Party administration of President Bill Clinton, the resident commissioner was given voting rights in the US Congress. This practice was rescinded when the Republican Party won the congressional elections of 1994 and took control of both the Senate and the House of Representatives.

6. Although island Puerto Ricans are not allowed to vote in US presidential or congressional elections, presidential primaries are held in Puerto Rico and both Democratic and Republican candidates actively campaign on the island for party convention delegates to support their nominations.

7. The statement "foreign to the United States in a domestic sense" is part of the Foraker Act, passed by the US Congress in 1900, which ended two years of North American military occupation and established a civil government in Puerto Rico. See Christina Duffy Burnett and Burke Marshall, eds., *Foreign in a Domestic Sense: Puerto Rico, American Expansion, and the Constitution* (Durham: Duke University Press, 2001). A more detailed discussion appears in Chapter 3 of this book.

8. For a detailed account of the long history of political status referenda or plebiscite bills introduced in the US Congress since the 1960s, see Juan Manuel García Passalacqua and Carlos Rivera Lugo, *Puerto Rico y los Estados Unidos: El proceso de consulta y negociación de 1989 y 1990*, 2 vols. (Río Piedras, PR: Editorial Universitaria, 1990, 1991); Marco Antonio Rigau and Juan Manuel García Passalacqua, *República Asociada o Libre Asociación: Documentación de un debate* (San Juan: Edi-

torial Atlántico, 1987); and Carmen Gautier Mayoral, ed., *Poder y plebiscito: Puerto Rico en 1991* (Río Piedras, PR: Centro de Investigaciones Sociales, University of Puerto Rico, 1990).

9. The term "Nuyorican" was adopted in the 1970s by New York–based Puerto Rican poets and artists. See Miguel Algarín and Miguel Piñero, eds., *Nuyorican Poetry: An Anthology of Words and Feelings* (New York: William Morrow, 1975); and Miguel Algarín and Bob Holman, eds., *Aloud: Voices from the Nuyorican Poets Cafe* (New York: H. Holt, 1994). Since the 1970s, the terms "Nuyorican" and "Neorican" have been frequently used, especially by island Puerto Ricans, to refer to US Puerto Ricans. The term "Diasporican" was introduced by poet Mariposa Hernández in her poem "Ode to the Diasporican." In some of the literature about Puerto Rican migration the terms "mainland" and "stateside" Puerto Ricans are used to distinguish the population living in the United States from that of the island. In this book we refer to island and US Puerto Ricans to differentiate both populations. Whether hyphenated or not, the term "Puerto Rican Americans" has been used by some North American scholars to describe the migrant population, such as Joseph P. Fitzpatrick, *Puerto Rican Americans: The Meaning of Migration to the Mainland* (Englewood Cliffs, NJ: Prentice-Hall, 1971). This term, however, did not have much appeal within the community and it is rarely used today. Some scholars argued that since Puerto Ricans are US citizens by birth the term was redundant. Others rejected it on political grounds as a sign of colonialism or cultural assimilation.

10. For example, the University at Albany's Puerto Rican Studies Program was initiated in 1970, and it became a full-fledged academic department offering a major in 1974. The department later evolved into the current Department of Latin American, Caribbean, and U.S. Latino Studies (LACS).

2

The Colonial Experience

The Spanish accounts of the indigenous "people who discovered Columbus" (Keegan 1992) during his voyages to the Caribbean islands, later to be known as the West Indies or the Antilles,[1] make a distinction between the peaceful Taino native inhabitants with whom they first came in contact and the reputedly warlike and cannibalistic Caribs, who frequently came to their coasts and raided their villages. However, some anthropologists have argued that the widespread dichotomy between the two Amerindian groups is the result of the colonizers' imagination, and that the distinction they made between the two indigenous groups mostly reflected Spanish self-interests, their less successful attempts at conquering and converting the Caribs than the Tainos, and the Caribs' fierce resistance to the European invaders (Sued-Badillo 1978). Notwithstanding, the questionable origin of the names attributed to each of the first two aboriginal groups mentioned in the European chronicles of the Spanish Conquest reaffirms the Manichean, or dualistic, nature of their initial characterization: the indigenous word "Taino," said to mean noble or good (Keegan 1992), and "Carib," standing for great warrior or referring to the group's alleged cannibalistic practices (Boucher 1992). Some anthropologists have rejected the original Taino/Carib dichotomy altogether and maintain that despite the conflictive relationship between these two aboriginal groups, they were not significantly different from one another, at least ethnically (Sued-Badillo 1978; Hulme 1986).

Two unfortunate circumstances limit our knowledge of these indigenous populations and their cultural practices. The first is that besides the symbols that appear in their stone carvings or petroglyphs, they did not leave a written historical record to rely upon. Second, their rapid extinction after the encounter with the Spaniards left little historical memory.

Most anthropologists of the pre-Columbian era, however, have been in agreement that the Taino indigenous population that inhabited Puerto Rico and much of the West Indies at the time of the Spanish Conquest migrated from the northern shores of the South American continent.[2] They have traced the origins of the Taino to the Orinoco Valley in Venezuela. Despite the very different methodologies employed in these studies, Rouse (1986) argued that the following consensus seems to have emerged:

> From a geographical point of view, the ancestors of the *Tainos* could have entered the West Indies via either the east coast of Venezuela, Trinidad, or the Guianas. The historic evidence favors Trinidad and the Guianas; Arawakan speakers were concentrated there during the Historic Age. Nevertheless, archeologists and, to a lesser extent, linguists have focused upon Trinidad and the east coast of Venezuela in tracing the ancestors of the *Tainos* back to the mainland. Having failed in this endeavor, they are now turning their attention to the Guianas. (154–155)

There seems to be little doubt that Amerindians traveled frequently across the chain of islands that make up the West Indies and that significant movement occurred between continent and islands, within the Caribbean island chain, and the circum-Caribbean area. Indigenous groups settled the islands of the West Indies and traversed the Caribbean Sea with considerable regularity, as indicated by the dispersion of their cultural remains. For them, territory was limited only by the technology of sea transport at the time. Anthropologists have even found evidence of Mesoamerican influence on West Indian aboriginal cultures, suggesting contacts by sea among different groups from more distant regions (Fernández Méndez 1972).

Regarding the Tainos, there has been a tendency to refer to them also as Arawaks, which is the name of an indigenous language family of South American origin, but some anthropologists (Rouse 1986, 1992; Keegan 1992) have contended that although there were linguistic similarities between Tainos and Caribs, they spoke a different language and exhibited some cultural differences from the South American Arawaks. Thus, Rouse (1986) suggested that when referring to the inhabitants of the West Indies at the time of contact with the Europeans, Tainos is more correct than Arawaks. In any event, there is at least sufficient evidence to establish that the Tainos occupied the islands of the Greater Antilles and that the Caribs settled in the Lesser Antilles; the latter were legendary for their frequent and belligerent incursions into the other islands, including Puerto Rico.

The rudimentary descriptions and accounts that we have of the lives of the Tainos were made by the Spanish, so we are left with a portrait of the conquered provided by the conqueror. One of these accounts, that of Spanish missionary Fray Bartolomé de las Casas, from 1552 (see Casas 1951, vol. 2, 356), mentions the daily visits of inhabitants of the eastern tip of Hispaniola, where Columbus first landed, to Puerto Rico, across the Mona passage, a route that is now frequently traveled by some Dominicans seeking entry, albeit on an undocumented basis, into Puerto Rico. Even today, it is not uncommon for overturned *yolas* (small wooden boats) to wash up on Puerto Rico's northwestern shores with little evidence of any occupants. And yet, the Dominican-born population of Puerto Rico now stands at over 100,000, further evidence of a strong migratory route through Puerto Rico that often ends in the United States.[3]

The presence of the Taino legacy in contemporary Puerto Rico is best represented in the remains of their pottery, stone artifacts, and symbols found in archeological sites, in the names of numerous towns and places, and in many commonly used words that were adapted from their native language into Spanish (Malaret 1955; Hernández Aquino 1969; Fernández Méndez 1972; Alvarez Nazario 1977). The physical appearance of a small percentage of the racially mixed Puerto Rican population still reflects the indigenous influence. Legends and myths about the Tainos, including their rebellions and subjugation by the Spaniards, also appear in the chronicles of the colonial era and have been recreated in the writings of Puerto Rican creoles, particularly throughout the nineteenth century, although they have continued to inspire many contemporary writers as well.[4] The symbols from Taino stone carvings, found largely in some of the towns around Puerto Rico's Cordillera Central mountain range, usually find their way into the island's visual arts, popular crafts, and tourist commodities. The island's Taino heritage is frequently celebrated in local festivities, such as in the annual mountain towns' Festival Indígena (Indigenous Festival) of the town of Jayuya and Festival Areyto (Indigenous Dance Festival) of the town of Villalba.

The original Taino villages were headed by *caciques* (chieftains). Their social and political structure is interesting because of their matrilineal tradition: Some women could inherit land and political power, and a few are referred to as *cacicas* in the Spanish chronicles. According to anthropologist Sued-Badillo (1979), Taino women from the upper social strata played a significant role in the community's political life, and there was a collective approach among the Tainos for incorporating women into many of their rituals and activities (41).

Rituals such as the *areyto* were described in colonial writings as a mixture of dancing and oral recitation, a way of preserving and passing along the native population's history and traditions. Taino religion was focused on worshipping nature and atmospheric phenomena: Guabancex, the great goddess of the earth; Yocahú, the god of heaven and father of life and death; and Huracán, who controlled the seasonal hurricanes that are so common in the Caribbean region.[5] The mountains of Puerto Rico inspired the religious *cemí*, the small stone idols that guarded the spirits of their tribal ancestors. These deities and other artifacts have been recovered in large numbers from archeological sites.

The myth about the docility of the Tainos contributed to the image of the "noble savage" that the Europeans frequently contrasted with that of the "barbaric" Caribs. Whether the Tainos were deserving of their peaceful reputation is subject to challenge, since there are some indications that they rebelled against the Spanish invader, as most indigenous groups did at some point. It is true that although colonization of Puerto Rico began in 1508, the Spanish could not establish control of the island until 1511, after subduing a major indigenous rebellion under the leadership of chieftain Agueybaná II. It was also recorded that the Taino population of the West Indies was almost extinct by the late 1500s.

Even though the Spanish conquest brought about the extermination of the indigenous Tainos, a Taino revival movement gained popularity during the 1990s. The Taino imaginary, or the recovery of the memory of an indigenous past, has been an important component of Puerto Rican national identity since the nineteenth century, but it has taken a new life in contemporary Puerto Rico, as well as among Puerto Ricans in the United States. On the island, it represents an important component of Puerto Rican cultural nationalism celebrated and propagated through state institutions, the media and advertising, local festivities, arts and crafts, and educational curricula. Within the Puerto Rican diaspora in the United States, Taino images and symbols also are a vibrant aspect of its cultural expressions and activities. Haslip-Viera (1999) claimed that the contemporary Taino revival movement should be seen in a broader context as "part of a much larger phenomenon in which disaffected or alienated individuals are attracted to alternative cultures and lifestyles because of prejudice, discrimination, poor living conditions, and severely limited economic and social opportunities" (6). Those critical of this revival movement have argued that the mythification of a long past Taino heritage tended to undermine the stronger and more visible African roots of Puerto Rican culture, and was another manifestation of the underlying racism and reluctance on the part of the cultural elites to accept the mulatto character of the Puerto Rican nation (Jiménez-Román 1999). Other scholars validated the notion that emphasizing the indigenous Taino heritage was a sign of cultural resistance and a way of counterbalancing the harmful effects of Spanish and US colonialism on Puerto Rican history and culture.[6] Despite this debate, it is clear that even after more than five centuries of the Spanish arrival in Puerto Rico, the influence of the Taino cultural roots is still a vital component of the Puerto Rican national imaginary and of any definition of the Puerto Rican nation put forth by the intellectual elites or other groups.

The Beginnings of Spanish Colonial Rule

The first encounter between the Spanish and the Taino indigenous population took place on November 19, 1493, during Christopher Columbus's second voyage to what became known as the New World. According to Spanish chronicles, the island's Taino name, Boriquén, meant "tierra del altivo señor" (land of the valiant warrior), an indication of the gallantry and respect conveyed by the native *caciques*. Columbus named the island Isla de San Juan Bautista in honor of St. John the Baptist, who became the island's patron saint. The indigenous name of the island was eventually adapted into Spanish as Borinquen, another name commonly used to refer to Puerto Rico. The terms *"borinqueños," "borincanos,"* and *"boricuas,"* for the island's native population, also appeared during the Spanish colonial period (Hernández Aquino 1969).

The territory of the island of Puerto Rico is only around 3,500 square miles; nearby are a few even smaller islands, two of which—Vieques and Culebra—are currently populated. The Spaniards therefore focused their early colonizing efforts on the larger neighboring islands of Hispaniola (present-day Dominican Republic and Haiti) and Cuba. Serious efforts to colonize Puerto Rico did not begin until 1508, more than a decade and a half after Columbus's arrival. It was then that Juan Ponce de León, who had accompanied Columbus during his second voyage, was sent to the island to lead the colonizing enterprise. Ponce de León established the island's first settlement, the Villa de Caparra, not far from the country's largest port, soon to be known as Puerto Rico. Early in the colonial period, the Spanish name of the island and that of its main port were interchanged.

Spanish colonization of the Caribbean islands brought about the rapid decimation of the indigenous population; it was almost extinct by the end of the century after the first contact. The effects of the Spanish *encomienda* system of land concessions relied on forced indigenous labor. These exploitative conditions, along with warfare, new diseases, and suicide, all contributed to what Fray Bartolomé de las Casas described as "the devastation of the Indies" (1552, 1974, 1992). By 1594, just over a century after the Spanish arrival, Puerto Rico's indigenous population, 1,545 inhabitants, had largely vanished (Sued-Badillo and López Cantos 1986, 85). According to estimates, this figure represents about 3 percent of the indigenous population at the time of the conquest.

The African Heritage

Enslaved Africans, especially from the West Sudan and the Bantu regions, were brought to Puerto Rico beginning in the early years of colonization, later in larger numbers, as the colonizers needed to replace the rapidly declining Taino labor force in agricultural and mining tasks (Alvarez Nazario 1974). In addition, the slaves were used for domestic service and the construction of roads, buildings, and military fortifications. The population of African origin, however, did not surpass that of the indigenous Tainos until the 1590s, when it rose to around 2,281 (Sued-Badillo and López Cantos 1986, 85). This figure was not to increase in any significant way until the late eighteenth and early nineteenth centuries, when Spain fostered immigration to Puerto Rico in order to promote economic development. The expanded economic activity increased the demand for enslaved labor. Thus, there was enough growth in the African-origin population throughout a good portion of the nineteenth century to begin altering the island's overall racial balance and profile. Miscegenation was common in most of the Spanish colonies, and Puerto Rico was no exception. The Spanish mixed with the indigenous Tainos and enslaved Africans, producing through the years new generations of mestizos and mulattos that constituted the island's creole population.[7]

The African heritage is often referred to as "the third root" (CEREP 1992) in the cultural and racial profile of the Puerto Rican nation. This important component of the island's heritage was essentially understated in the initial nineteenth-century historical narratives. These early attempts at documenting the history of an emerging Puerto Rican nation tended to give preponderance to the Spanish heritage over all others. Even after the 1873 abolition of slavery in Puerto Rico, the Spanish peninsular and creole elites were far from seeing blacks and mulattoes as equal; therefore racial prejudice was common, and through the years a handful of segregated communities developed on the island around some coastal areas and barrios of the larger cities. It is unquestionable that during the course of the nineteenth century Puerto Rico became more Africanized, both racially and culturally. But these changes were not readily acknowledged by the Europeanized intellectual and political elites, which, for the most part, did not consider the African heritage a significant component in their definitions of an emerging Puerto Rican nation. Nineteenth-century creole intellectuals were not totally oblivious to the traditional folklore and traditions of the racially mixed peasant population, which at the time represented the majority of the island's inhabitants, but they conceptualized the Puerto Rican nation from a Hispanophilic perspective, one that regarded the white Spanish-European component as representative of the essence of the island's creole culture.

Besides the obvious black and mulatto racial influence upon a substantial portion of Puerto Rico's population, indicators of the African heritage are quite evident in many of the island's cultural expressions—music, dance, literature, the visual arts, typical foods, and local festivities. The famous annual carnivals of the municipalities of Loíza, Ponce, San Juan, and Guayama recreate the traditional display of *vejigante* customs[8] and masks, as does Hatillo's Festival de las Máscaras (Festival of the Masks). The Spanish language of Puerto Rico reflects the African linguistic roots in some of its vocabulary and in the names of places and people (Alvarez Nazario 1974). The syncretism that took place between Catholicism and African religious traditions can be seen in the practice of *santería* and *espiritismo* among some Puerto Ricans. *Santería* rituals and invocations to Changó, the powerful god of fire, thunder, and lightning; to Oshún, the goddess of love; Yemayá, the goddess of the moon and seas; and many other deities still provide an expedient way of dealing with negative influences or evil spirits, or of ameliorating the whole gamut of human physical and spiritual ailments (González-Wippler 1973). Regarding the religious practices of *espiritismo*, some researchers have documented its practitioners' therapeutic psychological functions (Rogler 1972, 1985).

After the Spanish Conquest of the Indies, Puerto Rico remained an island with important connections to a continent or "mainland," in this case the European continent and the mainland of Spain.[9] Increased migration of Spaniards to other parts of the Americas when the scant gold deposits in Puerto Rico were exhausted meant that enslaved Africans eventually made up a growing part of the local labor force.

Racial mixture and cultural hybridity between Tainos, Africans, and the Spanish form the core of Puerto Rico's creole population. These three groups make up the basic racial and cultural profile of the Puerto Rican people, with the subsequent incorporation of new immigrant groups that came to the island at different times. For a long time Puerto Rican cultural nationalism tended to emphasize the superiority and dominance of the Spanish heritage, but since the final decades of the twentieth century, more attention has been given to the island's African roots and to its connections with other Hispanic and non-Hispanic Caribbean nations. Anthropologist Sidney Mintz noted that "a search for Africa in the Caribbean is among other things, an exploration of the nature of cultural disguise" (1974, 25). Without question, this statement applies to Puerto Rico, a nation where racism historically has been "camouflaged" by the myth of a racially harmonious society devoid of racism (Blanco 1942). Because of that, it has been said that Puerto Ricans suffer from "the prejudice of having no prejudice" (Betances 1972, 1973).

Puerto Ricans are not by any means immune to racial prejudice, but it is also fair to say that racial conflict has not manifested itself in modern or contemporary Puerto Rico in the same polarizing ways that it has in the United States or other countries torn by a deeply ingrained system of apartheid and a long history of racial tensions and violence. One of the main differences is that racial definitions and perceptions among Puerto Ricans are not largely determined by biological factors, as tends to be the case in the United States, where the racial optic is dominated by the notion that one drop of nonwhite blood makes someone a person of color. Among Latinos, racial perceptions are influenced by social status, multiple gradations of skin color, and other physical features (see Rodríguez 1974, 2000a). The popular expression *mejorar la raza*, meaning to improve the race by whitening it, also implies the degree of desirability and privilege attributed to being white, but there is a wider spectrum of physical and social factors embedded in the way Puerto Ricans and other Latinos perceive racial differences and racially define themselves.

The growing number of Puerto Ricans born or raised in the United States, the exacerbated forms of racial prejudice and discrimination they encounter, and the continuous back and forth migration between the island and the metropolis contribute to an increased awareness of race and racism among island Puerto Ricans. Simultaneously, the presence of Puerto Ricans and other Latinos in US society is changing its dichotomized black and white constructions of race by introducing new perspectives grounded in the racially mixed profile of Latinos and that of other groups frequently lumped into the "people of color" category.[10]

The Strategic but Neglected Spanish Colony

Despite its geographic strategic location as the "entrance and key to the Antilles,"[11] for almost three centuries Puerto Rico remained a neglected part of the vast Spanish New World empire. More attention was given to the larger colonies that could supply the precious mineral wealth and raw materials to support Spain's imperial hegemony, mercantile economy, and competition with other European powers. The larger colonies sustained the mercantile economy that helped finance the empire's religious and military ventures. Until the latter decades of the eighteenth century, Puerto Rico was not heavily populated, and the Spanish government received subsidies from the Viceroyalty of New Spain in Mexico to administer the colony. The island's creole population relied mostly on subsistence agriculture and contraband trade with neighboring non-Hispanic Caribbean islands to satisfy their basic needs (Morales-Carrión 1971). The population of Puerto Rico remained very small during the first three centuries of Spanish colonization; the stagnant population growth was reflected in the subsistence nature of most of Puerto Rico's agricultural productivity.

The initial neglect from Spanish authorities did not alter the importance of Puerto Rico's geographic location. In Spain's quest to hold on to its imperial glory, Puerto Rico was strategically important to counteract the growing commercial interests of the British, the French, and the Dutch in the Caribbean region. Competing European powers also recognized the island's strategic value and attempted to take it away from Spain. Puerto Rico was subjected to unsuccessful attacks from the British in 1595 and 1598 and the Dutch in 1625. The threat of foreign invasion motivated the Spaniards to build imposing military fortifications on the island and on its other Caribbean colonies. San Juan, the center of colonial administration and site of the country's major port, was eventually converted into a walled city. The fortifications surrounding the capital contributed to a sharp separation between the locus of colonial administration, where most of the peninsular population and the army resided, and a large portion of the sparse creole population, scattered throughout the island and mostly disconnected from the ruling authorities. As late as 1797, the British were, once again, fended off by the Spanish in another unsuccessful attempt to take over Puerto Rico.

Life in the colonies began to change after the modernizing French Bourbon dynasty came to occupy the Spanish throne in the early eighteenth century. Reforms were gradually introduced to foster economic development and commerce throughout the colonial empire. In took until 1765 for any reforms to reach Puerto Rico. That year, the Spanish Crown sent Field Marshall Alejandro O'Reilly to assess the island's socioeconomic conditions and potential for economic growth. O'Reilly's visit led to the implementation of wide-ranging reforms. These included relaxing the monopolistic Spanish trade, discouraging contraband, and promoting European immigration to increase Puerto Rico's population base. In the late 1700s and early 1800s, Puerto Rico was to witness a large influx of immigrants from Spain (primarily from the Balearic and Canary Islands and the provinces of Cataluña and Valencia), French Corsica, Germany, Italy, Holland, England, Scotland, and the United States. Most of these immigrants were attracted by land grants and other Spanish colonial government incentives given to individuals with enough capital to invest in agricultural development in different parts of the country (see Cifre de Loubriel 1975; Scarano 1981). Other immigrants, especially from Venezuela, Haiti, and the Dominican Republic, sought refuge in Puerto Rico in the early 1800s after the political turmoil generated by those colonies' respective wars of independence.

In addition to building Puerto Rico's defenses, the Spanish colonial government actively encouraged commercial agriculture, focusing on sugar, coffee, and tobacco production. These products became the island's main exports to Spain and would continue to be important in Puerto Rico's agricultural economy until the mid-twentieth century.

More substantial progress in Puerto Rico's conditions did not occur until the Spanish metropolis introduced the Real Cédula de Gracias (Royal Decree of Concessions) of 1815. The Real Cédula de Gracias was aimed at further expanding commerce and economic activity. Concurrently, it brought about the implementation of additional reforms to create an environment more favorable for cultural and social development, and less inviting for revolutionary insurgency at a time when the spirit of revolution was engulfing most of the European colonies in the Americas. Among the most significant economic changes were the introduction of new industrial machinery and the opening of trade between Puerto Rico and the United States.

This period of economic development was also supported by an increase in the importation of enslaved African labor. These factors contributed to a striking pattern of population growth that began in the late 1700s and continued into the 1800s. Puerto Rico's population almost tripled, from only 44,883 inhabitants in 1765 to 129,758 in 1795. Another significant population increase took place after the reforms implemented by the Real Cédula de Gracias. The island's population grew from 183,211 inhabitants in 1807; to 185,000 in 1812; 235,157 in 1824; 302,672 in 1828; and 443,000 by 1846 (Silvestrini and Luque de Sánchez 1988, 240; Scarano 1993, 412).

The majority of the Spanish New World colonies secured their independence in the years between 1808 and 1824, but revolutionary activity in Puerto Rico was largely discouraged by the repressive policies and authoritarian rule of the Spanish Crown's appointed governors. In 1809, Puerto Ricans were permitted for the first time to be represented in the Spanish Cortes, the main parliamentary body under the ruling monarchy, but this representation completely ceased in 1837 and was not to be restored until 1870. Political conditions in Spain had been in turmoil since the Napoleonic invasion of 1808, which had forced the Spanish people to take up arms against the French invaders and produced the liberal Cádiz Constitution of 1812. However, the return of King Ferdinand VII to the Spanish throne two years later nullified the progressive constitutional reforms, restored absolutist rule, and set the stage for a political confrontation between conservative supporters of the monarchy and liberals seeking representative government and the establishment of a Spanish republic. It was during this politically unstable period that there was an outbreak of wars of independence in the New World colonies and Spain lost most of its empire. Conditions in the Spanish metropolis deteriorated even further after the death of King Ferdinand VII in 1833. Serious divisions about the succession to the Spanish throne gave impetus to several wars (Guerras Carlistas) between conservative royalists and liberals, and these struggles dominated the metropolitan political landscape throughout the remainder of the nineteenth century.

Left with only the colonies of Cuba and Puerto Rico, Spanish officials ruled them with an iron hand. For many decades it was common practice for the Spanish colonial government to force advocates of liberal reforms or independence into prison or exile. A few clandestine revolutionary cells operated in Puerto Rico, trying to keep alive the separatist struggle and advocating the abolition of slavery, but the lack of freedom of expression and other political rights did not provide the necessary environment inside the island to incite revolution.

On September 23, 1868, Puerto Rico claimed its independence with the Grito de Lares armed revolt, but the insurrection was rapidly crushed by the Spanish army only a few days after it began. In contrast, the rebellion that started in Cuba with the Grito de Yara, only a couple of weeks after the Grito de Lares, signaled the beginning of the neighboring island's Ten Years' War of independence (1868–1878). The war in Cuba and the movement to liberate the two islands was sustained by the activities of Antillean political expatriates living in cities in Europe, the United States, or other Latin American countries. Mounting a revolution in Puerto Rico, however, was a daunting and dangerous endeavor. First, local political and social divisions did not facilitate the development of a strong and unified creole revolutionary movement that could incite the population to take up arms against the Spaniards. Second, the repressive practices of the Spanish colonial government curtailed all freedom of expression and civil liberties. Thus, while other Spanish colonies carried out wars of independence and became sovereign republics, Puerto Rico remained under Spanish control throughout the nineteenth century. This was also the case with Cuba, although the Cubans were able to keep their armed resistance alive during two separate wars of independence, the already mentioned Ten Years' War, and the Spanish-Cuban War that began with the Grito de Baire of 1895 and ended in 1898 with the US invasion of Cuba and Puerto Rico.

By the 1860s, liberals in Spain had again gained some political ground against supporters of the monarchy, which translated into a more open political climate in the colonies. In 1870 for the first time, Puerto Rico was given the right to form its own political parties, and nongovernment newspapers began to appear (Pedreira [1941] 1969). The first Spanish Republic was finally created in 1873; this major political change in the metropolis contributed to the abolition of slavery in Puerto Rico and Cuba that same year. The liberalizing political environment quickly came to an end with the restoration of the Spanish monarchy less than a year later and the gradual return to authoritarian rule for the colonies during the decades that followed. Political instability engulfed the Spanish metropolis as the remaining two island colonies continued to establish their claims for more civil liberties and control of their own affairs.

The political conditions described herein made it more difficult for the Puerto Rican creole propertied class to fulfill its ruling-class aspirations, which in the case of other colonies, was a key factor in galvanizing their respective struggles to rid themselves of colonial rule and secure their independence. Puerto Rico's creole propertied class was largely composed of hacienda owners involved in export mainly to Spain and the United States. By the mid-1800s the United States had become the island's main trade partner. The growing trade between Puerto Rico and the United States was mostly based on the exportation of sugar and, to a lesser degree, coffee, tobacco and other island agricultural products, and the importation of manufactured goods from an expanding North American economy seeking new foreign markets. The sugar industry boomed between 1815 and 1870, while coffee production began to replace it as the main export product during the decades between 1870 and 1900 (Quintero Rivera 1976a; Scarano 1993). The economic influence of the hacendados (hacienda owners) in this export-oriented agricultural economy, however, was severely limited by peninsular control of commerce and banking. Although the hacendados owned most of Puerto Rico's land, control of commercial transportation and financing was in the hands of Spaniards, who had the support of the colonial administrative structures. Acute class, racial, and political divisions within Puerto Rican society additionally impeded the emergence of a cohesive creole bourgeoisie and of a revolutionary consciousness capable of nourishing any claims for independence or of challenging the control of the ruling peninsular elites (see Quintero Rivera 1988; Picó 1990).

The influx of new immigrant entrepreneurs in the late 1700s and early 1800s has been considered another obstacle to the development of a strong creole bourgeoisie. In the first place, this population did not have strong nationalist loyalties toward Puerto Rico. Second, the new immigrant investors and proprietors began to erode the already limited economic power of the creole propertied class. Immigrant newcomers gained more access than creoles to certain sectors of Puerto Rico's economy, such as banking and financing, and even came to dominate the economic activity of certain regions of the islands. Together these factors contributed to thwarting the development of a strong creole national consciousness in nineteenth-century Puerto Rico.

The growth of the economic relationship between Puerto Rico and the United States during the course of the nineteenth century was another factor in shaping the propertied class's political views regarding the future of the island. It has been argued that the expanding commercial relationship between the two countries introduced Puerto Rico's propertied class to the "bourgeois" values of their North American neighbors and fueled aspirations among some members of this class for a possible future annexation of the island to the United States. According to Quintero Rivera (1976a):

> El sueño dorado de los terratenientes puertorriqueños respecto a la expansión comercial era el acceso al amplio mercado norteamericano. Era así, no sólo entre aquellos cuya producción comercial era fundamentalmente la caña de azúcar, cuyo principal campo de exportación eran los Estados Unidos aún dentro del patrón comercial del momento, sino también entre los productores de café, que añoraban penetrar ese mercado, el mayor para café en el mundo. La evidencia tiende a demostrar que buena parte de la lucha anti-española en el siglo xix conllevaba la aspiración de una futura anexión a los Estados Unidos. (25)
>
> [The golden dream of Puerto Rican landowners regarding commercial expansion was access to the expansive North American market. That was the case not only for those whose commercial production was fundamentally based on sugar, a product that at the time found its main export market in the United States, but also among coffee producers yearning to penetrate that market. The evidence tends to demonstrate that a considerable part of the nineteenth-century anti-Spanish struggle involved a desire for a future annexation to the United States.]

There is no doubt that the expanding commercial connections between Puerto Rico and the United States opened the doors for a large number of businessmen, professionals, skilled and semiskilled artisans, students, white-collar workers, and their families to come to the metropolis (Haslip-Viera 1996). Another important factor to consider is that during this initial period of contact between Puerto Rico and the United States, the prevailing view of the North American nation in the hemisphere was that of a republic firmly grounded on democratic principles and a successful free enterprise system. The United States was regarded as a model of the kind of democracy and progress that the former colonies in the Americas envisioned for their own countries after securing their independence. The intellectual and political elites and the entrepreneurial sector of the emerging Latin American nations were particularly drawn to the United States. The perception of a threat of North American imperialism did not really enter the Latin American discourse until the latter decades of the nineteenth century.

North American democracy contrasted with the more repressive environment that was found again in the Puerto Rico of the late 1880s during the infamous administration of Spanish Governor Romualdo Palacio. Reacting to the growing support for political autonomy among island creoles and to a series of boycotts they organized against the businesses of peninsular merchants, the colonial government decided to crack down on any challenges to their authority or the interests of the Spanish ruling class. The abuses of Governor Palacio's administration during the year 1887 came to be known as the *régimen del componte* (the "behave yourself" regime). Most of the prior modest gains that had been achieved in civil liberties, especially freedom of expression, were suspended. Nongovernment newspapers were closed, illegal searches became routine, and prominent liberal political leaders were arrested. The return to these despotic measures limited the political options of Puerto Rico's creole propertied class. Even with the more liberal environment found again in the 1890s, the unpredictable and unstable nature of the political situation in Spain, along with the authoritarian rule practiced by most colonial governors, forced creole political leaders to seek a moderate course of action for getting political concessions from the Spanish metropolis. Creole leaders chose to fight for reforms that would eventually allow the island to achieve a considerable degree of self-rule without a total separation from Spain.

The Partido Liberal Reformista (Liberal Reformist Party) had represented creole reform aspirations since its founding in 1870. Frustrations with the unpredictable and limited nature of Spanish colonial reforms eventually moved liberal creoles to claim political autonomy rather than independence. Under the leadership of Román Baldorioty de Castro, in 1887 the Liberal Reformist Party was replaced by the Partido Autonomista Puertorriqueño (Puerto Rican Autonomist Party). The new political entity sought a larger degree of administrative and economic decentralization with respect to the Spanish metropolis. Two years later, after Baldorioty's death, the reins of the Autonomist Party were taken over by Luis Muñoz Rivera, a prominent creole politician and journalist of the propertied class. Puerto Rico's Autonomists made a pact with Spain's Liberal Party members to merge with them, if they managed to win control of the metropolitan government. In exchange, Spanish liberals promised to grant political autonomy to the island. When the Liberal Party came to power in Spain in 1897, a Charter of Autonomy was finally granted to Puerto Rico. This new government endowed Puerto Rican creoles with the right to elect a governing cabinet and enjoy the political autonomy experienced by other Spanish provinces. The Autonomist Cabinet, headed by Muñoz Rivera, included prominent members of the creole propertied class and its political and intellectual elites. Autonomy was a welcome experiment in self-government for Puerto

24 *Puerto Ricans in the United States*

Rico, but also short-lived. The new government lasted less than a year; it came to an end with the US invasion of 1898.

The US takeover freed Puerto Rico from Spanish rule, but it also ended the brief autonomous government and marked the beginning of a new but also restrictive colonial relationship for the island. The creole propertied class's economic dependence on the United States and admiration of its achievements were major factors in this class's initial welcoming response to the arrival of the invading North American troops. The creole propertied class did not anticipate, however, that the new regime would open the doors so quickly to US investors, weakening the position of both Puerto Rico's landowning class and peninsular businessmen. US companies not only took control of Puerto Rico's economic production in a very short period of time but also shifted its focus. Most of the new North American capital was invested in the establishment of more modern and larger sugar mills, or *centrales*, numerous cigar factories, and needle industries. Control of shipping, the setting of trade tariffs, and replacing the Spanish national currency with the dollar were some of the immediate changes introduced by the new colonial rulers that mostly benefited North American investors.

At the time of the US invasion, agricultural production in the haciendas was dominated by coffee crops. With the new focus on sugar production and the control of the land in the hands of North American corporations, the local haciendas entered a stage of decline, being rapidly replaced by sugar as the main export product. The local hacendados' economic decline was accelerated by a reduction in the demand for coffee exports and a drop in the price of this product in the international market. The effects of hurricane San Ciriaco in 1899, which destroyed most of that year's coffee crop, only worsened the economic predicament of the hacendado class. It was clear once again that Puerto Rico's economy was to serve the interests of a new colonial metropolis at the expense of its national interests and those of its creole propertied class.

Notes

1. When Columbus first arrived at the New World islands in 1492, he believed he had reached parts of Asia or the Orient, then known as the Indies. Thus the term "Indies" has been used since Columbus's first voyage. Later on, the word "West" was added to the name to differentiate the New World islands from those of East Asia. The name "Antilles" also was used early in the colonial period to refer to the islands. The name was taken from the classical myth of the lost cities of Antillia.

2. Rouse argued that many of the islands in the Caribbean were settled by 5000 B.C. (1986, 108). The direction of the migratory flow, from a northwesterly direction from the Lesser Antilles to the Greater Antilles, was dictated by the movement of the ocean currents.

3. For more information about Dominican migration to Puerto Rico, see Jorge Duany, ed., *Los dominicanos en Puerto Rico: Migración en la semi-periferia* (Río Piedras, PR: Ediciones Huracán, 1990).

4. Nineteenth-century authors such as Alejandro Tapia y Rivera and Cayetano Coll y Toste frequently incorporated indigenous legends, myths, and historical events into their writings. For a compilation of these legends, see Cayetano Coll y Toste, *Leyendas y tradiciones puertorriqueñas* (Río Piedras, PR: Editorial Cultural, 1975). Alejandro Tapia y Rivera's legend *La palma del cacique*, his poem "El último borincano," and his opera script *Guarionex* all deal with indigenous themes. See Alejandro Tapia y Rivera, *Obras completas* (San Juan: Instituto de Cultura Puertorriqueña, 1968).

5. In *Art and Mythology of the Taino Indians of the Greater West Indies* (San Juan: Ediciones El Cemí, 1972), anthropologist Eugenio Fernández Méndez argued that Yocahú and Huracán might have been the same god. Sued-Badillo (1979, 25–26), however, believed that Huracán referred to the terrible storms and winds unleashed by the earth mother Guabancex as punishment for some violations of social norms.

6. The most complete analysis of different aspects of the Taino revival movement can be found in Gabriel Haslip-Viera, ed., *Taino Revival: Critical Perspectives on Puerto Rican Identity and Cultural Politics* (New York: Centro de Estudios Puertorriqueños, 1999).

7. The term "mestizo" has been used since the early years of the Spanish colonial period to refer to the racial mixture between white European and Indian. The term "mulatto" refers to the mixture between white European and African.

8. *Vejigantes* are the devilish masks used in Puerto Rican carnivals. The characters they represent often carry *vejigas* or filled animal bladders to strike anyone who bothers them.

9. The notions of island and mainland are curious, yet important. An island can be viewed as simply an extension of a larger continent that is divided by water. Yet islands are themselves peaks of larger land masses. While the geographical relationship between island and mainland can be fairly straightforward, it is the conception of the relationship on cultural, political, social, and economic grounds that is more relevant in terms of the colony-metropolis connection.

10. The label "people of color" is used mostly in the United States to refer to nonwhite or racially mixed populations or the populations of the Third World. This term is strongly contested, since, for instance, some Latinos are white, black, or racially mixed.

11. The island's Spanish Governor Fernando de Lando described Puerto Rico as the "entrance and key to the Antilles" in a 1534 letter to Emperor Charles V (King Charles I of Spain). See Eugenio Fernández Méndez, ed., *Crónicas de Puerto Rico desde la conquista hasta nuestros días*, 2 vols. (San Juan: Ediciones del Gobierno, 1957).

3

Migrations Before
World War II

The island of Puerto Rico has long played the role of a crossroads. It has served as the crossroads between the North and the South American continents, between old and new worlds, between memory and opportunity, and between native and newcomer. Puerto Ricans have always represented the emerging newness that arises from the blending and the synergy that occurs at a crossroads. This blending can be racial, a mixture of Amerindian, African, and Spanish. It is expressed in language, culture, religion, and civil society in the ways some Puerto Ricans "code switch" (switch languages) between Spanish and English and oscillate between the traditions, styles, and values of Puerto Rico and those of the United States. Political life is also part of this crossroads, as reflected by the back and forth swing of electoral mandates between the party that favors the current Commonwealth status and the proponents of statehood, and by the inability to reach a consensus about alternatives to the country's colonial dilemma. Scholars and creative writers have produced many metaphors that allude to the tenuous condition or ambivalence of being at the crossroads: "un barco a la deriva" (a ship adrift) (Pedreira 1934), a nation suffering from "cultural schizophrenia" (Seda Bonilla 1972; Carr 1984), a nation in "limbo" (Méndez 1997), or "la nación en vaivén" (the wavering or straddling nation) (Duany 2002). This crossroads also can be characterized by borders—borders that are sometimes easily traversed and other times serve as obstacles—as well as borders whose roles may be exclusionary and defensive or welcoming and encompassing.

The conception of "island," as land surrounded by water, can elicit thoughts of isolation. It can also give way to insular perceptions of events. In the 1930s, the prominent intellectual Antonio S. Pedreira wrote a classic treatise about the sense of *insularismo* (insularity) that he believed engulfed Puerto Rican life (Pedreira 1934). But the notion that Puerto Rico has simply been an island disconnected or isolated from the rest of the world is a misconception. At different times, Puerto Ricans have left their homeland seeking a more prosperous life, but Puerto Rico has served as a refuge for immigrants with similar aspirations or for those escaping political repression. It is also a return home for those Puerto Ricans who have lived afar for much of their working lives, and a temporary stay for others who continue to periodically gravitate between the island and the colonial metropolis.

Additionally, the conception of Puerto Rico and Puerto Ricans, from the perspective of an outsider, particularly from one unfamiliar with the Caribbean and its milieu, is fraught with contradictions and, in some sense, unfathomable. The island's ambiguous and unresolved political relationship with the United States and its uncertain path toward decolonization leaves most non–Puerto Ricans puzzled. Though not a sovereign nation, Puerto Rico displays attributes of nationhood and national identity. They are reflected in the enticing aromas of the typical *cuchifritos* (fried foods) stands in New York City; the bodegas (small grocery stores) of Lorain, Ohio; the flag-bearing pennants that hang from the rearview mirrors of well-worn automobiles that one sees in cities throughout the United States, as they are so obviously at the core of Puerto Rican cultural expressions (see Chapter 7). Cuban writer Antonio Benítez-Rojo, captured the contradictory realities that characterized the Caribbean in *The Repeating Island* (1989, 1997), and these could easily be applied to Puerto Rico:

> If someone needed a visual explanation, a graphic picture of what the Caribbean is, I would refer him to the spiral chaos of the Milky Way, the unpredictable flux of transformative plasma that spins calmly in our globe's firmament, that sketches in an "other" shape that keeps changing, with some objects born to light while others disappear into the womb of darkness; change, transit, return, fluxes of sidereal matter. (4)

As we stated in Chapter 1, the experience of migration has been and continues to be one of Puerto Rico's most constant historical realities. This has been the case since pre-Columbian times, when the indigenous Taino population migrated to the island from the northern shores of the South American continent, and persisted during the Spanish colonial period, when many Puerto Ricans left their homeland because of a variety of political or socioeconomic circumstances, or for similar reasons numerous foreigners came to its shores and made the island their home. But it was not until the US occupation of Puerto Rico, inaugurated on July 25, 1898, that migration became such a predictable and persistent occurrence in the lives of a significant portion of the island's population. This chapter provides a synthesis and analysis of the historical, socioeconomic, and political factors that contributed to the early waves of Puerto Rican migration to the United States, which began even before the US takeover of the island from Spain.

The Pilgrims of Freedom

The first indications of a Puerto Rican presence in the United States came in the second half of the nineteenth century when many individuals were forced to abandon the island to escape the tyrannical rule of the Spanish colonial authorities. As was noted in Chapter 2, political persecution and exile were a common destiny for those Puerto Ricans advocating liberal reforms or independence from Spain. These political émigrés have been appropriately named "the pilgrims of freedom" (Ojeda-Reyes 1992). Among them were leading members of the creole propertied class and the intellectual and political elites, but also self-educated artisans, especially *tabaqueros* (cigar industry workers) and typographers.

Puerto Rican political émigrés settled mostly in New York, although other cities like Philadelphia, Boston, New Orleans, Tampa, and Key West developed neighborhoods or settlements called *colonias* that attracted Cubans, Puerto Ricans, and other Latin Americans to those cities. Expatriates started coming to the United States during the early 1800s when the creole elites in the Spanish New World colonies began to stake their claims for independence from Spain and war broke out in some of these territories.

Most creole liberals in Puerto Rico were seeking political reforms at the time, hoping to achieve more participation in the island's government, representation in the Spanish Cortes, and increased civil liberties, especially freedom of expression and of the press. Others espoused more radical positions by supporting the abolition of slavery and complete separation from Spain. As early as the 1820s, Puerto Rican separatists, who supported independence, frequently were deported or pressured to leave the island. They mostly settled in cities in Spain or in other European or Latin American republics. Increased commercial relations between Puerto Rico and the United States allowed for a similar pattern to develop in later decades, shifting the point of destination to the North American nation.

In 1850, Puerto Rican liberal journalist Julio Vizcarrondo, publisher of the newspaper *El Mercurio* (The Mercury), was forced to leave the island because of his abolitionist views. He settled in Boston, married a North American woman, and lived there for four years. Shortly after returning to Puerto Rico, Vizcarrondo had to endure a second exile. This time he went to Madrid and continued his political activities there, creating the Sociedad Abolicionista Española (Spanish Abolitionist Society), collaborating with the newspaper *El Abolicionista Español* (The Spanish Abolitionist), and supporting the political efforts that led to the first Spanish Republic in 1868. Vizcarrondo kept advocating the abolition of slavery in Puerto Rico until it was finally granted in 1873.

Vizcarrondo's experience offers an early example of the back and forth pilgrimage faced by many Puerto Rican creoles during those years. Promoting any kind of liberal political ideas or inciting revolution in nineteenth-century Puerto Rico was considered subversive by the Spanish ruling authorities. Hence many supporters of either reforms or independence were exiled. These expatriates continued advocating political change from abroad, and Puerto Rican separatists, in particular, created their own organizations to carry on the fight for complete liberation. Some separatists came through New York City in the course of their exile and settled there for many years; others had briefer sojourns and later moved back to Puerto Rico or to other major Latin American or European cities.

Collaborations between Cuban and Puerto Rican separatists provided the impetus for the 1865 founding in New York of the Sociedad Republicana de Cuba y Puerto Rico (Republican Society of Cuba and Puerto Rico). The leading figure among Puerto Rican separatist émigrés was Ramón Emeterio Betances, a physician and a fervent abolitionist.[1] He and his friend and fellow abolitionist, Segundo Ruiz Belvis, sought refuge in New York after barely escaping from Spanish authorities back home. In the New York metropolis the two expatriates joined José Francisco Basora, another Puerto Rican separatist and abolitionist physician, and one of the original founders of the Sociedad Republicana, in forming the new Comité Revolucionario de Puerto Rico (Revolutionary Committee of Puerto Rico). Basora was also one of the editors of New York's Spanish-language newspaper, *La Voz de la América* (The Voice of America), published between 1865 and 1867 and aimed at advancing the separatist cause. It became a major source of information for reporting on events back on the islands and in other Latin American countries.

With the support of the growing Antillean separatist movement in exile, Betances and his comrades designed a plan to back up an armed rebellion in Puerto Rico. This plan included raising funds to bring a cargo of weapons to the island with the hope that the few clandestine revolutionary cells able to operate there could mount an insurrection. The first steps were taken when Betances left New York for the Caribbean island of St. Thomas in 1867. In November of that year, he issued from that neighboring island his "Diez Mandamientos de los Hombres Libres" (The Ten Commandments of Free Men), calling for the Puerto Rican people to take up arms against the Spaniards. Around the same time, he received news of the death of Segundo Ruiz Belvis, who had gone to Chile to garner support for the Antillean separatist cause and died there of illness shortly after his arrival. In a published tribute to him, Betances wrote: "Su sombra venerada vaga de uno a otro extremo de la Isla invitándonos a destrozar las cadenas de servidumbre que tienen a nuestra patria encorvada a los pies de sus mismos opresores" (His venerated shadow wanders from one end of the island to the other, inviting us to break away from the chains of servitude that hold our homeland bent over at the feet of the same oppressors) (Ojeda Reyes 2001, 113).

Enduring exile along with many other patriots and losing his loyal comrade in the struggle for the abolition of slavery and independence only served to strengthen Betances's resolve. He moved forward with his plans to have a ship deliver weapons to support an uprising in Puerto Rico, but the revolutionary plot was thwarted by an informer and the shipment was confiscated by St. Thomas authorities before leaving port, forcing Betances to escape to the Dominican Republic. He then left for Paris, where he had lived as a medical student in the 1840s and 1850s. A good portion of his exile was spent there practicing medicine, but his involvement in the separatist movement never wavered. In the 1890s he accepted a diplomatic post representing the expatriate Cuban provisional government, a position that also facilitated his efforts on behalf of Puerto Rico's independence. For more than four decades Betances lived in exile, although he was in continuous contact with other Puerto Rican and Cuban patriots in New York and other cities. This contact was essential in keeping the flame of freedom burning within the expatriate communities.

Betances's proclamation "Los Diez Mandamientos de los Hombres Libres" inspired, less than a year later, Puerto Rico's Grito de Lares separatist revolt of September 23, 1868, against Spanish colonial rule. Rebels took control of the mountain town of Lares and declared Puerto Rico an independent republic. However, Spanish troops were mobilized and within a few days were able to stop the insurgency from spreading to other towns.[2] More than two weeks later, on October 10, rebels in Cuba also proclaimed a free republic with the Grito de Yara, marking the beginning of Cuba's Ten Years' War of independence against the Spanish.

The arrival of Eugenio María de Hostos in New York in 1869 added another important Puerto Rican voice to the expatriate Antillean separatist movement. Hostos had come from Madrid, where he studied law and began a career as a journalist. A man with an impressive intellectual acumen, during his student years in Spain Hostos had been critical of Spanish colonialism and was a strong advocate of the abolition of slavery and other liberal reforms for Puerto Rico. His political beliefs became more radicalized after the unsuccessful Grito de Lares insurrection, so he left Spain for New York and joined the émigré separatist movement there. Shortly after his arrival in New York, Hostos was named editor of the Spanish-language newspaper *La Revolución* (The Revolution) published between 1869 and 1876 by the Junta Central Republicana de Cuba y Puerto Rico (Republican Central Council of Cuba and Puerto Rico). It did not take long for ideological differences between Hostos and Anglophilic separatists promoting the islands' annexation to the United States to surface. Because of his anti-annexationist views and the newspaper's refusal to declare itself against this particular political alternative, Hostos eventually decided to leave New York for South America. He spent the next decade liv-

ing in Venezuela, Colombia, Peru, Argentina, and Brazil, before finally settling down in the Dominican Republic in 1879. During his long pilgrimage in
Latin America, Hostos wrote his best-known essays about the future of the
Caribbean islands, continuing to defend their liberation and promoting the idea
of an Antillean federation of independent republics.[3] He returned to New York
for the last time in 1898 after the US takeover of Cuba and Puerto Rico with
the objective of creating the Liga de Patriotas (League of Patriots), an organization aimed at pressuring the United States to allow Puerto Ricans to hold a
plebiscite in order to decide the nature of their future political relationship
with the North American nation. But Hostos and his collaborators were unable
to persuade US authorities to allow Puerto Ricans to participate in this process.

José Martí, Cuban independence patriot and writer, was the central figure
of the émigré Antillean separatist movement. Also an exile, he lived in New
York from 1881 to 1895. At the time of his arrival he was twenty-eight years
old, so his New York years represented a significant portion of his adult life. It
was from being "in the belly of the beast," as he once stated, that Martí was inspired to write his most important essays about what he called *nuestra América*
(our America), referring to the new Latin American nations that had emerged
from the downfall of Spanish colonialism.[4] Living in the United States enhanced Martí's understanding of the North American expansionist drive, and he
foresaw its imminent threat to the young Latin American nations in the rest of
the continent. He also called for the new Latin American nations to promote a
unity and progress based, not on European or Anglo-American models, but on
an understanding of the multiplicity of cultures, races, and classes endemic to
each country (Acosta-Belén 1999). Thus the experiences in exile of Antillean
thinkers like Martí, Hostos, and Betances shaped their visions for the emanci-
pation of their respective islands and their future relationship with the United
States. In addition, they were among the most prominent voices warning Latin
Americans about the US imperialist threat in the hemisphere.

The émigré Puerto Rican separatist movement included members of the
creole elite as well as members of the working class. Both groups put out Spanish-language newspapers to advocate their ideals and outline their vision for the
future of their respective countries after independence. *Tabaquero* and labor activist Flor Baerga arrived in New York in the 1880s, after being involved for
many years in labor organizing in Puerto Rico.[5] In New York, Baerga, together
with Cubans Juan Fraga and Rafael Serra and others, founded the Club Los In-
dependientes (The Independents) in 1881. This particular organization aimed at
promoting the separatist cause among workers. The founding of multiple separatist clubs reflected existing political, national, class, and racial differences and
divisions within New York's Latino community, but all the separatists supported the fundamental notion of ending Spanish domination over the islands.
Their commitment to the movement was expressed in different forms. Some focused on proselytizing and fund-raising activities; others started newspapers or

wrote about their ideals; and more than a few eventually decided to take up arms and join the fighting rebel army in Cuba. Puerto Rican expatriate pharmacist Gerardo Forrest, for instance, started the separatist publication *Cuba and Puerto Rico* (1897) in New York before leaving to join the Cuban insurgency.

The alliance between Cuban and Puerto Rican separatists continued for several decades. The presence of José Martí strengthened those collaborations. Martí worked hard to bridge existing class, racial, and ideological divisions within the movement and, in addition, nurtured relations between Cubans and Puerto Ricans. The founding of the Partido Revolucionario Cubano (Cuban Revolutionary Party, PRC) in New York in 1892 was a significant moment, since the party platform included support for Puerto Rico's independence. The Club Borinquen was created that same year by Puerto Rican separatists to mark their official involvement in the party. This club was headed by Sotero Figueroa, a mulatto artisan typographer and journalist who had emigrated to New York in the late 1880s. Back in Puerto Rico, he had worked for and been mentored by the abolitionist patrician José Julián Acosta. Figueroa's book *Ensayo biográfico de los que más han contribuído al progreso de Puerto Rico* (Biographic Essay of Those Who Have Contributed to the Development of Puerto Rico, 1888) had won a prize in an island writing contest and been published by Acosta's press. An expression of a national consciousness that separated creole Puerto Ricans from their peninsular rulers, it was a pioneering contribution to Puerto Rican historiography.

After settling in New York, Figueroa started the Imprenta América, the press that printed the separatist newspaper *Patria* (Motherland) (1892–1898), founded by Martí. The role of Figueroa, who developed a close friendship with the Cuban leader, rapidly expanded beyond the newspaper's typographical production. He was named to the post of administrative editor and wrote many of the newspaper's editorials during Martí's frequent travels to Latino communities outside New York to garner financial and political support for Antillean independence.[6]

Another prominent member of the Club Borinquen was the Puerto Rican typographer, journalist, and poet Francisco Gonzalo "Pachín" Marín. Marín had been exiled from the island because of the publication of his liberal newspaper, *El postillón* (The Conductor, 1887). He arrived in New York in 1891 and a year later started publishing *El postillón* from there, but this time the newspaper described itself in more radical terms as "an unconditional voice of revolution." Pachín Marín also befriended Martí and other separatists. Although Martí left for Cuba in 1895 to fight in the Spanish-Cuban War and was killed by Spanish troops shortly after arriving in his homeland, his death inspired many émigré separatists to join the rebel army. Marín's brother, Wenceslao, also had lived in New York for a few years before deciding to follow Martí's footsteps and leave for Cuba. He was killed in the battlefield in 1896; this personal loss persuaded Pachín to trade his pen for a rifle and also go to Cuba. Less than a year later, he died of illness in the Cuban jungle, adding his name to the long list of separatists giving their lives in the struggle for Antillean freedom.

Also included among the many Puerto Ricans going to New York during this period was Arturo Alfonso Schomburg, a working-class Puerto Rican mulatto who migrated in the early 1890s. Born and raised in Puerto Rico, Schomburg lived in St. Croix for a brief period before going to New York. He had worked as an artisan typographer in a San Juan stationery shop and made friends with other artisans, especially typographers and *tabaqueros*. Schomburg brought with him from Puerto Rico a letter of introduction to Baerga and Serra, who helped him in his initial efforts to settle and find employment in the city. Schomburg, whose friendship with New York's Puerto Rican artisans drew him into the separatist movement, collaborated with Serra and others in the founding of the Club Las Dos Antillas (The Two Antilles Club) in 1892. He served as secretary of the club for four years.

Baerga was an avid collector of newspaper clippings and photographs that documented the presence and history of Puerto Ricans in New York City. The *tabaquero*'s dedication to this endeavor influenced a young Arturo Schomburg to develop a greater interest in history and in paying tribute to those individuals who had given their lives fighting for freedom (Des Verney Sinnette 1989). Years later, Schomburg would dedicate his life to collecting books and other materials that documented the history and experiences of peoples of African descent around the world (see Chapter 7).

Puerto Rican poet Lola Rodríguez de Tió and her journalist husband, Aurelio Tió, also lived in New York during their several exiles. They came to the city in 1892 and then, again, from 1895 to 1898, before returning to Cuba after the US invasion. In New York, the poet and other women separatists engaged in fund-raising and proselytizing activities. Women separatists gathered around the Club Mercedes Varona (Mercedes Varona Club), the first women's club of the PRC, which was founded in 1892 and presided over by Inocencia Martínez de Figueroa, Sotero Figueroa's wife. Another important women's club was the Hermanas de Ríus Rivera (Sisters of Ríus Rivera), named after the Puerto Rican general that had distinguished himself fighting in the two Cuban wars of independence. This club was established in 1897 by Juan Ríus Rivera's Honduran wife, Aurora Fonts, along with Rodríguez de Tió, Martínez de Figueroa, and a few other women committed to advancing the separatist cause.[7]

Rodríguez de Tió published some of her best-known patriotic poems in the newspaper *Patria*. Her revolutionary poetry was a source of inspiration for the independence struggle; some of her poems also promoted Antillean unity. The famous verses of her poem "A Cuba" (To Cuba), symbolize this ideal: "Cuba y Puerto Rico son / de un pájaro las dos alas / reciben flores o balas / sobre el mismo corazón" (Cuba and Puerto Rico are / the two wings of one bird / they receive flowers or bullets / in the very same heart).[8]

In 1895, only a few months after Martí's death, a Sección de Puerto Rico (Puerto Rico Section) of the PRC was established. But the absence of the prominent separatist leader gave other Cuban leaders who succeeded him the opening to set a different course to end the Spanish-Cuban War. The idea of US intervention in the conflict and the possibility of the two islands' annexation by the United States began to take a new life among the more Anglophile and conservative commercial and professional sectors of the Antillean separatist movement. Although some Cuban and Puerto Rican separatists took the US imperialist threat seriously, others viewed the North American nation as a symbol of democracy and modernity. They saw the promise of a future for Cuba and Puerto Rico without the political instability and socioeconomic hardships that were afflicting most of the new Latin American republics after their independence. The Sección de Puerto Rico to some extent reflected the increased support among separatists for US intervention in the Spanish-Cuban War and the annexation of the islands. The Sección was headed by Julio Henna, a Puerto Rican physician and supporter of annexation. Other members included annexationist physicians Roberto H. Todd and Manuel Besosa, and anti-annexationists Sotero Figueroa, Pachín Marín, Antonio Vélez Alvarado, Juan de Mata Terreforte, and Gerardo Forrest. For a brief period, the Sección published the newspapers *Cuba y Puerto Rico* (1897) and *Borinquen* (1898). After the outbreak of the Spanish-Cuban-American War, Todd and Henna played a leading role in encouraging US officials to invade Puerto Rico, providing them with information about the location of Spanish military installations and troops around the island.[9]

From Paris, Ramón Emeterio Betances kept writing articles in Spanish- and French-language newspapers and sending letters to comrades laying out his revolutionary agenda, including his vision for the creation of a postindependence Antillean federation of sovereign republics. He also expressed his opposition to those separatists favoring US intervention in the Spanish-Cuban War and the possible annexation of Cuba and Puerto Rico by the United States. For many years, Betances's pronouncement "Las Antillas para los antillanos" (the Antilles for the Antilleans) alerted the world to US imperialist ambitions in the Caribbean and affirmed the islands' right to become independent nations.[10] Little did Betances know that only several weeks before his death in 1898 his worst fears were to become a reality with the outbreak of the Spanish-Cuban-American War and the US invasion of the islands.

The "Splendid Little War"

The Spanish-Cuban-American War was provoked by the mysterious explosion of the battleship *Maine*, a US naval vessel stationed at the port of Havana. Claiming that the explosion was an act of sabotage, the North American press

New York Herald

Just as the "Remember the Alamo" catchphrase galvanized public opinion in favor of the Mexican-American War (1846–1848), "Remember the Maine" provided a justification for the Spanish-Cuban-American War of 1898.

accused the Spanish government of responsibility and rapidly promoted a "Remember the Maine" mentality. That slogan evoked the "Remember the Alamo" frenzy that half a century earlier had led to a declaration of war against Mexico, and to the annexation of almost half of the territory of Mexico by the United States. In response to mounting public pressures and its own expansionist designs, the US Congress declared war against Spain and invaded Cuba and Puerto Rico. The war ended with the Treaty of Paris (1899), which transferred the remainder of Spain's colonial empire—Cuba, Puerto Rico, and the Pacific territories of the Philippines and Guam—to the United States.

The Spanish-Cuban-American War brought the Antillean separatist movement to an end. Few of the most militant separatists returned to Puerto Rico. Schomburg stayed in New York and eventually diverted his attention to his bibliophilic and historical interests. Schomburg's ties to leading African American intellectuals and the Pan-African movement, his marriage to an African American woman, his move to Harlem, and the racism he often felt within his native culture contributed to his becoming distanced from the Puerto Rican community. A sign of this estrangement was his Anglicizing his first name to Arthur. In 1911, Schomburg was among the founders of the Negro Society for Historical Research, and in later years he presided over the American Negro Academy. Schomburg sold his collection of books and materials to the New York Public Library; it formed the nucleus of the Schomburg Center for Research on Black Culture of the New York Public Library, opened in 1927. The collection and the center became focal points during the years of the Harlem Renaissance. From 1930 to 1932, Schomburg had a brief academic career as a lecturer and bibliographer at Fisk University, helping this institution develop its black collection, but he eventually left to accept the post of curator of his own collection at the New York Public Library. Two years before his death, he wrote the column "Our Pioneers" for the New York newspaper *Amsterdam News,* giving him the opportunity to celebrate the achievements of notable black personalities from different parts of the world, including Hispanic countries.[11] In this regard, he played a pioneering role in documenting the experiences of African peoples in many different countries.

The US invasion of Cuba brought an end to the Spanish-Cuban War, which some scholars believe was close to being won by the rebels (Foner 1972; Pérez 1998). Nonetheless, the international press focused its attention on glorifying the battlefield histrionics of Colonel Theodore Roosevelt and his Rough Riders in the liberation of Cuba and in putting an end to Spanish tyrannical rule in the Americas. Little credit was given to the Cuban rebel army and its considerable battlefield accomplishment, weakening the Spanish army during almost three years of fighting prior to the US intervention. In a letter to Roosevelt, US Ambassador to England John Hay characterized the US conflict with Spain as "a splendid little war."[12] After all, this war had made the United States an imperial power and more determined than ever to replace its European counterparts and consolidate its hegemony in the American hemisphere. The war also made Teddy Roosevelt a legendary hero and facilitated his winning the US presidency in the 1904 election.

Puerto Rican General Juan Ríus Rivera, one of the commanders in the Cuban rebel army, was appointed civil governor of Cuba under US occupation but resigned from the post after the North American nation introduced the Platt Amendment into Cuba's new constitution, affirming its power to intervene in the island's affairs. Cuba was finally given its independence by the United States in 1902, but Puerto Rico was kept as "an unincorporated territory" under US jurisdiction, the beginning of a colonial political status that will be examined in more detail in Chapter 4.

Many of the pilgrims of freedom were condemned to spend a good portion of their lives abroad or to die away from their Puerto Rican homeland. For years they had been able to defend their separatist and abolitionist ideals by

Minneapolis Journal

"Will Wear the Stars and Stripes"
Uncle Sam: "Here, sonny, put on these duds."

writing for Spanish-language newspapers and participating in the political and cultural organizations that were created in New York City and the other Latino émigré communities (see Chapter 7). They frequently corresponded with their families and friends on the island and with other patriots and intellectual figures of their time. As we have seen, the experience of exile often involved moving from one country to another in an endless pilgrimage, with the possibility of intermittent returns to Puerto Rico during the brief and infrequent periods when Spanish colonial authorities allowed a few civil liberties, but some émigrés never returned to the island.

The US–Puerto Rico connection intensified after the Spanish-Cuban-American War of 1898. The North American invasion put an end to the autonomous government that Spain had granted Puerto Rico the year before. The Charter of Autonomy had been regarded by some island leaders as an important step toward the creation of a Puerto Rican sovereign state. Nonetheless,

"Americanization": A cartoon by Puerto Rican artist Mario Brau Zuzuárregui, meant to criticize the policies of the new US colonial government in Puerto Rico, such as the imposition of the English language. From the collection of Mario Brau Zuzuárregui, Colección Puertorriqueña del Sistema de Bibliotecas de la Universidad de Puerto Rico.

these political accomplishments were totally undermined by the new rulers. In fact, most of the initial US colonial policies, which were based on patronizing and disparaging views of the Puerto Rican people and of their former Spanish rulers, aimed at Americanizing the island and manufacturing the necessary consent among the population to justify North American control.

Among the most controversial Americanization policies were the implementation of English as the official language of Puerto Rico and of its school system, the use of island schools to inculcate US values and accelerate the adoption of English, the undermining of Puerto Rican history, culture, and the Spanish language, and the religious proselytizing by Protestant missionaries among a population that was primarily Catholic (see Negrón de Montilla 1971; Silva Gotay 1997). The new colonial government even changed the official name of the island to "Porto Rico."[13] These Americanization policies generated strong opposition from some sectors of Puerto Rican society. The

New Porto Rico: This postcard heralds Puerto Rico's transformation under the new US regime. The colonial government used the name "Porto Rico" rather than "Puerto Rico" on all its official documents until the 1930s. Postcards Collection, Archives of the Puerto Rican Diaspora, Centro de Estudios Puertorriqueños Library and Archives, Hunter College.

creole intellectual elite, in particular, was highly critical of these policies, which were viewed as a concerted attempt at "denationalizing" Puerto Ricans by diminishing the importance of their native language and cultural patrimony and espousing the superiority of the Anglo-American way of life. But there were segments of the population that believed that the US presence was bringing progress and democracy to Puerto Rico and that the island was better off under the new US colonial regime than under Spanish rule.

From the beginning, the US colonial administration was headed by military officials with little knowledge of island affairs. Soon it became evident that creole political leaders were not expected to play any prominent role in shaping most of the policies and decisions that were initially implemented. Puerto Rico and Cuba were becoming pawns in a larger plan to consolidate US military and geopolitical interests and its hegemonic power in the Caribbean region and over the rest of the hemisphere. This primary goal superseded any local considerations. Cuba was allowed to become an independent republic in 1902, but its constitutional sovereignty was limited by the US-instigated Platt Amendment, which gave the United States free rein to intervene in Cuban affairs whenever it deemed necessary to maintain political and economic stability and to protect US strategic interests. The United States in fact used its Platt Amendment prerogatives and intervened and dictated the course of Cuba's government several times in the decades that followed and even after the 1959 Cuban Revolution. But independence was not an alternative offered to Puerto Rico. Its designation as "an unincorporated territory" relegated the island to a powerless colonial status under the jurisdiction of the US Congress.

The Beginnings of Labor Migration

A more nuanced understanding of the history and evolution of Puerto Rican migration to the continent is closely related to the complex subordinate colonial relationship that developed between Puerto Rico and the United States once the latter took possession of the island. But there is also a wider context that must be considered in dealing with all transnational migratory movements of workers. This context is directly related to the development of capitalism as a mode of production and the power relations it engenders, particularly relations among the more-industrialized and less-developed nations.

Bonilla and Campos (1986) provided a useful summary of the evolving patterns of Puerto Rican migration before and after the US takeover vis-à-vis the shifts in the relations of capital and their effects on the island's labor force. Their study divided the migratory process into three major phases, each phase responding to the international dynamics of capitalist development, the displacement and reshuffling of workers it produced throughout the world, and how these processes in turn influenced the specific local factors and conditions leading to Puerto Rican migration. The colonial relationship between Puerto Rico and the United States generated its own particular set of circumstances because of the island's inherent subordinate condition, and we give due attention to these factors as well in our discussion.

According to Bonilla and Campos (1986), the first phase of Puerto Rican migration ran from 1873 to 1898, dates that referred to two main events in the island's history: the abolition of slavery and the US invasion. The years in between these two events marked the expansion of hacienda-based production in Puerto Rico and a significant increase in export trade and commercial ties between the island and the United States. The US occupation of Puerto Rico initiated a second migration cycle, which ended in 1929 with the capitalist crisis of the Great Depression. During this period, the island's economy witnessed the transition from hacienda-based production to US-controlled agricultural plantation capitalism, which prompted the decline of economic activity in the local haciendas. The third phase, the post–World War II period known as the Great Migration, covered Puerto Rico's transition from an agricultural to an industrial economy also dominated by US capital. This latter cycle continued throughout the 1950s and 1960s.

More than fifty years after the beginning of the mid-twentieth-century Great Migration, new and different migration patterns have been developing among Puerto Ricans. These trends were first documented by Rivera-Batiz and Santiago (1994) in their perceptive analysis of what they described as "the changing reality" of Puerto Ricans in the United States, a process that started in the 1980s, became more defined in the 1990s, and has continued into the present. These post–World War II migrations are discussed in more detail in Chapter 4.

As we have seen, the early migrations were propelled by the socioeconomic changes taking place in Puerto Rico, still a Spanish colony, during the last few decades of the eighteenth and the early part of the nineteenth century. It was during this period that the island began to move from subsistence agriculture, a pervasive contraband economy, and the stagnant monopolistic mercantile practices that characterized the initial three centuries of the Spanish colonial regime to the hacienda economy that came to dominate most of the nineteenth century. Hacienda production was largely in the hands of creole and immigrant landowners. Sugar was the dominant export product from the mid-1820s to the mid-1870s, and the United States was the main market. But sugar's place in the island's economy was to be replaced by coffee for the remainder of the nineteenth century. Tobacco was also among the few export products. The largest portion of the coffee and tobacco exports, however, went to Spain and Cuba, rather than the United States.

Puerto Rico's hacienda mode of production relied on the labor of *agregados* (tenant farmers) and day laborers, and before the abolition of slavery in 1873, on the labor of enslaved Africans. The demand for workers in the expanding agricultural sector had prompted the colonial government to implement in 1849 the Reglamento de Jornaleros (Day Workers' Regulations), a purported antivagrancy measure that forced large numbers of peasants to work for the meager wages that the hacendados were willing to pay them. Nontenant and landless peasant workers were compelled to carry an official *libreta de jornaleras* (worker's journal) as a record of their daily employment in order to avoid heavy fines from the ruling authorities. This system was in effect for twenty-four years—until 1873.

As seen in Chapter 3, economic activity on the haciendas intensified in the nineteenth century with the growing demand for agricultural products for export to the US market. The expanding trade relationship with the United States exposed the island's hacendados, merchants, other professionals, and students to North American ways and to the expanding world of bourgeois capitalism (Quintero Rivera 1980). Nevertheless, Puerto Rican emigration was still relatively low, with the US Puerto Rican population less than two thousand people in 1900.

The US takeover of Puerto Rico immediately generated several official reports and books about Puerto Rico and the other new North American possessions. The bulk of the early publications describing the acquired territories tend to glorify the benevolent and expansionist role of the United States in the Americas and other parts of the world as a model of democracy and civilized progress. Titles such as *Our New Possessions* (White, 1901), *Our Islands and Their People* (Wheeler and de Olivares 1899) and *America's Insular Possessions* (Forbes-Lindsay 1906) began to set the tone for the colonial discourse that introduced Puerto Ricans, Cubans, Filipinos, and Guam's Chamorros to a US audience. These books contained the first images and descriptions of the Puerto Rican people to be embedded in the minds of the US public: a destitute, racially inferior island population redeemed from Spanish tyrannical rule and ready to be introduced to democracy, enlightened civilization, and prosperity by the benevolence of the great North American nation. From all these publications a uniform and belittling composite of the nature, character traits, and ways of life of the Puerto Rican population through the eyes of the US colonizer began to emerge.

According to a 1899 report by military governor General George W. Davis, the following were some of the prevailing conditions in Puerto Rico at the time of the US occupation:

> Nearly 800,000 of the 960,000 population (260 to the square mile) could neither read nor write. Most of these lived in bark huts and were, in effect, the personal property of the landed proprietors. ... They were poor beyond the possibility of our understanding and if they were so fortunate as to have for the current hour, they were content. (War Department 1902, 669)

These first impressions of the island's population were accompanied by descriptions of early North American efforts to build better roads, more

"SOME PORTO RICANS AS OUR ARTIST SAW THEM. This view was taken in one of the streets of Aguada, near the spot where Columbus landed. It is the custom for the little children to go naked, even to school. Some of those whose parents are well-to-do wear shoes and stockings, but nothing else." (Original quote accompanying this photograph when it was first published in the book *Our Islands and Their People*, 1899, 334.)

schools, and deal with the numerous health problems afflicting Puerto Rican peasants, who at the time constituted the majority of the island's population. Among the most pressing problems were numerous tropical diseases, widespread malnutrition, and a high mortality rate. The presence of US enterprises with business interests throughout the Caribbean and Latin American region was also immediately felt, as many companies began to send recruitment agents to Puerto Rico to hire contract laborers. This practice soon turned into the main conduit for the migration of workers.

After two years of military rule, Charles Allen was appointed as the first US civil governor of Puerto Rico under the new colonial regime. Governor Allen made reference to the emigration of Puerto Rican workers in his first report about the state of island affairs, submitted to Congress in 1901. In this document Governor Allen noted that "emigration has been almost unknown" on the island and that Puerto Ricans seemed to be "essentially home-loving people, and remarkably attached to their native land" (History Task Force 1982, 14). The North American governor then referred to the devastation caused by hurricane San Ciriaco in 1899 and the severe unemployment and destitution it wrought on the peasantry. He viewed these conditions as favorable for emigration agents to induce Puerto Rican peasants to work in the sugarcane fields of Hawaii or the iron mines in Cuba, places where US companies were having an immediate demand for low-wage labor. He also believed that the island could easily dispense with these workers:

> Most of the emigrants are of the very poorest class of laborers, many of them without a box or a bundle or anything whatever more than the scanty apparel in which they stand upon the wharves. Very few of them have the least rudiments of education. In other words, these emigrants comprise the least desirable elements of this people. (History Task Force 1982, 15)

The colonial government used emigration as a tool to alleviate the poverty and unemployment among the majority peasant population and get rid of "the least desirable elements" of Puerto Rican society. This initial migration strategy coincided with a strong demand by US investors for low-wage labor for their companies in the acquired territories and elsewhere in the hemisphere as well as in the expanding industrial sector in the continental United States. Thus US companies were encouraged to recruit workers from Puerto Rico to work in agriculture, manufacturing, and service industries.

Migration of Puerto Rican workers to other countries, as we have mentioned, had occurred at a much slower pace under the Spanish colonial administration and only began to show a perceptible growth pattern after the US takeover. Desperate conditions of poverty and the lack of employment opportunities for many peasants, artisans, and other day laborers had prompted the former Spanish rulers to foster emigration, especially after the abolition of slavery, which created a surplus of unemployed workers (History Task Force 1982). During those years, Puerto Rican workers were encouraged to leave the island for the Dominican Republic, Cuba, Panama, and Venezuela, countries with need for agricultural workers or other forms of manual labor.

Not only working-class workers left during this early period. The limited educational opportunities for Puerto Ricans under Spanish rule had motivated the island's most affluent families to send their male offspring to Spain or other European countries to receive an advanced education. With the expanding commercial connections between Puerto Rico and the United States, the focus began to shift toward the end of the nineteenth century to North American universities. Since then, many island Puerto Ricans have sought professional training in the metropolis, coming into contact with the various Puerto Rican or Latino communities in several US cities.

There is no question that the North American occupation of Puerto Rico propelled the second migration phase. The rapid flow of US investment capital into Puerto Rico after the takeover was the main catalyst for the development of full-fledged agrarian capitalism under the control of large absentee-owned sugar trusts that purchased most of the island's cultivable land. The large-scale sugar production shifted the focus of and monopolized the island's agricultural economy. More than half the available agricultural land was soon concentrated in the hands of a few North American corporations, which built large and more technologically advanced sugar mills or *centrales*. This land concentration reduced the number of smaller farms owned by the local hacendado propertied class. The shift from coffee production, which was the heart of the hacienda economy, to sugar plantation production further debilitated the economic power and social position of the hacendados and increased unemployment among peasant workers. According to Quintero-Rivera (1980), the consolidation of US-led agrarian capitalism had multiple effects in reshaping social and political relations in Puerto Rican society. These included: (1) the emergence of "a dependent anti-national bourgeoisie" (14) whose main role was to fulfill the island's needs for importing consumer products from the United States; (2) the concomitant growth of a sector of "intermediary professionals" (17) that saw the North American nation as the conduit to bringing progress and modernity to Puerto Rico; and (3) the proletarianization of the island's labor force, which faced the trials and tribulations of "wage-labor capitalist relations" (22) and the exploitation of their labor by US companies. This new proletariat was also caught in the contradictions stemming from their rejection of the seignorial and paternalistic relations of the hacienda economy and the old Spanish colonial order, and their admiration for North American liberal democracy with its promise of more civil liberties and worker protections than they had experienced before. Thus, Quintero Rivera (1976a, 1976b, 1980) emphasized that the Puerto Rican workers' movement developed an internationalist socialist outlook in their struggles, rather than assuming anti-American positions or subscribing to the Hispanophilic nationalistic stance of a creole propertied class being stripped from its limited economic power by the US corporations.

The general decline in hacienda production created a surplus of peasant workers, who were forced to look for employment in the new US-controlled sugar, tobacco, and needle industries being established on the island. However, these sectors of economic activity did not generate enough job opportunities to ameliorate the rising agricultural unemployment.

The desperate economic conditions that developed during the latter years of Spanish rule and the early years of the US occupation motivated workers to organize. Numerous workers, especially from the artisan sector, joined the Federación Libre de los Trabajadores de Puerto Rico (Free Federation of

Puerto Rico's Workers, FLT), the island's largest labor union, which had been founded in 1899. Two years after its founding, the FLT became an affiliate of the American Federation of Labor (AFL). For the next four decades the FLT was led by Santiago Iglesias Pantín, a Spanish émigré carpenter who had come to Puerto Rico from Cuba in 1896. He left Puerto Rico for New York in 1900 and developed ties with US workers affiliated with the AFL. He became an AFL labor organizer and was instrumental in getting the FLT to affiliate with the larger and stronger North American union. The connections between the FLT and the AFL, along with the class antagonisms between workers and the creole hacendado class, which had been exploiting their labor since the years of Spanish rule, contributed to the workers' support for the US presence in Puerto Rico and for the possibility of a future statehood for the island.

In 1915 the FLT founded the Partido Socialista (Socialist Party, PS), which became the FLT's political arm in challenging the control of local politics by creole landowners. The *tabaqueros,* men and women who worked in the island's tobacco factories and shops, were the largest and most vocal group among the artisans and within the wider Puerto Rican labor movement. Men concentrated on cigar making, while women were largely relegated to stripping the tobacco leaves. The needlework industries, another active sector in the labor movement, employed mostly women.[14]

Growing numbers of workers migrated to the United States during these early decades of US domination. In 1910 the total US Puerto Rican population was 1,513; it had increased to almost 11,811 by 1920, and 52,774 by 1930 (Wagenheim 1975). Because of its affiliation with the AFL, Puerto Rico's FLT actually encouraged workers to migrate to the United States rather than to other countries with lower wages and fewer worker protections.

The economic debacle produced by the Great Depression slowed down Puerto Rican migration, but a growth pattern continued. By 1940 the US migrant population had increased to 69,967, which was 33 percent higher than the previous decade. This increase, however, was much lower than the larger percentage increases of the 1910s and 1920s.

There was another economic change that characterized this second phase of Puerto Rican migration. Puerto Rico was exporting a few agricultural products needed in the metropolis but was becoming a major consumer of US manufactured goods. A noted scholar captured this dependent relationship in simpler terms when he stated that Puerto Rico "produces what she does not consume and consumes what she does not produce" (Lewis 1963). The ultimate result of this pattern was an enduring condition of economic dependency that underwent various stages of development throughout the twentieth century but that, in a broader sense, would remain unchanged in some concrete ways. The consistency of the pattern is clear: Under US rule, Puerto Rico was to serve the specific industrial and investment interests of North American companies, and the Puerto Rican labor force would be used to solve labor shortages in the metropolis or forced to migrate in order to make a living. A major consequence of this manipulation of Puerto Rico's labor force has been the increased dependency of the island's government on the influx of federal funds from the US Congress to provide essential social services to the poor and unemployed and to support public agencies and other aspects of the island's infrastructure. This reliance on federal assistance on the part of the local government, which intensified after the 1940s, only added to the island's colonial dependency.

Economic dependency lay side by side with political subordination and the limited political power for self-government granted to Puerto Ricans by the US Congress. Two major congressional acts have guided Puerto Rico's relationship with the United States: the Foraker Act of 1900 and the Jones Act of 1917.[15] The Foraker Act provided a civil government for the island after the initial two years of military occupation, establishing a government headed by a North American governor and an Executive Council of North American officials appointed by the president of the United States. Puerto Rican participation in the ruling structures was limited to an elective House of Delegates. The Jones Act granted US citizenship to Puerto Ricans and eliminated the US-appointed Executive Council. Instead, it introduced an elective Senate, which provided Puerto Ricans with an additional level of participation in running the insular government. The citizenship decree also introduced compulsory military service. This meant that before the draft was abolished in the 1970s, Puerto Rican men were compelled to serve in the US armed forces. This happened for the first time during World War I and from then on, in all subsequent US armed conflicts.

The changes in the island's political and socioeconomic conditions engendered by US colonial authority and the international economic forces and labor needs that propelled Puerto Rican migration must be examined in more detail in order to better understand the specific characteristics and differences between each of the major migratory phases. It is important to point out that in making Puerto Rico a territorial possession, the United States acquired a country confronting severe conditions of poverty, malnutrition, and unemployment. Politically, the island was just beginning to develop after having been a neglected colony for most of the Spanish colonial period, and then having faced the burden of authoritarian rule throughout the nineteenth century, before finally being granted autonomy by Spain in 1897.

The socioeconomic and political dislocations produced by the initial US occupation of Puerto Rico and the North American nation's subsequent control over island affairs can be correlated with the pace and magnitude of the various migratory waves. As the United States came out of the Great Depression and entered World War II, migration began to intensify. This was due, on the one hand, to the increasing demand for labor during wartime; and on the other, to the industrial revolution that changed Puerto Rican society and the focus of its economy. Thus, the great majority of Puerto Rican migration studies have focused on the postwar Great Migration period (mid-1940s to mid-1960s), the third phase in Bonilla and Campos's (1986) periodization. A shortcoming of many of the early migration studies was that they tended to emphasize push-pull socioeconomic factors that caused Puerto Ricans to leave their homeland and settle in the United States, but they did not pay enough attention to the fundamental dynamics and contradictions of the colonial relationship between the two countries, which made migration such a viable, controlled, and attractive government tool for dealing with the island's economic problems. At many different times, both US ruling authorities and the local political leadership have consented to this particular manipulation of the Puerto Rican labor force.

Early arguments to explain migration showed a propensity to overemphasize Puerto Rico's extreme poverty and overpopulation problems, a situation that the US colonial regime dealt with by introducing new population control and family-planning policies that became part of the development discourse of the 1940s and 1950s. In fact, the overpopulation argument was at the forefront of all explanations about the island's high levels of poverty, and migration and population control were seen as the two most expedient solutions to this problem.

It is not then surprising that population pressure on the island has been commonly cited as the main rationale for the drive to foster Puerto Rican migration. The idea that was promoted generally emphasized the dual objectives of economic development and growth. The notion of an "overpopulated" impoverished island lacking in natural resources was reiterated in most of the early migration studies. Mills, Senior, and Goldsen dramatized this perspective in the opening line of *The Puerto Rican Journey* (1950): "If the United States were as crowded as Puerto Rico, it would almost contain all the people in the world" (3). In an earlier study, Chenault (1938) had expressed a similar view by stating, "One important factor which can cause migration from a country as crowded as Puerto Rico is the lack of natural resources to support its growing population" (12). The irony is that while these assertions were being made to justify migration, especially by North American researchers and public officials, Puerto Ricans were migrating in large numbers to New York City, a city with a population density almost a hundred and fifty times higher than that of Puerto Rico at the time (History Task Force 1979, 20). The stress on an overpopulation problem implied that Puerto Rico had neither the natural nor the human resources to sustain its growing population and thus migration was the most logical alternative to alleviate this condition. This view, however, obfuscated the structural economic factors that created the conditions that encouraged the migration of workers, in this case the development of US-controlled capitalism on the island and the ways in which colonialism shifted the balance of power and social and economic relations within Puerto Rican society, making Puerto Rico a subordinate entity under the complete authority of the United States.

Other common explanations for increased migration to the United States were the island's persistent high rates of unemployment and illiteracy. At the time of the US takeover, about 60 percent of Puerto Rico's population could not read or write. Another factor often cited for increased migration is the granting of US citizenship to Puerto Ricans in 1917, because this allowed for unrestricted movement of workers to the metropolis, although it had been relatively easy for Puerto Ricans to do so since 1898. The geographic proximity of the island to the United States and, since the 1940s, the availability of air travel and inexpensive airfares between Puerto Rico and several US major cities were also cited as important factors in facilitating mass migration.

A fixation on the push-pull factors summarized above, said to have a causal effect on Puerto Rican migration, often understated the weight of the planning efforts of US and Puerto Rican policymakers and government agencies. At different times they have used migration as an escape or safety valve to deal with some of the island's harsh socioeconomic conditions and to provide a source of low-wage labor for manufacturing and agricultural employers in the US metropolis.

Migration, however, was not the only tool for dealing with Puerto Rican poverty and population growth. Many government policies aimed at population control and reducing the birthrate relied on the use of various contraceptive methods. The push for population control was facilitated by the introduction of oral contraceptives to the island. Moreover, US pharmaceutical companies used Puerto Rican women for testing "the pill" before it was introduced to the US market (Ramírez de Arellano and Seipp 1983). Another popular method fostered by the government was the massive sterilization of women through the surgical procedure that became known as *la operación*.[16] These population control practices intensified during the rapid industrialization period of the 1950s, and Puerto Rico currently has one of the highest sterilization rates of women in the world. About 35 percent of all Puerto Rican women are sterilized, compared to 30 percent in the United States (Vázquez Calzada 1973; Presser 1980). Between 1950 and 1970 the fertility rate on the island declined by 48 percent, from 5.2 to 2.7 children per woman.

Puerto Rican migration continued at a steady pace and reached one of its highest levels after World War II, a direct consequence of *Operación Manos a la Obra* (put your hands to work), known in English as Operation Bootstrap, a government development program aimed at industrializing the island's economy. These conditions are analyzed in greater detail in Chapter 4.

Migration to Hawaii

The migration of agricultural workers to the sugarcane plantations of Hawaii in 1900–1901 was the first large exodus of contract labor out of Puerto Rico, but Hawaii was not the only destination. During the first decade of US occupation, workers also were recruited to work in the Dominican Republic and Cuba to support the expansion of North American sugar trusts there (History Task Force 1982).

Puerto Ricans leaving for Hawaii were desperately searching for any sources of employment following the devastating effects on agricultural production of hurricane San Ciriaco in 1899. Workers were recruited for the sugarcane fields of the Hawaiian Islands, and entire families traveled there in the course of eleven expeditions beginning in November 1900 and ending a year later.

Early 1900s advertisement for steamship travel from San Juan to New York and San Juan to New Orleans, frequent destinations for Puerto Rican contract workers. Archives of the Puerto Rican Diaspora, Centro de Estudios Puertorriqueños Library and Archives, Hunter College.

The journey from Puerto Rico to the Hawaiian Islands was long and onerous, since it involved going to the port of New Orleans by ship and then by train to San Francisco in order to board another ship to the final destination. Many agricultural workers were uninformed about the ordeal they were to face on their journey to Hawaii, but changing their minds was not a feasible option, since they were constantly under the surveillance of the employing company's agents. A description of the initial voyage summarizes some of the hardships:

> The first group of 114 men, women and children came on the S.S. Arkadia to New Orleans where they were loaded onto two tourist cars of the Southern Pacific Railway and began a slow and eventful journey via a southwest route across the United States to San Francisco. Overcrowding in the cars led to much discomfort. The lightweight clothing worn by the people, while suitable for Puerto Rico and Hawaii, was not warm enough for the winter trip. The trip was a slow one as the agents wanted to time the arrival of the train to San Francisco to coincide with the departure of the S.S. City of Rio de Janeiro for Honolulu, so that the passengers could be put on the ship immediately and be on their way to Hawaii. (Camacho Souza 1986, 27)

Even with the watchful attention of the agents of the Hawaii Sugar Planters' Association, which paid for their transportation, worker defections did occur, as only fifty-six Puerto Ricans landed in Hawaii on the first voyage. Some of the dropouts managed to stay in New Orleans or San Francisco; their defections led to small concentrations of Puerto Ricans in these localities.

The working conditions of Puerto Rican workers in the sugar fields were harsh indeed, whether in Puerto Rico or Hawaii. A 1903 government report spoke disparagingly about the Puerto Ricans who were transported to Hawaii:

> They have brought with them a criminal element which may take time to eliminate, but will find the islands a decidedly discouraging field of operations, and they have faults and weaknesses which it may require a generation or two fully to correct. They are somewhat given to drinking, gambling, and carrying concealed weapons, and are more quarrelsome and vindictive than the other inhabitants. (US Department of Labor 1903, 361)

The report went on to minimize the potential contributions of Puerto Ricans to Hawaiian society by stating:

> The ultimate effect of the Porto Rican immigration upon the islands will probably be unimportant. Those who remain will doubtless amalgamate more or less with the Portuguese during their transition into Hawaiian Americans. They and their descendants will in all probability be vastly better off than they had any prospect of being in their own country. (361)

The conditions of Puerto Rican laborers were significantly less idyllic than those described by US officials in Hawaii, and the tone of the discourse was consistent with US colonial policies and practices at the time. That entire families were transported halfway across the globe under deplorable conditions, in winter, to work in a society and culture that was alien to them, particularly linguistically, can explain some of the defiant behavior of Puerto Ricans in their new environment. What was described as indolence by the North Americans was most likely a form of resistance.

This motivation of Puerto Ricans to leave Puerto Rico in search of employment or better economic opportunities was shared by succeeding generations. There was another contract labor wave of Puerto Rican migration to Hawaii in 1921, again motivated by economic necessity. Puerto Ricans have integrated into the larger Hawaiian society through intermarriage with native Hawaiians, Japanese, and other ethnic groups on the islands. Nonetheless, the Puerto Rican community there maintains important aspects of its own island culture. Various civil associations have emerged to sustain Puerto Rican culture, language, and traditions. The experience of Puerto Ricans in Hawaii represents the first organized movement of Puerto Ricans following the Spanish-Cuban-American War. Moreover, many of its features foreshadowed the wider Puerto Rican experience in the United States: the underlying economic motivation for the risky journey, the need to maintain community and cultural heritage, the desire to cling to one's native language, the openness to interaction with the surrounding society, and the celebration of one's heritage.

The early migrations of Puerto Ricans to certain US localities like Hawaii only began to be researched in the 1970s. Some of the descendants of Hawaii's *Borinkis* (Puerto Ricans in Hawaii) started the Puerto Rican Heritage Society of Hawaii in 1980 to promote the process of documenting their presence and contributions. Several important studies also were released in the 1980s detailing the formation and evolution of this particular community (Rosario Natal 1983; Camacho Souza 1986; Carr 1989). The number of self-identified Puerto Ricans residing in the state of Hawaii was over 30,000 in 2000, according to the US census. This figure constitutes 2.5 percent of the total population of the islands and less than 1 percent of the total Puerto Rican population residing in the continental United States.

The presence of those Puerto Ricans who stayed in San Francisco on their way to Hawaii or who settled there on their way back from the islands is revealed by the existence of community organizations such as the Club Puertorriqueño de San Francisco (Puerto Rican Club of San Francisco), founded in 1912. The influx of Puerto Ricans to other parts of California continued to expand over the decades as they settled in cities such as San José, Los Angeles, San Diego, and Union City (see Chapter 4). Another community organization, the Liga Puertorriqueña de California (Puerto Rican League of California) was established in 1922. More than half a century later, in 1973, the Western Region Puerto Rican Council was founded to draw attention to the needs of Puerto Ricans in that part of the country and to their presence there since the early decades of the twentieth century. These organizations served important social and cultural functions and, in addition, gave the community a voice in dealing with other more pressing group needs and civil rights issues.

A pattern of Puerto Rican labor migration to closer destinations, in the neighboring Caribbean islands, developed after the United States purchased the Virgin Islands from Denmark in 1917. A preferred destination was the island of St. Croix (Santa Cruz), where Puerto Ricans were hired to work in agriculture and stock farms. This exodus intensified after 1927, but an exchange of agricultural workers between Puerto Rico's eastern island municipality of Vieques and St. Croix had existed since the nineteenth century. With the large expropriation of almost two-thirds of Vieques's territory by the US Navy in 1941, migration of *viequenses* from Puerto Rico to St. Croix intensified. Migration from other Puerto Rican towns to St. Croix continued to grow in later years. In the year 2000 there were about 20,000 Puerto Ricans living in St. Croix, representing one-third of that island's total population.

The Growth of the New York Community

The New York Puerto Rican community was the largest and fastest growing one during the early decades of the twentieth century, but according to the US census, it numbered a little less than 2,000 in 1910. A notable growth began during the World War I years, since many of the war industries relied on immigrant contract labor and Puerto Ricans were one of the groups that fulfilled this demand. Besides New York, Puerto Ricans also were recruited for industries in New Orleans; Wilmington, North Carolina; Charleston, South Carolina; and Brunswick and Savannah, Georgia. Some of the contract labor was gender specific, as illustrated by the recruitment of Puerto Rican men for agricultural work in upstate New York and New Jersey, and women for work in the cordage factories of St. Louis, Missouri, and New York's garment industry (History Task Force 1982).

The granting of US citizenship to Puerto Ricans in 1917 encouraged the island's largest labor union, the FLT, to point out the advantages and protections that Puerto Rican workers would gain if they sought employment in the United States rather than going to other countries. But despite the linkages between the FLT and the AFL, North American companies were not deterred from exploiting Puerto Rican contract workers or forcing them to work in conditions less favorable than those of other US workers. Thus, in the United States, Puerto Ricans became part of an underprivileged working class and a major source of low-wage labor that supported the country's manufacturing and service sectors.

Census data from the 1920s and 1930s showed that New York City was becoming the preferred point of destination for Puerto Rican migrants. Puerto Rican barrios were forming in Manhattan's Lower East Side, Upper West Side, and Chelsea area, and along the Navy Yard and Atlantic Avenue sections of Brooklyn. The Chelsea area was the site of more than 500 Hispanic-owned tobacco factories and shops (Sánchez Korrol [1983] 1994). The socialist *tabaqueros* were an important sector of the community, since they tended to be active in grassroots organizing and in the creation of organizations and publications that empowered community members to speak out and denounce the injustices endured by migrants in the workplace or in the society at large. The largest concentration of Puerto Ricans was in the eastern section of Harlem which soon became known as Spanish Harlem, or "El Barrio." After the postwar Great Migration years, Puerto Ricans began to concentrate in the South Bronx and the Williamsburg sections of Brooklyn later known as "Los Sures" (the southern section).

Among the migrants there were a large number of displaced agricultural workers, but there were also factory workers, skilled artisans, businessmen, professionals, students, writers, and artists. Regarding the various types of occupations held by Puerto Rican migrants during the early stages of migration, Rodríguez stressed the importance of recognizing "the diversity and richness of the migrant population" (1989, 2). Rodríguez also noted, "Migrants brought nontransferable skills" and "transferable skills that were not transferred" (1989, 2), statements that underscored the predicament for newcomers; they had "to accept whatever jobs were available" (Handlin, 1959, 70). The working-class nature of Puerto Rican migration was, therefore, unquestionable, with a large representation in the manufacturing sector, agricultural employment, and service areas. The overrepresentation of Puerto Rican workers in semiskilled, low-wage manufacturing and agricultural employment was not to change until the 1980s (see Rivera-Batiz and Santiago 1994; Chapter 5).

Women migrants were a major source of labor for New York's garment industry. This particular industry not only reflected a gendered division of labor but also historically had relied on the labor of various immigrant groups, such as Jewish and Eastern European women, and mirrored the prevalent ethnic and racial pecking order in US society at a given period. White workers, in particular, were resistant to letting Puerto Rican women into the International Ladies' Garment Workers' Union (ILGWU), and when they did, they denied them equal access to work in the best shops or leadership positions (Ortiz 1996). Other sectors of women's employment were meatpacking, tobacco, and confectionery work, domestic service, clerical work, and other kinds of manufacturing and service industry jobs. Puerto Rican women who did not work outside the home frequently engaged in child care, home-based needlework, or took in boarders to contribute to the household income. The few migrants with higher levels of education held positions as teachers, librarians, nuns, social and health workers, and wrote for newspapers. Sánchez Korrol ([1983] 1994) emphasized the diversity and importance of women's "informal networks" to the early community, since they facilitated the exchange of vital information about finding housing, employment, schools for their children, medical and social services, and places to shop or to find cultural enrichment or social entertainment.

During the 1920s important Puerto Rican organizations emerged that fostered a sense of community cohesiveness and facilitated the early migrants' incorporation into the host society. The Hermandad Puertorriqueña en América (Porto Rican Brotherhood of America) was founded in 1923 to promote "unity, brotherhood and mutual aid among Puerto Ricans" (Sánchez Korrol [1983] 1994, 147). Coming out of this organization was the idea of establishing an umbrella federation for different Latino nationalities to combine their goals and efforts in a unified front. In this way, they could have a more effective voice around pressing community issues. One issue was the negative image and coverage Puerto Ricans received in the mainstream press. Promoting this kind of unity also was important in dealing with civil rights violations and other injustices perpetrated against community members. These concerns were also behind the creation of the Liga Puertorriqueña e Hispana (Puerto Rican and Hispanic League) in 1927. The *Liga* initiated the publication of a biweekly bulletin, which lasted for six years. The bulletin was an informative educational tool and included social commentary on a variety of community-related issues.

A few workers' organizations also emerged during this period. Two of the most active were Alianza Obrera (Workers' Alliance) and Ateneo Obrero (Workers' Atheneum). Many hometown clubs, another way of fostering communal ties, were established in New York and other cities with large concentrations of Puerto Ricans. The New York clubs included the Club Caborrojeño, Mayagüezanos Ausentes, and Hijos de Camuy, all of them bearing the name of a Puerto Rican town (see Sánchez Korrol [1983] 1994). They provided a social and cultural atmosphere for migrants to feel at home and share their experiences with others. In addition, the clubs helped sustain their connections with the Puerto Rican homeland.

The proliferation of small businesses, a characteristic of New York City's ethnic enclaves, occurred also in Puerto Rican neighborhoods. The Puerto Rican Merchants' Association was founded in the 1940s to promote and protect the interests of small businesses. Small entrepreneurs started bodegas, restaurants, travel agencies, banks and finance companies, record stores, beauty parlors, barber shops, auto dealerships, dry cleaners, clothing stores, moving companies, and *botánicas* (shops that sold herbal remedies). The latter are very common in Puerto Rico, so their presence in the US barrios made available to migrants the popular herbal remedies and other traditional concoctions and recipes to deal with physical or emotional ailments.

As we discuss in Chapter 7, the writings of grassroots activists and journalists Bernardo Vega and Jesús Colón, who migrated to New York in 1916 and 1918 respectively, provided a detailed record of this earlier stage of community formation, describing the many pioneer organizations and newspapers that were created during those years, the array of functions they served, and their most prominent leaders. These outlets facilitated the process of settlement and adaptation of a primarily working-class migrant community to a culturally different and largely unwelcoming environment. They also contributed to enriching the migrants' cultural and social life, engaging them in issues that influenced their collective well-being, and helped strengthen communal ties.

The Poverty-Stricken Island

Conditions in Puerto Rico during the years before and after the Great Depression were precarious, to say the least, in both economic and social terms. The sugar plantation economy that developed during the early years of the US regime significantly changed the lives of the Puerto Rican working class. The decline of production in the coffee haciendas, in particular, created a surplus of unemployed rural workers that could not be absorbed by the jobs generated by the now-US-controlled sugar industry or by the new tobacco and needle industries. The seasonal nature of work in the monopolizing sugar industry intensified the precariousness of employment for agricultural workers and was also a major catalyst for migration from mountain to coastal and urban areas, to the slums of the island's capital of San Juan, or to the United States. The situation deteriorated even further when sugar and tobacco production continued to decline in the early 1920s, as the prices of these products in the international market began to plummet. This downturn in local production foreshadowed the broader economic crisis that was to come in 1929 with the Great Depression. As if dreadful economic conditions were not enough, the forces of nature brought added desolation to Puerto Rico with two devastating hurricanes: San Felipe in 1928 and San Ciprián in 1932.

The island's socioeconomic plight during the Great Depression years was captured in the song "Lamento borincano" (A Puerto Rican Peasant's Lament, also known as "El Jibarito"), written by Puerto Rico's most famous composer, Rafael Hernández. The song, which dramatized the dismal conditions of the composer's poverty-stricken homeland, touched the hearts and souls of the Puerto Rican people. It recounted the tale of a peasant riding his mare to the city's market, hopeful that he could sell his scant agricultural produce in order to support his family. But the *jibarito* (peasant) did not find any buyers and was forced to return home empty-handed, overwhelmed by sadness and hope-lessness, lamenting his fate, and wondering what the future would bring to the country, to his children, to his home. The sense of hopelessness in the song's lyrics "todo está desierto y el pueblo está muerto de necesidad" (everything is barren and the people are dying of deprivation), accompanied by the poignant image of the destitute Puerto Rican peasant, will be forever ingrained in the minds of the generations of Puerto Ricans that witnessed the wretched socio-economic conditions and despair that engulfed the island during those years. Perhaps even more so, it was meaningful to those who migrated in the hope of a better future in the United States. Rafael Hernández was one of those mi-grants (see Chapter 7).

Once again, after three decades of US rule, Puerto Rico found itself a neg-lected colony, just like it had been during the first three centuries of Spanish rule. The capitalist economic collapse that shattered the lives of so many workers in the United States and other parts of the world during the Great De-pression was only magnified in the deplorable socioeconomic conditions that prevailed in the Puerto Rico of the 1930s and 1940s. *Porto Rico: A Broken Pledge* (1931), by Bailey W. Diffie and Justine Whitfield Diffie, captured the realities that burdened the majority of Puerto Ricans then. The authors searched for answers to explain why, after more than three decades of US rule, the government had failed to reduce poverty or significantly change the stan-dard of living of the masses. They concluded that the answers were rooted in the conditions created by colonialism and imperialist rule:

> The problem of the United States in Porto Rico, in the opinion of the authors, revolves itself into one question: can we govern the Island for its own best interests? As long as the United States Government has the ultimate word in policies, the Island will be governed for the good of those interests consid-ered "American." Porto Rico is at once the perfect example of what eco-nomic imperialism does for a country and of the attitude of the imperialist to-wards that country. . . . Its land owned by absentee capital; its political rights resting in the hands of the United States Government; its people in the depths of deprivation, it has been told to help itself. That is the "remedy" which the President [Hoover] prescribes—imperialism's answer to problems of its own creation! No solution further than a policy followed for the last thirty-three years—a policy which has not solved Porto Rico's problems. Porto Rico can hope for no relief under the existing system. (220)

Diffie and Diffie's chastising assessment of the island's state of affairs contradicted President Herbert Hoover's statement to the press about being "well satisfied" with the conditions he found in Puerto Rico after a brief visit in 1931. That the US president said this in the midst of the Great Depression, which was having severe consequences in his own country, is an indication of the neglect and indifference that most US officials have shown toward Puerto Rico through the years. A decade later, prosperity was still an illusive dream for Puerto Ricans. The island's last appointed North American governor, Rexford Guy Tugwell, a trusted and influential member of President Franklin Delano Roosevelt's New Deal Brain Trust, who was governor from 1941 to 1946, referred to the island as "the stricken land" in a book that underscored Puerto Rico's socioeconomic and political predicament during those years, and that recounted the efforts of his administration to turn things around (Tugwell 1947).

But turning things around in an island engulfed by poverty was also a daunting challenge for a new generation of liberal Puerto Rican leaders, most of them educated in the United States, who made their presence felt on the island's political scene. They shared the view that relying on short-term federal emergency assistance was not sufficient to deal with the economic crisis and with the hold that US corporations had over Puerto Rico's land and its overall agricultural economy. Instead, they were envisioning a wide-ranging project of national reconstruction. Governor Tugwell, the first North American governor of Puerto Rico to openly acknowledge that several decades of US presence had had little effect in changing the dire social and economic conditions endured by most of the island's population, reached out to this younger generation in seeking solutions to some of the major problems. Poverty was still high, unemployment and underemployment remained unchecked, malnutrition and tropical diseases had deleterious consequences on the population's welfare and kept mortality rates high, the network of schools, hospitals, and other service institutions was still limited, and most agricultural land was concentrated in the hands of a few US corporations and creole landowners.

Tugwell's first visit to Puerto Rico was in 1934, when he was an assistant secretary of agriculture, seven years before his appointment to the island's governorship. This visit allowed him to learn firsthand of the country's conditions and to engage in discussions with Puerto Rican political leaders, reaching out to those with progressive views who were pushing for social and political reforms. Some of the New Deal emergency measures aimed at getting the United States out of the depression had been transferred to Puerto Rico, where the Puerto Rico Emergency Relief Administration (PRERA), a federal agency popularly known as "la Prera," was established in 1933. The PRERA offered food and other essentials to the most indigent Puerto Ricans but represented just a provisional response to serious conditions requiring more permanent solutions.

Among the new leaders was Carlos Chardón, an outspoken advocate of radical reforms, including the government's taking land away from large absentee corporate landowners to redistribute among small Puerto Rican farmers and workers. At the time, Chardón was the chancellor at the University of Puerto Rico, the country's largest university. In order to develop a comprehensive reconstruction plan, Chardón enlisted the collaboration of other local leaders, among them Luis Muñoz Marín, the son of the former autonomist leader Luis Muñoz Rivera. Muñoz Marín was then serving in the island's Senate as a member of the Liberal Party and was well connected with members of the US Congress and of the Roosevelt administration.[17] Chardón, Muñoz Marín, and others articulated a plan for getting the country out of its economic crisis and accelerating the process of national reconstruction. It was in 1934, the year of Tugwell's visit to Puerto Rico, that what was named the Plan Chardón (Chardón Project) was being formulated.

The Plan Chardón was the first major initiative coming out of a new generation of native politicians, policymakers, and technocrats clearly committed to significant social and economic change. The document noted: "The economic problem of Puerto Rico, in so far as the bulk of the people is concerned, may be reduced to the simple term of progressive landlessness, chronic unemployment and implacable growth of the population" (Maldonado 1997, 36). Calling for land reform and economic reconstruction, the plan stressed the need to reduce population growth on the island (12). Some of the measures relied on the active involvement and support of the state to carry on the massive reconstruction initiative. The measures proposed included the government's expropriation and purchasing of lands from large landowners, to be divided in parcels and distributed among small farmers. Other proposals included the creation of a state-owned cement company to build government buildings and public housing, and putting controls on the levels of sugar production, the prices paid to sugar growers by the corporations, and on the salaries of sugar industry workers. As a result of these proposals, in 1935 the Roosevelt administration authorized the creation of another federal agency—the Puerto Rico Reconstruction Administration (PRRA)—and placed at its helm another North American New Deal liberal, Ernest Gruening. Prior to this appointment, Gruening had been in charge of the US Department of the Interior's Territories and Insular Possessions Division, so he was quite familiar with Puerto Rico's problems. PRRA tried to implement some of the proposals in the Plan Chardón and stimulate the economy by expanding employment in the public sector. This project provided the initial steps for the process of change that was to overtake the island during the 1940s and 1950s.

Between Reform and Revolution

While the majority of Puerto Rico's population was dealing with basic survival issues, two major developments were overtaking the political arena. Political realignments in Puerto Rico during the 1930s were to influence US policies and shift the balance of power among the major local political parties during the decades that followed. Since the early years of the US occupation, island politics had been controlled by the opportunistic alliances between the three major parties—Unionists, Republicans, and Socialists—and the political personalism and patronage practices of their longtime leaders. But the island's political landscape was about to take a major turn.[18]

First, under the leadership of Pedro Albizu Campos, a charismatic Harvard-educated mulatto lawyer, the Partido Nacionalista Puertorriqueño (PN, Puerto Rican Nationalist Party), originally founded in 1922 after the Unionist Party had drifted away from supporting independence, was revitalized in 1930 as the main front of local opposition to US colonialism. Second, a populist political movement was also taking shape; it presented itself as a new and more viable political option for change, offering the poverty-stricken peasantry and other working-class Puerto Ricans the dream of *"pan, tierra, y libertad"* (bread, land, and liberty). The leader of what became, in 1938, the Partido Popular Democrático (PPD, Popular Democratic Party), also known as the Populares, was Luis Muñoz Marín. The PPD had been formed after Muñoz Marín and the left wing of the Partido Liberal (former Unionists) were expelled from this organization because of their strong opposition to the party's decision to eliminate the independence option from its platform.

Puerto Rican Nationalists began to gain visibility by denouncing the US imperialist presence in Puerto Rico; they found a receptive audience among some members of the island's intellectual elite and the struggling working class. Albizu's political rhetoric denounced the illegality of the Treaty of Paris that had forced Spain to cede an autonomous Puerto Rico to the United States. He also condemned the usurping of Puerto Rican land and the exploitation of workers by the large North American sugar corporations, and lamented the decline of the creole propertied class. He called for the liberation of Puerto Rico through any means, including armed struggle. The Nationalists' main credo was "La patria es valor y sacrificio" (the Motherland signifies courage and sacrifice). The party organized the paramilitary group Cadetes de la República (Cadets of the Republic), whose members marched in political rallies dressed in military garb. The group was inspired by the Sinn Fein Irish liberation movement (see Silén 1996), which fought against British colonialism and eventually secured the creation of the Irish Republic in 1921.

Despite its initial growing appeal, the Nationalist Party had a conservative and essentialist vision of Puerto Rico as a Catholic Hispanic country struggling against the colonizing forces of Americanization and seeking to recover "the nation of landowners" that existed prior to the arrival of the North American troops. This particular vision did not resonate with the impoverished Puerto Rican masses, who believed that the Spanish past, with all its social and political divisions—including those between the landowning hacendado class and the landless peasants—was not a utopia to return to. The Nationalist movement, however, was more successful in planting the roots for the strong cultural nationalism that was to be subsequently reaffirmed by Puerto Rico's intellectual elite, and ultimately spill over to other sectors of the population intent on resisting colonialism and the forces of Americanization. Even those

Puerto Ricans currently favoring statehood for Puerto Rico, who are often referred to as "pitiyanquis" (an adaptation of the French "petit yankee"), endorse an *"estadidad jíbara"* (nativist statehood), rejecting assimilation into Anglo-American culture and affirming their belief that Puerto Rico's cultural and linguistic distinctiveness and patrimony have to be preserved under this status.

The increasing Nationalist activism in Puerto Rico from the 1930s to the 1950s and the threat to the United States of having the island's political situation develop into another Ireland contributed to the determination of both federal and local authorities to destroy the party and its leaders. A sustained campaign of persecution, blacklisting, and violent confrontations between Nationalists and the Puerto Rican police sealed the fate of the movement. The killing of four Nationalist University of Puerto Rico students by the Río Piedras police in October 1935 pushed members of the party to seek retribution in the month of February 1936 by assassinating the North American chief of the island's police force, Colonel Francis Riggs. Two Nationalists, Hiram Rosado and Elías Beauchamp, were arrested for the murder, taken to police headquarters, and, in retaliation, shot to death while they were under police custody.

Colonel Riggs was an old friend of Blanton Winship, the island's US-appointed governor at the time. Without hesitation, Governor Winship immediately unleashed a series of repressive measures carried out systematically by US and Puerto Rican officials and government agencies, all aimed at eradicating the Nationalist Party. Albizu and some of his followers were arrested and accused of conspiring against the United States. His first trial, which had a majority of Puerto Rican jurors, ended in a hung jury. A new jury composed mostly of North Americans in his second trial found Albizu guilty; he spent the next decade of his life in a federal prison in Atlanta, Georgia.

Albizu's imprisonment did not deter the Nationalists from continuing their political activities. In 1937, the Puerto Rican police denied permission to the party to hold a rally in the southern city of Ponce, Albizu's birthplace. The event, organized to commemorate the abolition of slavery, was to be on Palm Sunday. Nationalists refused to cancel the rally, and government authorities mobilized the police. During the scheduled demonstration, shooting broke out, leaving nineteen Nationalists and two policemen dead, and close to a hundred people injured. This incident was later to be known as la Masacre de Ponce (Ponce Massacre).

The escalating political violence in Puerto Rico and the international denunciations of colonial oppression against the United States led the US Congress to consider granting independence to Puerto Rico. The violence of those years was even characterized as "dynamite on our doorstep" in the title of a popular book written by a North American who went to Puerto Rico in 1936 to teach English (Brown 1945). US Senator Willard Tydings enlisted Ernest Gruening's help in introducing a bill to let Puerto Ricans decide if they wanted independence from the United States. The proposed Tydings Bill, however, did not offer any economic benefits for Puerto Rico during the transition to independence and eventually faded, but not without causing serious divisions and realignments within the local political parties.[19]

The politically charged environment made it easier for the reform movement initiated by Muñoz Marín and his followers to gain popular support. What the Populares were proposing would indeed "revolutionize" the country, but this was couched as a "peaceful revolution," a contrast from the armed struggle being espoused by the Nationalists.

Muñoz Marín's charismatic and populist style of campaigning brought him to the desolate Puerto Rican countryside, where he was in direct contact with the poor peasantry and learned about their conditions and needs. He emphasized his connection with the impoverished peasant by choosing the image

Political campaign photo of Luis Muñoz Marín in the 1940s with a superimposed image of a Puerto Rican *jíbaro*. Records of the Office of the Government of Puerto Rico in the United States, Centro de Estudios Puertorriqueños Library and Archives, Hunter College.

Vergüenza Contra Dinero (Dignity Versus Money): An anonymous 1940 campaign poster bearing the logo of the Partido Popular Democrático (Popular Democratic Party) and showing a *jíbaro* with a typical straw hat and the words "Bread-Land-Liberty." Below the image is the caption "Voting like this you elect an honest and decent government that will remove hunger and misery from all of our homes." Reprinted with author's permission from Teresa Tió, *El Cartel en Puerto Rico* (Mexico City: Pearson Educación, 2003), 38.

of a *jíbaro* with a straw hat as the symbol of his new party and the slogan "Jalda arriba va avanzando el popular" (the Populares are moving uphill and forging ahead), which signified the push for meaningful change. The leader persuaded peasants not to "sell" their vote to the old political parties and to believe that each vote, even the votes of people who could not write or read, was important and could give the PPD the opportunity to transform Puerto Rican society.

The PPD campaigned vigorously for land reform by limiting to five hundred acres the amount of land that any corporation or landowner could own and by distributing free *parcelas* (land parcels) to the poor. The party also made a pledge to bring running water and electricity to every home, even those in isolated rural areas, make food and health services available for the indigent, build more public schools and provide better access to higher education, and improve the country's infrastructure to support economic development. All these promises resonated with the masses, who were tired of the political alliances among the old political parties that benefited only their leaders and the privileged elites.

Many of Muñoz Marín's early proposals reflected the socialist and proindependence ideals of his youth and were characteristic of the social policies of a welfare state. However, he modified his views because of the limitations and the political compromises he had to make in order to secure the support of the US Congress and other officials to carry out the envisioned socioeconomic and political reforms (see García Passalacqua 1996). More than anything else, this meant believing and accepting that without the continuation of US assistance and private investment capital, the PPD would not be able to execute its ambitious agenda to modernize and transform Puerto Rican society.

Although the PPD did not gain an outright win in the first election in which it participated, in 1940, the close results gave the Populares enough political power and control of Puerto Rico's legislature to start trampling over the opposition and take control of local politics. Their victory placed Muñoz Marín at the head of the Puerto Rican Senate and gave a mortal blow to the grip that the old parties had had on island politics for over two decades and to their shady coalitions. President Roosevelt's 1941 appointment of Rexford Tugwell as Puerto Rico's governor made it possible for the younger generation of local politicians to push their reform proposals and feel hopeful about securing changes in the island's relationship with the United States. But Governor Tugwell's term was not devoid of controversy. He was perceived by the local political opposition to be a supporter of the PPD's agenda. Some members of Congress considered his reform proposals to be too socialistic because of their heavy reliance on state support. Clearly Tugwell's administration was an important period for Puerto Rican society, although there is no doubt that the bulk of the reforms that were enacted during his term could not have happened without the major role played by the new PPD's political leadership. Decades later, Tugwell's governorship was hailed as "the administration of a revolution" (Goodsell 1965), and he was commended for his role in providing a "turning point from colonial misery and decay to self-government and astounding economic progress," which perhaps would not have come to fruition if it were not for his efforts "in breaking through established routines and his willingness to foster native forces that were ready to take over" (Friedrich 1965, vii–viii). Unquestionably, Tugwell was the most receptive and successful of a long line of North American appointed governors of Puerto Rico, but the driving forces that eventually carried out the country's socioeconomic and political transformation of the 1940s and 1950s were in the hands of Muñoz Marín and his inner circle of policy advisers and technocrats.

Toward the end of his tenure, Tugwell recommended to President Harry Truman that he appoint a Puerto Rican to succeed him as governor. The president accepted the recommendation and in 1946 appointed Jesús T. Piñeiro, a member of the PPD, as the island's first Puerto Rican governor. Another major US concession was the passage of a law allowing Puerto Rican voters to elect their own governor in 1948, for the first time. As the PPD's candidate for the governorship, Muñoz Marín was elected to the post by an overwhelming 61.2 percent of the voters.

By the end of the 1940s, Muñoz Marín's position regarding Puerto Rico's political status had shifted considerably from his younger years, when he was an ardent defender of independence. After graduating from Georgetown University he had worked as a journalist, wrote poetry, and moved to New York's Greenwich Village with his North American poet and journalist wife Muna

Lee. During those years, Muñoz Marín wrote for various US newspapers and had been critical of North American colonialism.[20] He shuttled between New York, Washington, DC, and Puerto Rico for most of the 1920s. In 1930 he finally settled on the island in order to follow in his father's footsteps and pursue a career in politics. Only a few years after his return, Muñoz Marín began to publicly modify his views about Puerto Rico's relationship with the United States. He continued to defend his socially progressive positions but started to question the feasibility of achieving his social and economic goals for the island without the financial support of the United States. Thus, from the PPD's inception, its political agenda did not attempt to challenge US jurisdiction over Puerto Rico, as the Nationalists did. Instead, the Populares formulated a vision for a new political arrangement that would guarantee self-government but allow the United States to maintain territorial and military control over Puerto Rico, allow Puerto Rico to continue to receive the flow of federal assistance, and attract US investors.

Since the early years of occupation, island political leaders had been lobbying the US Congress to give Puerto Rico a larger degree of self-government. The idea for a new political status labeled "Estado Libre Asociado (ELA)" and modeled after the Free State of Ireland had floated around congressional corridors since the early 1920s.[21] This old political formula was revived by the Populares seeking an innovative solution to the denunciations of colonialism against the United States made by Nationalists and other independence supporters. Under the proposal for an Estado Libre Asociado, to be officially known as "Commonwealth" in English, Puerto Rico was to be granted the right to enact its own constitution but would remain a territory "in permanent union with the United States." This meant that the US Congress and the Pentagon were not willing to relinquish their territorial control over the island, and Puerto Rico would not have its own citizenship or enjoy the international rights accorded to a sovereign state. Thus when applied to Puerto Rico, the term "Commonwealth" may be considered a misnomer, since it has little relationship to the Commonwealth agreement established by the British government with some of its former colonies.

Several decades earlier, Pedro Albizu Campos, the main leader of the Nationalist movement, had been found guilty of conspiring against the US government in Puerto Rico and, along with many of his closest allies, condemned to a federal prison in 1936. It has been well documented that during almost a decade-long incarceration in an Atlanta prison, he was subjected to mistreatment and torture, including radiation experiments (Maldonado-Denis 1972; Ferrao 1990; Silén 1976). These caused Albizu to develop severe health problems, notably the stroke that eventually shortened his life.

The sensationalist media coverage of the violent incidents involving clashes between Puerto Rican Nationalists and government authorities in Puerto Rico and the United States reached its peak during the 1950s. On October 30, 1950, there was a Nationalist revolt that began in Puerto Rico's mountain town of Jayuya and spread to a few other island municipalities, prompting Governor Muñoz Marín to mobilize the National Guard. That same day there was a shooting at the entrance to La Fortaleza, the governor's official residence, an incident that ended with the death of five Nationalists. Two days later, there was an attempt to assassinate President Harry Truman when two party members tried to shoot their way into Blair House, his Washington, DC, temporary residence at the time. One of the perpetrators, Oscar Collazo, was arrested and the other, Griselio Torresola, was killed. A North American security guard also was killed during this attempt. Albizu was arrested, accused of fostering subversive activities against the government, and, for the second time, condemned to a long prison sentence. He was pardoned by Governor Muñoz Marín in 1953 but was arrested and sent to prison again in 1954 after three armed Nationalists entered the chambers of the US House of Representatives and started shooting. Five members of Congress were injured. Nationalists Lolita Lebrón, Andrés Figueroa Cordero, and Irving Collazo were arrested for the attack on Congress and spent the next three decades of their lives in a federal prison. Albizu, who was already imprisoned in Puerto Rico, suffered a stroke, which caused him some paralysis. Because of his deteriorating health, he was pardoned by Muñoz Marín again, in 1965, and died in a hospital a few months later.

The incidents involving Puerto Rican Nationalists not only drew international attention to Puerto Rico's colonial condition but also increased negative feelings from the wider US population toward the growing presence of Puerto Ricans during the peak years of the Great Migration. In order to deal with the backlash produced by these incidents, US and Puerto Rican authorities initiated an all-out offensive to discredit and crush the Nationalist movement. Puerto Rican Nationalists were summarily labeled fanatics and terrorists by the media, and their use of violence was swiftly condemned by US officials and Puerto Rico's Commonwealth government. Officially sanctioned surveillance and blacklisting against Puerto Rican Nationalists intensified as a result of these incidents, and these practices were also applied indiscriminately to other independence advocates. The Ley de la Mordaza (Gag Law), enacted by the Puerto Rican legislature in 1948, basically prohibited any expression of dissent challenging US authority over Puerto Rico or perceived to be a threat to the stability of the insular government. This law was used to justify Albizu's incarceration and that of his supporters (Acosta 1987, 1993).

The US position of wanting to keep territorial jurisdiction over Puerto Rico was directly linked to its strategic military importance in the Caribbean region and the rest of the hemisphere, a role that had intensified during World War II, the subsequent Cold War period, and the post–Cuban Revolution years. What this meant in simpler terms was that the various branches of the US armed forces have been infamous for interfering with any congressional proposals for

Mass arrests of suspected Puerto Rican Nationalists by the police and National Guard during the 1950 revolt that began in the town of Jayuya. The Ruth M. Reynolds Collection, Centro de Estudios Puertorriqueños Library and Archives, Hunter College.

granting more autonomy to Puerto Rico or putting an end to its colonial status. By settling for the limited Commonwealth arrangement, the leadership of the PPD remained hopeful that this status would eventually evolve into the creation of a real "free state" without severing the island's economic and military "association" with the United States. Those critical of the Commonwealth argued that the purported "new" status was nothing new. Its most ardent critics described it as a fiction, a farce, or a meaningless cosmetic makeover of the colonial relationship that did not remove some of the basic stipulations or limitations of the Foraker and Jones Acts, or the overriding power of the US Congress over Puerto Rico (Géigel Polanco 1972; Maldonado-Denis 1972). Although the colonial nature of the Commonwealth is now acknowledged by a large majority of Puerto Ricans, that was not the case for many decades after its creation.

A retrospective analysis of this outcome raises a fundamental question: Why did Luis Muñoz Marín accept such an imperfect political status compromise when his party had the overwhelming support of the great majority of Puerto Ricans, the only time in the island's history when any politician has been able to command such a popular mandate? The answer lies, at least partially, in the weight of family history. Just like his father, Luis Muñoz Rivera, a few decades earlier, Muñoz Marín believed that the benefits of maintaining the links with the colonial metropolis outweighed those of Puerto Rico's being a sovereign state. Thus, he did not use his populist movement to challenge or denounce US colonial authority. Instead, he succumbed to practicing the politics of *posibilismo*, that is, striving to achieve only those goals that were perceived within the realm of real possibilities or settling for what were perceived as pragmatic alternatives to the colonial condition. With his vision for the political future of Puerto Rico, Muñoz Marín was, indeed, choosing the ambiguity of autonomy with the United States rather than the unpredictable consequences and irrevocability of independence without it. Once again, the Puerto Rican political elites were settling for a limited share of political power and maintaining the country's dependence on the colonial metropolis, rather than envisioning a national sustainable development project that responded to the needs and self-interests of the Puerto Rican people or that envisioned the island's independence.

This snapshot of the socioeconomic and political conditions of Puerto Rico sets the stage for the events that accelerated the pace of migration to the United States during the 1940s and 1950s.

From the Steamship *Embarcados* to the Transnational *Guagua Aérea*

Until the 1940s, the principal mode of transportation for Puerto Ricans to travel to the United States was the steamship. A few of the ships were given familiar Puerto Rican names, including those of island towns—*Borinquen, San Juan, Ponce, Coamo*. The steamship *Marine Tiger* was so identified with transporting Puerto Rican migrants during the early years that for a while Puerto Ricans were often called the "Marine Tigers." The Puerto Rican expression *"se embarcó"* (s/he took a ship) was the commonly used phrase to refer to someone leaving the island for the United States. The expression continued to be used even after air travel became the primary mode of transportation.

Earlier in this chapter we documented the largely neglected pioneer migrations of Puerto Ricans to the United States prior to the mid-twentieth-century Great Migration. The truth is that for many decades, Puerto Rican migration was primarily identified with the mass exodus to the United States in the aftermath of World War II. That is partially explained by the fact that Puerto Ricans were the first and, to this date, the largest airborne group of migrants to come to the United States. As air travel became available in the 1940s and the jet engine was introduced in the early 1960s, the character of the migratory movements of workers from developing countries seeking employment in the highly industrialized societies like the United States began to change. In Puerto Rico's case, US airlines were encouraged by government authorities to introduce special low-fare flights from San Juan to New York. One of the airline commercials luring Puerto Ricans to the metropolis coined the slogan "En el Jet 55, a Nueva York en un brinco" (Board Flight 55 and take a leap to New York) for a low fare of fifty-five dollars. Fifty-five referred to both the flight number and the low-cost fare. As the Puerto Rican migrant population continued to spread to other major US cities like Chicago and Philadelphia, low fares were extended to those destinations as well.

Puerto Ricans came from a country in the Americas and, like Mexicans and other Latino groups in their migratory experience, there were historical events and relations that connected the United States with their respective countries of origin. This was a major deviation from the patterns established by prior immigrants, the vast majority of whom had come to North American shores from a distant Europe or Asia, leaving behind their native countries and facing limited possibilities of ever going back again. For Puerto Ricans, who were already US citizens, the geographic proximity between the island and the continent and the access to air travel created a transnational bridge that fostered bidirectional cultural, socioeconomic, and political exchanges between both communities. This uninterrupted *"ir y venir"* (back and forth movement) that Puerto Ricans have with their homeland has introduced a new model of immigrant assimilation and relationship to Anglo-American society that differs from the traditional "melting pot" ideology. Currently, a more flexible multicultural perspective is taking hold; it is based on an individual's capacity to function in more than one culture and language and a sense of identity that straddles different cultural spaces *"aquí y allá"* (here and there). US Puerto Ricans share a strong sense of ethnic identity, whether they are first-generation migrants or were born or raised in the United States. But whether this is a symbolic or an actual connection to the homeland does not preclude them from valuing their rights as US citizens or from a sense of affiliation to North American society.

Puerto Ricans often use the popular phrase *"brincando el charco"* (jumping over the puddle) to reflect the normality of a nation constantly transcending its island borders *"para buscárselas"* (to seek fortune) in numerous US cities and localities. Similarly, some Puerto Ricans continue to return to the island after spending some portion of their lives in the United States, although except for a few years in the late 1960s and early 1970s, the rate of reverse migration to the island was much lower than the number of those emigrating to the metropolis (Hernández 1967; see also Chapter 4).

Prominent Puerto Rican author Luis Rafael Sánchez, who has spent many years living between Puerto Rico and New York, invented the metaphor *"la guagua aérea"* (the airbus). Sánchez described Puerto Rico as a nation "flotante entre dos puertos de contrabandear esperanzas" (floating and smuggling hopes between two ports) (Sánchez 1994, 22). Others have referred to Puerto Ricans as straddling two cultures and languages (Flores 2000) or an island constantly on the move or caught up in a *vaivén* (coming and going; fluctuation) (Duany 2002). There is no disagreement that the commuting relationship between the island and the metropolis constantly introduces new realities and patterns, some of which are now quite evident, others are in flux, and some, as we will see in later chapters, cannot be predicted with any comfortable degree of certainty.

Notes

1. For one of the most complete sources of biographical information about Betances, see Félix Ojeda Reyes, *El desterrrado de París: Biografía del Doctor Ramón Emeterio Betances* (San Juan, PR: Ediciones Puerto, 2001).

2. One of the best-documented accounts of the events surrounding the Grito de Lares is found in Olga Jiménez de Wagenheim, *Puerto Rico's Revolt for Independence: El Grito de Lares* (Boulder: Westview, 1985).

3. See Eugenio María de Hostos, "Manifiesto de la Liga de Patriotas Puertorriqueños," *Patria*, September 10, 1898. Most of Hostos's writings about the struggle for independence have been collected in Eugenio María de Hostos, *América: La lucha por la libertad*, ed. Manuel Maldonado Denis (México: Siglo Ventiuno, 1980).

4. For an extensive analysis of Martí's writings about *nuestra América*, see Phillip S. Foner, *Our America by José Martí* (New York: Monthly Review Press, 1977); Andrés Sorel, ed., *José Martí en los Estados Unidos* (Madrid: Alianza Editorial, 1968); and Jeffrey Belnap and Raúl Fernández, eds., *José Martí's "Our America": From National to Hemispheric Cultural Studies* (Durham, NC: Duke University Press, 1998).

5. For a detailed discussion of the activities of the *tabaqueros* in Puerto Rico, see Angel Quintero Rivera, "Socialista y tabaquero: La proletarización de los artesanos," *Sin Nombre* 8.4 (1978); and Gervasio García and Angel Quintero Rivera, *Desafío y solidaridad: Breve historia del movimiento obrero puertorriqueño* (Río Piedras, PR: Ediciones Huracán, 1982). Bernardo Vega mentioned the involvement of Flor Baerga and other *tabaqueros* in the separatist movement in his *Memoirs of Bernardo Vega*, ed. César Andreu Iglesias (New York: Monthly Review Press, 1984), first published in Spanish as *Memorias de Bernardo Vega* (Río Piedras, PR: Ediciones Huracán, 1977).

6. Some of Figueroa's writings in *Patria* include the six-part essay "La verdad de la historia," *Patria*, March 19, 1892, April 3, 1892, April 16, 1892, May 21, 1892, June 11, 1892, and July 2, 1892. Also see Josefina Toledo, *Sotero Figueroa, Editor de Patria* (La Habana: Editorial Letras Cubanas, 1985); and Edgardo Meléndez, *Puerto Rico en Patria* (Río Piedras, PR: Editorial Edil, 1996).

7. For a more detailed account of Inocencia Martínez de Figueroa's contributions to the separatist movement and to the founding of the Club Mercedes Varona, see "Síntesis biográfica de Inocencia Martínez Santaella," in Josefina Toledo, *Sotero Figueroa, Editor de Patria: Apuntes para una biografía* (La Habana: Editorial Letras Cubanas, 1985), 119–151. Mercedes Varona was a Cuban separatist killed in 1870 in a confrontation with Spanish troops during the Ten Years' War.

8. A complete collection of Lola Rodríguez de Tió is available in *Obras completas*, vols. 1–4 (San Juan: Instituto de Cultura Puertorriqueña, 1968).

9. Roberto H. Todd made this claim in *La invasión americana: Cómo surgió la idea de traer la guerra a Puerto Rico* (San Juan: Cantero Fernández, 1939). Todd also wrote a long essay about Henna. See Roberto H. Todd, *José Julio Henna, 1848–1924* (San Juan: Cantero Fernández, 1930).

10. For a collection of Betances's writings, see Carlos M. Rama, ed. *Las Antillas para los antillanos* (San Juan: Instituto de Cultura Puertorriqueña, 1975).

11. For a biography of Schomburg see Victoria Ortiz, "Arthur Schomburg: A Biographic Essay," in *The Legacy of Arthur Arturo Schomburg: A Celebration of the Past, A Vision for the Future* (New York: Schomburg Center for Black Culture, 1986); Elinor Des Verney Sinnette, *Arthur Alfonso Schomburg: Black Bibliophile and Collector* (Detroit: New York Public Library and Wayne University Press, 1989); and Flor Piñeiro de Rivera, *Arturo Schomburg: Un puertorriqueño descubre el legado histórico del negro* (San Juan: Centro de Estudios Avanzados de Puerto Rico y el Caribe, 1989).

12. See Frank Freidel, *The Splendid Little War* (Boston: Little, Brown, 1958).

13. The name "Porto Rico" was adopted by the US colonial government as the official name for the island and had been used as such in world maps of earlier periods. The official name was not changed to Puerto Rico until the late 1930s.

14. For detailed information about women's employment during this period, see Caroline Manning, *The Employment of Women in Porto Rico* (Washington, DC: Government Printing Office, 1934). For a focus on employment in the needle industries, see María del Carmen Baerga, ed., *Género y trabajo: La industria de la aguja en Puerto Rico y el Caribe* (San Juan: Editorial de la Universidad de Puerto Rico, 1993).

15. The Foraker Act was named after Joseph Foraker, the US senator from Ohio who introduced the bill in Congress on January 9, 1900. The Jones Act was named after Representative William Jones of Virginia. A more detailed discussion of the Foraker and Jones Act can be found in Benjamin B. Ringer, *"We the People" and Others: Duality in America's Treatment of its Racial Minorities* (New York: Tavistock Publications, 1983).

16. The documentary film *La operación* (1982), directed by Ana María García, focused on how government policies for population control and economic development in Puerto Rico relied on the massive sterilization of women, especially between the 1930s and the 1960s.

17. Muñoz Marín's contacts in Washington's power circles during the Roosevelt administration were facilitated by a prominent North American journalist, Ruby Black, a close friend of his first wife Muna Lee, and of First Lady Eleanor Roosevelt. See Teresita Santini, *Luis Muñoz Marín 1898–1998* (San Juan: Universidad Interamericana and Fundación Francisco Carvajal, 1998).

18. In 1924 the Partido Unión Puertorriqueña, also known as the Unionistas (Unionists), whose supporters advocated either autonomy or independence for Puerto Rico, and the pro-statehood Partido Unión Republicana (Republicanos) formed a coalition known as La Alianza for that year's legislative elections. The Alianza was aimed at counteracting the electoral strength of the workers' Partido Socialista. In response, the pro-statehood Partido Socialista joined a dissident group of pro-statehood Republicanos to form another coalition, named La Coalición. These arrangements lasted until 1932. The Partido Unionista dissolved that year and reconstituted itself into the Partido Liberal. A new electoral coalition aimed at defeating the Partido Liberal was formed by the Partido Socialista and Partido Unión Republicana that same year. See Bolívar Pagán, *Historia de los partidos politicos puertorriqueños* (San Juan: M. Pareja, 1972); and Robert W. Anderson, *Party Politics in Puerto Rico* (Stanford, CA: Stanford University Press, 1965).

19. Disagreements about the status issue and the Tydings Bill produced a split in Puerto Rico's Partido Liberal between its elderly leader Antonio R. Barceló, who represented the more conservative wing of the party, and a young Luis Muñoz Marín and his more radical followers. The Muñoz Marín faction supported Puerto Rico's independence with some economic guarantees from the United States. This faction split from the Partido Liberal in 1937 and founded the PPD.

20. In the 1920s, Muñoz Marín published some articles in the *Nation,* the *New Republic,* and the *American Mercury.*

21. In 1922 Representative Philip Campbell and Senator William King introduced a bill to Congress seeking to provide an autonomous government to be known as the Associated Free State of Puerto Rico, but the bill never made it to the floor of the House or Senate. See Benjamin B. Ringer, *"We the People" and Others: Duality in America's Treatment of its Racial Minorities* (New York: Tavistock Publications, 1983), 1030–1036. The original idea was revived decades later, and under a new constitution, the island officially adopted the name Estado Libre Asociado de Puerto Rico in 1952.

4

Postwar
Migration Patterns

The conspicuous presence of Puerto Ricans in New York City during the late 1940s and 1950s led some observers to refer to them as "newcomers" (Handlin 1959), but as we have seen, the postwar massive influx was a continuation of a process that had started over half a century before. What is known as the Great Migration marks the period when mainstream US society became more aware than before of the Puerto Rican presence in New York, its surrounding urban areas, and a few other parts of the country. But the most obvious contradiction about this massive migration influx to the United States is that it occurred at a time when Puerto Rico was being showcased as a successful model of industrial capitalist development, modernization, and democratic rule. The island became an example for the rest of the Caribbean, Latin America, and other developing countries of what an undeveloped country could achieve with the assistance and tutelage of the United States. In order to understand this basic contradiction, we must examine the interplay of the political conditions and colonial power relations under which Puerto Rico's mid-twentieth-century socioeconomic transformation took place.

After their electoral victory of 1948, the Populares took over the reins of the island's government with overwhelming support of the large majority of the population, making Luis Muñoz Marín the first Puerto Rican governor elected by popular mandate. Allowing Puerto Ricans to elect their own governor was the most significant political concession that the United States had made to the island since the Jones Act in 1917 granted US citizenship to Puerto Ricans, and a major catalyst for the inauguration of the Constitution of the Estado Libre Asociado (ELA), or Commonwealth of Puerto Rico, on July 25, 1952. Paradoxically, the date was picked in commemoration of the US invasion of Puerto Rico half a century earlier, perhaps indicating the ambivalent and problematic nature of the new status. Supporters called the new ELA a celebration of freedom, but it was "freedom with a long chain," as Muñoz Marín himself once referred to it in private (Maldonado-Denis 1972). The ELA was far from freeing

Puerto Rico from the territorial jurisdiction of the US Congress, but it at least allowed Puerto Ricans an acceptable degree of self-government.

After the PPD took over the insular government, debates within the party revolved around, among other issues, whether emphasis should be placed first on alleviating social ills, enhancing the island's political status, or whether a strong program of industrialization should take precedence.[1] Teodoro Moscoso, a member of the party's upper echelon, championed an "industrialization-first" perspective. Shortly thereafter, he was named chief administrator of Fomento (to foster), the government's main agency to promote industrial economic development. Moscoso became the chief architect and driving force behind the Operation Bootstrap industrialization initiative that would modernize Puerto Rico.[2] One of the landmark documents that promoted the determination to move toward an "industrialization first" development strategy was the Plan Chardón (see Chapter 3).

Several crucial elements were required to achieve the increases in per capita income that the massive industrialization process of Operation Bootstrap was intended to produce. First, population growth had to be reduced. Second, goods manufactured in Puerto Rico needed a substantial market abroad. Third, US manufacturers needed an incentive to locate their operations on the island. Fourth, a stable political environment was necessary. Finally, island wages had to remain competitive and flexible.

All those conditions were rapidly met in Puerto Rico by the new Muñoz Marín administration. Family planning and population control initiatives to reduce births on the island and accelerated migration to the United States were given high priority. Access to the US domestic market was key to achieving

Cien Industrias Nuevas (100 New Industries). A 1950s poster by Rafael Ríos Rey, released by the Commonwealth government's Industrial Development Administration (Fomento) heralding the proliferation of more than 100 industries on the island during the early Operation Bootstrap years. Reprinted with the author's permission from Teresa Tió, *El cartel en Puerto Rico* (Mexico City: Pearson Educación, 2003), 22.

economies of scale; thus a corporate federal tax exemption program was introduced and became a powerful instrument to attract US industrial capital. With the repression of the Nationalist movement and the imprisonment of most of the party's high-profile leadership, the Puerto Rico–US political relationship provided a stable and welcoming environment for North American businesses. Added to all of these was the incentive of having Puerto Rico supply a steady source of low-wage labor, so minimum wage boards were established on the island to set up industry-wide minima below the US statutory minimum wage level.[3] Moreover, the Muñoz Marín administration negotiated with the leaders of the island's major labor unions to foster an environment of "industrial peace" in order to attract more US investors. This meant avoiding strikes and settling for Fomento's policies for the new industrial labor force.

The debate over the need for a comprehensive migration policy to forestall population pressure had strong proponents and detractors. Given the Catholic church's opposition to a state-sponsored plan of birth control on the island, many policymakers felt that large-scale migration was the best mechanism to control population growth. However, opponents argued that Puerto Rico would experience a brain drain and that the migrants would return when economic conditions improved, further exacerbating population pressure.

A *jíbaro* on his horse contemplating a departing plane, a symbol of the 1950s airborne mass migration to the United States and the transformation of Puerto Rico from a rural to an urban society, a process that began in the post–World War II years. Archives of the Puerto Rican Diaspora, Centro de Estudios Puertorriqueños, Hunter College.

Maldonado (1997) summarized the outcome of these debates in the following manner:

> Like so much in island politics, the debate over migration became a question of semantics. Muñoz insisted that the government's migration policy was neutral. But when a government makes it as easy as possible for its people to migrate, when it trains them, gives instructions in new living conditions, provides basic English classes, battles the airlines to keep the fares low, and establishes employment offices at their destination, isn't it in effect sponsoring a policy that encourages migration? (146)

The use of migration as an instrument of economic development and, more specifically, of industrialization was becoming fashionable in intellectual circles as well. Development economists were gradually more interested in the transition from agriculturally based societies to industrial ones as they scanned the international development landscape in the aftermath of World War II. Moreover, labor migration from rural to urban areas in the less-developed countries was to serve as a low-cost impetus to the early stages of rapid industrialization. Thus, development models with such labels as "surplus labor," "disguised unemployment," and "underemployment" were in vogue (Lewis 1954; Jorgenson 1961; Fei and Ranis 1964; Sen 1966). These intellectual currents simply confirmed the development strategy that had already been launched by policymakers in Puerto Rico and Washington, DC—industrialization was to be based on the migration of labor from rural to urban parts of the island and, subsequently, exported to the United States.

The first official recognition that migration was to be part of the social and political reforms and policies designed by the new Muñoz Marín administration was the establishment by the island's Department of Labor of the Oficina de Puerto Rico en Nueva York (Office of Puerto Rico in New York, later to be known as the Migration Division, or Commonwealth Office) in New York City. The main purpose of this agency was to facilitate the migrant's transition into US society. Because promoting contract labor was part of the new administration's development strategies and there was a significant demand for low-wage labor coming from many industries in the continental United States, it was logical for the Puerto Rican government to try to manage the migration process through an agency that provided employment and housing information, job training, and referral services to potential workers. The Migration Division also promoted cultural activities, and its services were especially aimed at recent arrivals. Branches of this agency were started in other US cities with large concentrations of Puerto Ricans, such as Chicago and Philadelphia. However, the office frequently reflected the priorities of island-based planners and policymakers or US Puerto Rican professionals, without paying enough attention to the views of grassroots organizations that existed in the various Puerto Rican barrios or to their leadership (see Chapter 6).

Contract workers inside a decommissioned cargo plane with improvised seating, leaving for the United States in 1946. Archives of the Puerto Rican Diaspora, Centro de Estudios Puertorriqueños, Hunter College.

In Puerto Rico, it was clear that population growth was viewed as a real constraint on economic development. High fertility rates, particularly in rural areas, kept productivity and hence per capita income very low. At the time, it seemed obvious that the number of jobs being created under Operation Bootstrap would never keep pace with the employment needs of the growing population. The general view was that both unemployment and underemployment would continue to rise in the absence of a population "safety valve" in the form of migration and birth control. This perspective was supported by many influential figures in the Puerto Rican government as well as US policymakers.

These concerns led to the government-sponsored policy of migration from Puerto Rico to the United States. What the proponents failed to imagine was the extent to which migration would lead to massive numbers of people moving from the island's countryside to urban areas, and later to the continental United States. Maldonado (1997) described the events in the following terms:

> The hope of industrialization had ignited a full-fledged "revolution of rising expectations" throughout Puerto Rico, setting into motion a massive migration from the country to the cities and grotesquely inflating the horrid slums that had appalled the Roosevelt New Dealers fifteen years earlier; the migration grew so huge that it spilled over the Atlantic to the slums of New York City. (75)

The process that would fundamentally transform the island and lead to the emergence and growth of Puerto Rican communities throughout the United States had been unleashed.

The determinant of the size of the US Puerto Rican population is the size and growth of the Puerto Rican population on the island. In this respect, the population of Puerto Rico grew substantially over the twentieth century (see Table 4.1), with an average annual growth rate of 1.4 percent (from 1899 to 2000). But this statistic conceals the fact that population growth on the island was especially high during the period before the Great Migration.[4] During the first half of the twentieth century, birthrates were extremely high on the island

Table 4.1   Population and Population Growth in Puerto Rico, 1899–2000

	Total Population	Increase in Population from Preceding Census	
		Number	Percentage
1899	953,243	154,678	19.4
1910	1,118,012	164,769	17.3
1920	1,299,809	181,797	16.3
1930	1,543,913	244,104	18.8
1940	1,869,255	325,342	21.1
1950	2,210,703	341,448	18.3
1960	2,349,544	138,841	6.3
1970	2,712,033	362,489	15.4
1980	3,196,500	484,487	17.9
1990	3,522,037	325,537	10.2
2000	3,808,610	286,573	8.1

Sources: 1980 US Census of Population and Housing: Characteristics of the Population, Number of Inhabitants: Puerto Rico, Table 1; *1990 US Census of Population and Housing: Summary Social, Economic, and Housing Characteristics,* Table 1; *Census 2000 Summary File 1 (SF1): Profile of General Demographic Characteristics.*

while mortality rates were declining slowly, thus producing dramatic increases in population. Mortality dropped because of key interventions such as inoculations, improved sanitary conditions, a more expansive health delivery system, and the extension of potable water to most communities. Although such declines in mortality generally precede declines in fertility, planners were not willing to wait for this change. This process of population growth and change is described by Rivera-Batiz and Santiago (1996) in the following terms:

> Mortality rates started to drop precipitously in Puerto Rico in the 1930s. Between 1930 and 1950, the number of persons who died each year dropped from 20 per thousand to fewer than 10 per thousand. This reduced death rate was linked to improved health conditions and better nutrition. During the same time period, the birth rate stayed more or less constant, fluctuating around 40 births per thousand. The stable birth rate, combined with the sharply declining death rate, led to booming population growth. (24)

All the conditions described above set the stage for the perception, both in Washington, DC, and in San Juan, that migration was a major component of any economic strategy aimed at remedying the impoverished conditions many Puerto Ricans faced on the island during those years.

There is little doubt that Puerto Rican emigration to the United States during the 1950s represents one of the largest outflows of people relative to the size of the island's population base.[5] It is estimated that a net figure of 470,000 people, out of a population of approximately 2.2 million people, left the island during the decade of the 1950s (see Table 4.2). This represents a remarkable 21 percent emigration rate, one of the highest in modern times. Although net emigration has remained sizable since 1960, it clearly has not approached the

Table 4.2   Net Emigration from Puerto Rico, 1900–2000

	Net Number of Out-Migrants
1900–1910	2,000
1910–1920	11,000
1920–1930	42,000
1930–1940	18,000
1940–1950	151,000
1950–1960	470,000
1960–1970	214,000
1970–1980	65,817
1980–1990	116,571
1990–2000	96,327

Sources: The data for 1900–1970 are from José Vázquez Calzada. 1988. *La población de Puerto Rico y su trayectoria histórica.* Río Piedras, PR: Universidad de Puerto Rico, Escuela de Salud Pública, 1988; the data for 1970–1980, 1980–1990, and 1990–2000 are derived from the 1980, 1990, and 2000 *US Census of Population and Housing: Puerto Rico.*

levels of the 1950s. Some variation in the size of the migration flow will be expected as Puerto Rican economic conditions change in relation to the US business cycle (and global changes as well). But it is unlikely that migration will play as overwhelming a role in Puerto Rican population change in the future as it did in the immediate post–World War II era.

As migration plays a diminished role in population change in Puerto Rico and in the numbers of Puerto Ricans residing in the United States, fertility and mortality will substantively influence the future growth of both of these populations (see Table 4.3). Note that net migration in each location appears as opposite of the other. The data suggest that in Puerto Rico as well as among Puerto Ricans residing in the United States, the natural increase in the population will be driving population growth in the future. Thus, the determinants of fertility and mortality are the key elements in the future size of both populations. Factors such as age structure, the average age of marital unions, and the extent to which women participate in the labor force and their level of educational attainment will be particularly important in determining the rate of population growth.

Table 4.3 Population Growth in Puerto Rico and Among US Puerto Ricans: Natural Increase Versus Net Migration, 1970–2000

Component of population change in Puerto Rico	1970–1980	1980–1990	1990–2000
Natural increase of the population	550,300	442,108	382,900
Net migration	–65,813	–116,571	–96,327
Total change in population	484,487	325,537	286,573
Component of population change among Puerto Ricans residing in the United States	1970–1980	1980–1990	1990–2000
Natural increase of the population	527,824	467,371	689,499
Net migration	+65,813	+116,571	+96,327
Total change in population	593,637	583,941	785,826

Sources: Figures for population change are as determined by the decennial census of Puerto Rico (see Table 3.1). Data for births and deaths in Puerto Rico are as supplied by the US Bureau of the Census (quoted in *Statistical Abstract of the United States*, 1992, supplemented with information from the Planning Board of Puerto Rico, *Informe Económico del Gobernador*, 1992) and the various annual publications of the National Center for Health Statistics.

Note: The natural increase in the population is the difference between births and deaths, as determined by the geographic Register of the Puerto Rico Department of Health. Net migration figures are calculated as a residual.

This issue also brings up an interesting perspective on the relative numbers of Puerto Ricans residing in the United States vis-à-vis the island's total population.[6] The 2000 US Census indicated that 3.4 million Puerto Ricans were residing in the United States (see Table 4.4). Less than half that number (42 percent) were born in Puerto Rico. According to Table 4.1, 3.8 million people were residing in Puerto Rico in the year 2000. Although fewer Puerto Ricans reside in the United States than on the island, the former figure is growing at a faster rate than the latter. Thus, should current trends continue, before the end of the decade it is likely that there will be more Puerto Ricans residing in the United States than the total population of Puerto Rico (see Figure 4.1). This change is driven, in good measure, by the relatively younger age of Puerto Rican migrants compared to the average age of residents of the island. Hence, the Puerto Rican population in the United States is younger than the population residing in Puerto Rico and more likely to be of childbearing age.

Earlier writings by Kal Wagenheim (1975) suggested that the US Puerto Rican population would surpass the island population by the year 2000. Part of the reason for Wagenheim's premature estimate was the assumption that the migration from the island would continue at an accelerated rate, as it had in the past. This proved incorrect, largely because net migration, which responds to so many different forces, is always a difficult variable to forecast. Nonetheless, given that Wagenheim made his prediction about twenty years ago, he really was quite close to the mark.

A more recent study by Falcón (2004) suggested that the number of Puerto Ricans residing in the United States already surpasses the number of Puerto Ricans residing on the island. Falcón applied the percentage of Puerto

Table 4.4   Puerto Rican Population in the Continental United States and Percentage Born Elsewhere, 1910–2000

	Total Population	Percent Change (Ann. Avg.)	Number Born Outside the US	Percent Born Outside the US
1910	1,513	—		
1920	11,811	20.5	—	—
1930	52,774	15.0	—	—
1940	69,967	2.8	—	—
1950	301,375	14.6	—	—
1960	892,513	10.9	—	—
1970	1,442,774	4.8	777,881	53.9
1980	2,036,411	3.4	1,031,054	50.6
1990	2,620,352	2.5	1,210,352	46.2
2000	3,406,178	2.6	—	—

Sources: 1960 US Census of Population and Housing, Puerto Ricans in the United States, subject report PC(2)-1D, Table A, p. viii; 1970 US Census of Population and Housing, Puerto Ricans in the United States.

Figure 4.1   Population of Puerto Rico and Puerto Ricans Residing in the United States, 1910–2030

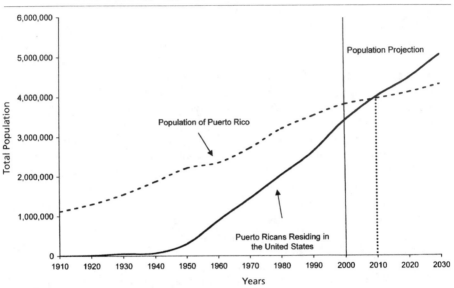

Ricans living on the island based on the 2000 US Census to the annual estimate of the Current Population Survey (US Bureau of the Census 2003) and
compared his estimate to the CPS count of Puerto Ricans in the United States.
Whereas the decennial census provided a more accurate count than the CPS,
one can reasonably conclude that the next census count (2010) will show that
the number of Puerto Ricans residing in the United States surpasses both the
total Puerto Rican population of Puerto Rico and the total island population,
which also includes a large contingent of Dominicans and Cubans.

The implications of this change in the US–Puerto Rico population balance
are potentially significant. For example, if US Puerto Ricans were to have a
political voice in the periodic plebiscites that are conducted on Puerto Rico's
future political status and its economic relationship with the United States,
their votes could determine the outcome. The fact that US Puerto Ricans continue to identify with their geographic, cultural, and linguistic roots despite
their dispersion across the fifty states has been commented on by numerous
writers, both on the island and the metropolis, and arguments have been made
about the importance of seeing them as part of a single Puerto Rican nation.
Indeed, if the US Census Bureau decided to combine their counts of the island-
and US-based Puerto Rican populations in a decennial census, the number of
Puerto Ricans would double from almost 10 percent of the total US Latino
population to approximately 18 percent, far outnumbering other groups, with

the exception of the Mexican/Chicano population, which in the year 2002 represented over two-thirds of all US Latinos.

The Growing Geographic Dispersion

Puerto Ricans are an extremely mobile population. Rivera-Batiz and Santiago (1994) claimed, based on the 1990 census, that 33.8 percent of Puerto Ricans residing in the United States moved from one residence to another in the previous five years. This compares with 25.9 percent for the population at large. What makes the Puerto Rican experience unique is not solely the volume of mobility—the number of people that move frequently—but also the *pattern* of that mobility. Not only is there evidence of continuous migration between the island and the United States—often referred to as commuter migration, back and forth migration, or circular migration—but there is also a growing *geographic dispersion* of the Puerto Rican population throughout the continental United States.

Historically, New York City has been the primary destination point for Puerto Ricans. Even before the mid-twentieth-century Great Migration, 80 percent of the Puerto Rican population residing in the United States lived in metropolitan New York City (López 1980). New York City is certainly not the closest in geographic distance between San Juan and the continental United States. Miami, for instance, might have been conceived as a destination of closer proximity. But New York City is an urban center that has historically absorbed wave after wave of immigrants from different parts of the world—Western, Eastern, and Southern Europe, the Caribbean, Latin America, Asia, and so on. It is also "closer" to Puerto Rico in terms of the ability of people to travel (costs of migration) between San Juan and New York City.

As Puerto Ricans settled in New York, families were concentrated in specific areas and communities that arose in various parts of the city. In the 1930s Puerto Ricans were settling into the Upper East Side of Manhattan in East Harlem, which became known as Spanish Harlem, or "El Barrio" (López 1980, 321; Rodríguez 1989). Dispersion and subsequent concentration then occurred throughout the metropolitan area, so that by 1970 Puerto Ricans were a majority of the population in Washington Heights, East Harlem, and the Lower East Side in Manhattan, Williamsburg and Greenpoint in Brooklyn, and the South Bronx. These communities were also characterized as areas with a high percentage of economically disadvantaged families.[7]

Another component of the Puerto Rican migration stream that has received much less attention was the seasonal workers that came from the island to work on farms in the Northeast. This work was transitory in nature, and both the working and living conditions were precarious at best. Between the 1940s

English class for recent migrants. Archives of the Puerto Rican Diaspora, Centro de Estudios Puertorriqueños, Hunter College.

and the 1960s the Puerto Rican government facilitated the movement of this labor force between the island and agricultural areas of New Jersey, upstate New York, Connecticut, Pennsylvania, and Massachusetts. Pay was low, housing was often substandard, and these workers had fewer rights and benefits than other workers since unionization was almost nonexistent.

Puerto Ricans have been largely concentrated in the Northeast of the United States, where over 80 percent of the migrant population resided in 1970 (see Figure 4.2). Another 9 percent lived in the Midwest, mostly in Chicago and parts of Ohio. This settlement pattern changed dramatically between 1970 and 2000. A major rupture from earlier patterns of settlement occurred during the 1970s in the aftermath of New York City's fiscal crisis. New York City's default in 1975 had a devastating impact on the socioeconomic status of the Puerto Rican and African American population, especially because of the simultaneous decline in the city's manufacturing sector.

Between 1970 and 2000 Puerto Ricans gravitated to the South, moved within the Northeast, maintained their presence in the Midwest, and were found in every state of the union (see Figure 4.3). Migration from Puerto Rico, which used to be primarily aimed at New York City, now flows directly to

Figure 4.2   Geographic Distribution of the Puerto Rican Population, 1970 and 2000

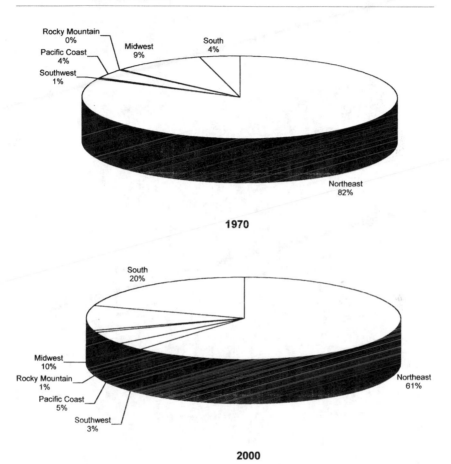

1970

2000

other parts of the country. The traditional San Juan to New York City and back migratory route is now a multidestination one, with individuals staying in two or more locales and sometimes not returning to the point of origin. The significant mobility of Puerto Ricans should not be characterized as a movement of a homogeneous group of people who travel for identical reasons. The character of the movement to the Southeast is often different from the movement of Puerto Ricans within the Northeast. In the former case, there is a movement of more educated individuals seeking employment within Florida's growing economy. Throughout the Northeast we often see Puerto Ricans moving from

Figure 4.3 US Puerto Rican Population by State, 2000

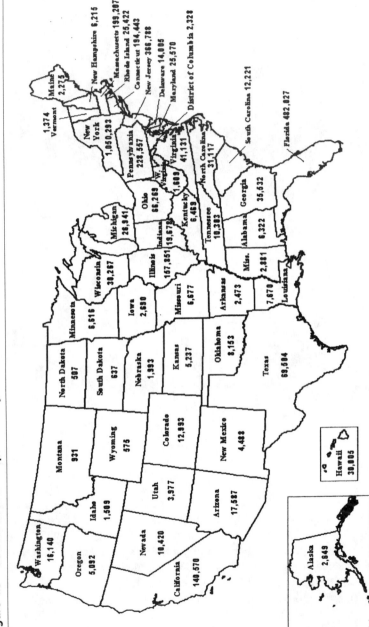

Source: US Census, DP-1 Profile of General Demographic Characteristics: 2000: Census 2000 Summary File (SF1) 100 Percent Data.

large cities with more expensive housing to midsize cities with a more afford-able housing stock. This differentiated process of dispersion was highlighted first by Rivera-Batiz and Santiago (1994) when they claimed that Puerto Rican mobility and its socioeconomic character "is not necessarily based on the tra-ditional urban-suburban patterns observed among other groups in the popula-tion. Rather, a number of Puerto Rican communities are plagued with poverty and joblessness in midsize urban areas of the Northeast, while at the same time there exist many affluent, booming communities in the Southern and Western United States" (viii).

In 1970, over 80 percent of the Puerto Rican population in the United States was concentrated in only three states—New York, New Jersey, and Illi-nois (see Figure 4.4). In 2000, a similar proportion of the Puerto Rican popu-lation resided in New York, Florida, New Jersey, Pennsylvania, Massachu-setts, Connecticut, Illinois, and California. Most noteworthy was the growing percentage of the Puerto Rican population residing in Florida, Pennsylvania, Massachusetts, and Connecticut and the declining percentage of the popula-tion residing in New York and Illinois.

But these changes do not tell the whole story. We need to place the change in Puerto Rican population by state in the context of broader changes in each state's population. For example, between 1990 and 2000, the Puerto Rican population of Florida increased by 235,017 people, the largest increase in the number of Puerto Ricans of any state (see Table 4.5). However, Florida's total population grew by over 3 million during the same period, so Puerto Ricans made up only 8 percent of Florida's population growth. In contrast, the num-ber of Puerto Ricans in Connecticut increased by 47,601 during the period covered by the 2000 census, yet Connecticut's total population grew by only 118,449, so Puerto Ricans contributed to Connecticut's total population growth by over 40 percent from 1990 to 2000, a significantly higher level than in Florida.

While the growth of the Puerto Rican population in Florida has received significant attention in the media because of its sheer size compared to Puerto Rican population growth elsewhere, the real story is the impact of this popu-lation growth in some areas of the Northeast. Although the West and the Southeast continue to attract large numbers of people, the Northeast has been a net loser of population. Thus, since general population growth has been rel-atively slow in the Northeast, Puerto Ricans have become an important con-tributor to population growth in these states.

Since the 1970s the states that have benefited most from Puerto Rican population growth have been in the Northeast (see Figure 4.5). Connecticut stands out with 25 percent of its population growth from 1970 to 2000 consist-ing of Puerto Ricans. As we will see, much of this growth occurred in midsize urban centers such as Hartford, Bridgeport, Waterbury, New Haven, and New

Figure 4.4 Distribution of the Puerto Rican Population by State, 1970 and 2000

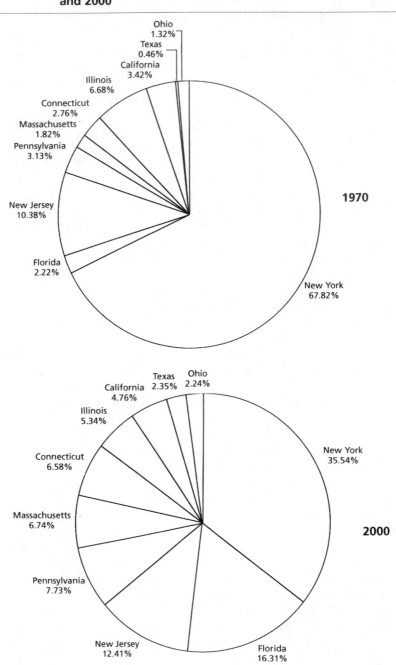

Ohio 1.32%
Texas 0.46%
California 3.42%
Illinois 6.68%
Connecticut 2.76%
Massachusetts 1.82%
Pennsylvania 3.13%
New Jersey 10.38%
Florida 2.22%
New York 67.82%
1970

Texas 2.35%
Ohio 2.24%
California 4.76%
Illinois 5.34%
Connecticut 6.58%
Massachusetts 6.74%
Pennsylvania 7.73%
New Jersey 12.41%
Florida 16.31%
New York 35.54%
2000

Table 4.5 Contribution of Puerto Ricans to State Population Growth, 1980–2000

	Change in Total State Population (1)		Change in Puerto Rican Population (2)		% Puerto Rican Contribution to State Population Growth (2) Divided by (1)	
	1980–1990	1990–2000	1980–1990	1990–2000	1980–1990	1990–2000
New York	432,383	986,002	100,212	−36,308	23.2	−3.7
Florida	3,191,602	3,044,452	152,235	235,017	4.8	7.7
New Jersey	365,365	684,162	76,593	46,655	21.0	6.8
Pennsylvania	17,748	399,411	57,186	79,569	322.2	19.9
Massachusetts	279,388	332,672	74,743	48,014	26.8	14.4
Connecticut	179,540	118,449	58,481	47,601	32.6	40.2
Illinois	4,084	988,691	16,894	11,792	413.7	1.2
California	6,092,119	4,111,627	33,379	14,153	0.5	0.3
Texas	2,757,319	3,865,310	20,043	26,523	0.7	0.7
Ohio	49,485	506,025	13,411	20,416	27.1	4.0

Source: US Census Bureau, *Census 2000.*

Figure 4.5   Contribution of Puerto Rican Population Growth to the Growth of Selected States, 1970–2000

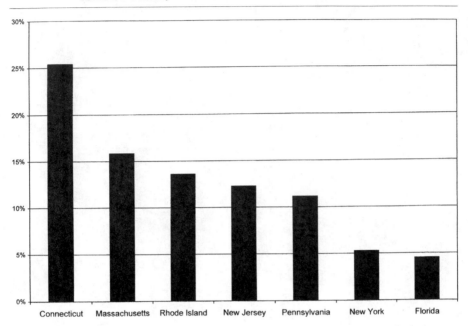

Britain. But even in the states of Massachusetts, Rhode Island, New Jersey, and Pennsylvania, Puerto Ricans have become an important contributor to state population growth over the three decades.

The Urban Character of the Communities

Puerto Ricans in the United States have, by and large, resided in urban areas. This concentration would be expected in light of the significant and directed migration that occurred right after World War II. For several decades New York City was the great hub of destination. As relative newcomers to the New York City immigrant population, Puerto Ricans generally lived in the more economically depressed parts of the city, often residing in substandard housing. Differences in climate, unfamiliar surroundings, and an uncertain economic environment all posed real challenges to the newcomers.

Not only did Puerto Ricans find themselves in a disadvantaged position with respect to housing in New York City, but they also made up the growing low-wage labor force in the city. They began filling the ranks of the city's workers in the service sector and also increasingly made up the labor force in the light-manufacturing sector, especially in the garment district. The early

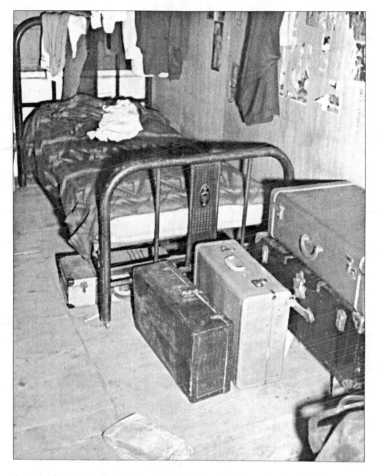

A typical migrant worker's grim housing at a farm in the Northeast. These rooms generally lacked heating and plumbing. Archives of the Puerto Rican Diaspora, Centro de Estudios Puertorriqueños, Hunter College. Photo by Tony Rodríguez.

large-scale migration of Puerto Ricans to New York City, Chicago, and the Northeast coincided with a sustained period of economic change in these areas. There was increasing evidence that the United States was embarking on a process of economic structural change, later to be referred to as "deindustrialization," which culminated in New York City's fiscal default in the mid-1970s. For Puerto Ricans this played out in very unfortunate ways.

Despite all these changes, New York City still has the greatest concentration of Puerto Ricans. According to the 2000 US Census, 789,172 Puerto Ricans resided there (see Table 4.6). Chicago, with a Puerto Rican population of

Table 4.6   US Cities with Largest Concentrations of Puerto Ricans, 1980–2000

	Puerto Rican Population			Growth Rt. (Ann. Avg.)	Growth Rt. (Ann. Avg.)
	1980	1990	2000	1980–1990	1990–2000
New York City, New York	860,552	896,763	789,172	0.4	−1.3
Chicago, Illinois	112,074	119,866	113,055	0.7	−0.6
Philadelphia, Pennsylvania	46,587	67,857	91,527	3.8	3.0
Newark, New Jersey	39,732	41,545	39,650	0.4	−0.5
Hartford, Connecticut	24,615	38,176	39,586	4.4	0.4
Springfield, Massachusetts	12,298	23,729	35,251	6.6	4.0
Bridgeport, Connecticut	22,146	30,250	32,177	3.1	0.6
Jersey City, New Jersey	26,830	30,950	29,777	1.4	−0.4
Boston, Massachusetts	18,899	25,767	27,442	3.1	0.6
Cleveland, Ohio	12,267	17,829	25,385	3.7	3.5
Paterson, New Jersey	24,326	27,580	24,013	—	−1.4
Camden, New Jersey	*	22,984	23,051	—	0.0
Rochester, New York	10,545	16,383	21,897	4.4	2.9
Milwaukee, Wisconsin	*	14,028	19,613	—	3.4
Reading, Pennsylvania	6,957	11,612	19,054	5.1	5.0
Waterbury, Connecticut	5,819	12,080	18,149	7.3	4.1
Yonkers, New York	*	14,420	18,097	—	2.3
New Haven, Connecticut	*	13,866	17,683	—	2.4
Allentown, Pennsylvania	4,279	9,670	17,682	8.2	6.0
Tampa, Florida	4,038	9,863	17,527	8.9	5.7
Buffalo, New York	6,865	12,798	17,250	6.2	3.0
Worcester, Massachusetts	5,433	12,166	17,091	8.1	3.4
Orlando, Florida	*	7,035	17,029	—	8.8
Lawrence, Massachusetts	5,726	14,661	15,816	9.4	0.8
New Britain, Connecticut	5,358	10,325	15,693	6.6	4.2
Holyoke, Massachusetts	*	12,687	14,539	—	1.4
Lancaster, Pennsylvania	5,967	10,305	13,717	5.5	2.9
Los Angeles, California	13,835	14,367	13,427	0.4	−0.7
Vineland, New Jersey	*	11,672	13,284	—	1.3
Perth Amboy, New Jersey	*	13,531	13,145	—	−0.3
Miami, Florida	12,320	12,004	10,257	−0.3	−1.6
Ft. Lauderdale, Florida	1,218	2,209	2,801	6.0	2.4

Source: US Census Bureau, Census 2000.
Note: * Data not available for the geographic designation or locale not among the top cities for 1980.

113,055, and Philadelphia with 91,527, had the next largest numbers. But whereas the size of the Puerto Rican population declined in New York City between 1980 and 2000 and remained relatively constant in Chicago over that period of time, the Puerto Rican population of Philadelphia almost doubled. Other large cities that have experienced substantial Puerto Rican population growth over the past two decades are Boston, Cleveland, and Milwaukee. Clearly, the largest urban centers that historically served as the prime destinations for Puerto Rican migrants, such as New York City and Chicago, are no longer fulfilling that role, but this does not imply that the fundamentally urban character of Puerto Rican settlements in the United States has changed.

Demographic data confirm that the initial concentration of Puerto Ricans in urban centers has changed and that the population has become more dispersed over time. The thirty-two cities with the highest concentration of Puerto Ricans contained 63 percent of the total US Puerto Rican population in 1980 (Table 4.6). But in the year 2000, these same cities contained only 46 percent of the total. This phenomenon was particularly driven by the fortunes of New York City and the decline in its Puerto Rican population base. By the year 2000, New York City was home to only 23 percent of the total US Puerto Rican population (see Table 4.7). This contrasts sharply with the nearly 43 percent of the Puerto Rican population that resided in New York City in 1980 (and even more sharply with the nearly 60 percent in 1970).

Another important observation is that many midsize US cities with a Puerto Rican population of around 20,000 people in 1980 showed considerable growth over the two decades that followed. Most noteworthy are Hartford and Bridgeport, Connecticut; and Jersey City, New Jersey. Puerto Rican population growth in these cities can be directly attributed to the movement of people from New York City to outlying areas. In addition, new areas of settlement that are not confined to a particular part of the country have become quite pronounced since the 1980s. These newer Puerto Rican communities include those within the general proximity of New York City such as Yonkers, New York; New Haven, Connecticut; and Camden, Vineland, and Perth Amboy, New Jersey. They also include the phenomenal growth of the Puerto Rican population in Orlando and Tampa Bay, Florida.

While the decline in the New York City resident Puerto Rican population during the decade of the 1990s certainly fueled some of the population growth in surrounding cities, there is little evidence to suggest that Puerto Ricans simply moved from the largest metropolis in the country to a nearby smaller city. The ring of sizable Puerto Rican communities within a 100-mile radius of New York City did not change appreciably in relative terms from 1980 to 2000. For example, the cities with the largest concentrations of Puerto Ricans within a 100-mile radius of New York City made up approximately 10 percent of the total US Puerto Rican population in both 1980 and 2000. This does not mean that Puerto Ricans were not moving into these communities but, rather, that the growth of the Puerto Rican population in these cities was proportional to the growth of the Puerto Rican population overall. This also suggests that despite the influx and outflow of people, these communities exhibited considerable stability in terms of population.

It also seems clear that Puerto Ricans have been opting for a more suburban lifestyle if they have the economic means to do so. Whether it is for better housing, better schools, more affordable communities, or simply a change in lifestyle, there is little doubt that Puerto Ricans are following the path of

Table 4.7   Percent of Total US Puerto Rican Population in Selected Cities, 1980–2000

	1980	1990	2000
New York City, New York	42.729	32.876	23.169
Chicago, Illinois	5.565	4.394	3.319
Philadelphia, Pennsylvania	2.313	2.488	2.687
Newark, New Jersey	1.973	1.523	1.164
Hartford, Connecticut	1.222	1.400	1.162
Springfield, Massachusetts	0.611	0.870	1.035
Bridgeport, Connecticut	1.100	1.109	0.945
Jersey City, New Jersey	1.332	1.135	0.874
Boston, Massachusetts	0.938	0.945	0.806
Cleveland, Ohio	0.609	0.654	0.745
Paterson, New Jersey	*	1.011	0.705
Camden, New Jersey	*	0.843	0.677
Rochester, New York	0.524	0.601	0.643
Milwaukee, Wisconsin	*	0.514	0.576
Reading, Pennsylvania	0.345	0.426	0.559
Waterbury, Connecticut	0.289	0.443	0.533
Yonkers, New York	*	0.529	0.531
New Haven, Connecticut	*	0.508	0.519
Allentown, Pennsylvania	0.212	0.355	0.519
Tampa, Florida	0.200	0.362	0.515
Buffalo, New York	0.341	0.469	0.506
Worcester, Massachusetts	0.270	0.446	0.502
Orlando, Florida	*	0.258	0.500
Lawrence, Massachusetts	0.284	0.538	0.464
New Britain, Connecticut	0.266	0.379	0.461
Holyoke, Massachusetts	*	0.465	0.427
Lancaster, Pennsylvania	0.296	0.378	0.403
Los Angeles, California	0.687	0.527	0.394
Vineland, New Jersey	*	0.428	0.390
Perth Amboy, New Jersey	*	0.496	0.386
Miami, Florida	0.612	0.004	0.003
Ft. Lauderdale, Florida	0.060	0.001	0.001

Source: US Census Bureau, *Census 2000.*
Note: * Data not available for the geographic designation or locale not among the top cities for 1980.

earlier immigrant groups in New York City. It is also the case that Puerto Ricans have been moving from the Northeast to parts of Florida. In Chapter 5, we explore how these migratory patterns are related to a growing Puerto Rican middle class, which is associated with a rising standard of living.

Finally, with respect to the mobility of Puerto Ricans, in certain communities where their numbers have been growing rapidly, their percentage of the city's total population has increased, in effect, significantly increasing the Puerto Rican presence in these communities. This is particularly so in the

Northeast, where population growth overall has slowed. The rather dramatic changes mean that Puerto Ricans now constitute over 20 percent of the total population in twelve different midsize cities (see Table 4.8). This is all the more remarkable in that twenty-five years ago the Puerto Rican presence did not reach 20 percent in any of these cities, but in the year 2000 over 30 percent of the population of Holyoke and Hartford was Puerto Rican. This change

Table 4.8   Puerto Rican Presence in Midsize US Cities with Greatest Concentrations, 1980–2000

	Percent of Total City Population That Is Puerto Rican		
	1980	1990	2000
Holyoke, Massachusetts	*	29.0294	36.4953
Hartford, Connecticut	18.08	27.3195	32.5602
Camden, New Jersey	*	26.2698	28.8484
Perth Amboy, New Jersey	*	32.2420	27.7889
Lancaster, Pennsylvania	10.90	18.5505	24.3434
Kissimmee, Florida	*	8.5790	23.6583
Vineland, New Jersey	*	21.3070	23.6072
Reading, Pennsylvania	8.84	14.8150	23.4635
Springfield, Massachusetts	8.07	15.1156	23.1789
Bridgeport, Connecticut	15.54	21.3500	23.0612
Lawrence, Massachusetts	9.06	20.8825	21.9536
New Britain, Connecticut	*	13.6771	21.9366
Waterbury, Connecticut	5.63	11.0865	16.9188
Allentown, Pennsylvania	4.12	9.2016	16.5823
Paterson, New Jersey	17.63	19.5754	16.0921
Lorain, Ohio	10.65	13.1686	15.3470
Newark, New Jersey	12.07	15.0951	14.4948
New Haven, Connecticut	*	10.6274	14.3036
Bethlehem, Pennsylvania	*	10.8137	14.1541
Jersey City, New Jersey	12.00	13.5427	12.4042
Elizabeth, New Jersey	*	10.9653	10.7732
Rochester, New York	4.36	7.0727	9.9635
Worcester, Massachusetts	3.36	7.1666	9.8993
New York City, New York	12.17	12.2466	9.8545
Yonkers, New York	*	7.6669	9.2291
Orlando, Florida	*	4.2716	9.1578
Providence, Rhode Island	*	4.4529	7.3218
Philadelphia, Pennsylvania	2.78	4.2796	6.0312
Buffalo, New York	1.92	3.9004	5.8945
Tampa, Florida	1.49	3.5223	5.7760
Miami, Florida	0.006	0.004	0.003
Ft. Lauderdale, Florida	0.001	0.001	0.001

Source: US Census Bureau, *Census 2000.*
Note: * Data not available for the geographic designation or locale not among the top cities for 1980.

raises the question whether the increased presence of Puerto Ricans in midsize cities has translated into their greater political participation and representation in these communities. Much of the cursory evidence suggests that it has not yet, but the potential remains for greater influence in these communities as their numbers increase.

A Tale of Three Cities: New York City, Hartford, and Orlando

New York City, Hartford, and Orlando are very different cities with considerably different historical origins. They vary in size, with over 8 million inhabitants in the immediate New York City area and over 18 million in the wider metropolitan area; Hartford has over 100,000 people residing in the city and 1.1 million in its metropolitan area; and Orlando has nearly 200,000 people in its city and approximately 1.7 million in the metropolitan area (all data as of the 2000 census). These three cities also represent different facets of the Puerto Rican experience in the United States. The establishment of Puerto Rican communities in these cities occurred at different times and was motivated by different socioeconomic forces. In many respects, they also represent different phases of expansion in a long-term process of Puerto Rican population concentration and dispersion.

New York City's Puerto Rican population expanded dramatically via direct migration from the island in the 1950s. During the 1960s, net migration from Puerto Rico to the United States declined compared to the previous decade. Although the net immigration flow was still in the direction of New York City, return-migration patterns were already being felt, thus reducing the rate of growth of the Puerto Rican population in New York City compared to the 1950s (Hernández Alvarez [1967] 1976). In 1970, the Puerto Rican population (844,303 people) made up approximately 11 percent of the New York City population, but it had declined to 9.8 percent by 2000 (789,172 people). The growth in the number of Puerto Ricans living in New York City between 1980 and 2000 was extremely low, compared to previous decades. Despite the relative constancy of the percentage of New York City residents that are Puerto Rican, an upsurge in Puerto Rican migration during the 1980s did not translate into a significantly larger Puerto Rican–born New York City population.

The initial growth of the Puerto Rican population in New York City was driven exclusively by migration from Puerto Rico. Since the 1970s, however, it has been the natural increase in the population—that is, births minus deaths—that is determining population growth. While Puerto Ricans remain a relatively younger group than the rest of the city's population, the gap in age structure is closing fast. In 1970 approximately 75 percent of Puerto Ricans residing in New York City and 53 percent of the whole city's population were younger than thirty-five, a 22 percentage point gap that shrank by half to an 11 percentage point gap in 1990.

Behind these changes in the age structure of the Puerto Rican population in New York City lie several demographic factors. First, they reflect the decline in Puerto Rican migration to the city. Second, they correspond to an upsurge in new, younger immigrants from the Dominican Republic, Central America, Mexico, and Asia. As younger immigrants arrive in the city, the demographic profile of Puerto Ricans more closely approximates that of the city at large. Third, the exodus of Puerto Ricans from New York City has been disproportionately of the younger population, particularly women of childbearing age. This has the effect of immediately shifting the age distribution upward and reducing birthrates in the years to come. It is important to keep these demographic trends in mind when considering the changing socioeconomic and political conditions of the Puerto Rican population in New York City.

Puerto Rican presence in the city of Hartford shares similar origins with those of New York City and in some respects can be viewed as a microcosm of the larger metropolis and in others as a site of important differences (Cruz 1998). New York City certainly served as a feeder of Puerto Rican population to Hartford, but the latter also received direct migration from the island. Hartford began to see an influx of Puerto Ricans in the 1950s. They came to work in the agricultural farms in the surrounding region, particularly in the tobacco-growing areas. Many of these workers did not return to the island but, rather, remained in Hartford, where they found a growing community. Some light manufacturing took place in Hartford, the home of the Royal Typewriter Company, another source of employment for Puerto Ricans, but the city would suffer a decline in its manufacturing base in the 1970s, as did much of the Northeast.

The increase in the Puerto Rican population in Hartford became particularly noticeable during the decade of the 1980s, when the population grew by 55 percent. This growth was prompted by renewed migration from the island as well as an influx of Puerto Ricans from neighboring cities in the Northeast, including New York City. This period also saw considerable growth in the number of Puerto Ricans throughout Connecticut, as communities expanded in Bridgeport, Waterbury, New Haven, and New Britain. Whereas the 1950s was the decade of substantial growth in the numbers of Puerto Ricans in New York City, for Hartford the decade of most rapid growth was the 1980s (Cruz 1998).

The growth of the Puerto Rican population in Connecticut during the 1980s coincided with a period of relatively slow population growth in the state. As we have seen, this translated into a greater presence of Puerto Ricans within many cities in Connecticut, but none more so than Hartford. With Puerto Ricans representing 32 percent of Hartford's population, the city is one of a handful of US localities with a Puerto Rican mayor. The relationship between the Puerto Rican community and the wider Hartford citizenry has gone through tumultuous periods, as Puerto Ricans sought greater representation and improvements in housing, education, health services, and the like.[8]

Chapter 5 explores the issue of socioeconomic progress among Puerto Ricans in Hartford. Hartford represents a good example of the community's political enfranchisement and use of identity politics for empowerment (Cruz 1998). Hartford, the city with the largest concentration of Puerto Ricans in 2006, was the only major city in the United States with a Puerto Rican mayor. The question remains whether the aspirations of the Puerto Rican community for representation have been adequately met in light of their presence in this city.

Orlando provides a strikingly different Puerto Rican experience from that of New York City or Hartford. The Puerto Rican population of Orlando grew substantially during a period of rapid and remarkable population growth throughout Florida. Orlando also has a much smaller Puerto Rican population than Hartford, but it has been growing at a much faster rate. The Puerto Rican percentage in Orlando was similar to that of New York City in 2000 (around 9 percent) but less than a third of that of Hartford (32 percent). As in Hartford, the growth in Orlando's population has been fueled by direct migration from Puerto Rico as well as by migrants from New York City and other parts of the Northeast. While 39 percent of all Puerto Ricans who left New York City between 1985 and 1990 returned to the island, 14 percent moved to Florida—many to Orlando (Rivera-Batiz and Santiago 1996, 148). However, migration from Puerto Rico is contributing to Orlando's Puerto Rican population growth to a much greater extent than it is in New York City or Hartford.[9]

The concentration of Puerto Ricans in the city of Orlando is noticeable but actually much smaller than the concentration of Puerto Ricans in the neighboring city of Kissimmee. In Kissimmee approximately 24 percent of the city population was Puerto Rican as of the year 2000. Many of Florida's cities have an Hispanic flavor to them, as may be seen in restaurants, markets, and social clubs, but Kissimmee's have a noticeable Puerto Rican taste.

What has drawn Puerto Ricans to central Florida, Orlando and Kissimmee in particular, is the economic boom that the state experienced during the 1990s and the employment opportunities that became evident as tourism and other sectors flourished. Puerto Ricans seeking to retire and leave the colder Northeast and the bustle of life in Puerto Rico also have moved to central Florida. All in all, a heightened quality of life has been an inducement for many to resettle in Florida. An educated, professional, and middle-class Puerto Rican family is also likely to move to Florida in search of employment and educational opportunities. The income and labor market characteristics of Puerto Ricans in Orlando and other parts of central Florida also attract this more affluent segment of the US Puerto Rican population (as will be discussed in Chapter 5).

New York City, Hartford, and Orlando present just three different demographic snapshots of the Puerto Rican experience in the United States. They also represent communities with different trajectories and experiences. New York City remains the most significant destination for the majority of Puerto Ricans, and their experiences do not deviate significantly from the more traditional New York City immigrant one. Hartford, in contrast, better represents the experiences of Puerto Ricans struggling in cities whose economic heyday has long passed and that are coping with an economy where skills and knowledge-based jobs are most highly prized. The advantage that Puerto Ricans have in this setting is that they are a growing presence and have real opportunities to convert their numbers into greater political representation. Finally, Orlando encapsulates the more recent migratory experience, moving into areas of growth. There a more highly educated Puerto Rican population, the core of an emerging middle class, is making inroads in such communities, although their impact is still at a nascent stage.

Other Migration Destinations

Despite the growth of the Puerto Rican population in cities like Hartford and Orlando, Chicago and Philadelphia still remained, after New York, the cities with the second and third largest percentages of the total US Puerto Rican population in the year 2000, respectively holding 3.3 and 2.6 percent. The arrival of Puerto Rican newcomers to these two cities took place during the postwar Great Migration period.

Elena Padilla (1958) was one of the first researchers to study Puerto Rican migration to Chicago and compare it with that of New York. She noted that the declining manufacturing base in both cities pushed a large number of Puerto Ricans into nonindustrial service and menial jobs. In later studies, Félix Padilla (1985, 1987) documented in more detail the evolution of the Chicago Puerto Rican community. According to him, as the Puerto Rican population continued to grow during the late 1950s and early 1960s: "Puerto Ricans became ever-more conspicuous, and the indifference with which they had been regarded in the early years changed to hostility. Ethnic tensions, police brutality, and the rise of a racist doctrine, which whites applied to Puerto Ricans, began to determine the status of the city's Puerto Rican population" and "accelerated the growth of a Puerto Rican ethnic consciousness" (1985, 60). Padilla also noted that despite the initial dispersal of Puerto Ricans in several areas of the city, by 1960 there was a Puerto Rican enclave taking shape in the Westtown/Humboldt Park area of Chicago, also known as the Division Street area.

Part of the tumultuous history of the US civil rights movement manifested itself in the rioting that took place in many of the ethnic enclaves of the nation's largest cities. During 1966, Chicago's Puerto Rican riots were a response to segregation, racial conflicts, and the overall socioeconomic marginality experienced by the community. But some of the anger and frustration against the white-dominated power structures was channeled through social and political activism, as Puerto Ricans began to create new organizations to fight for their rights and foster social change (see Chapter 6). These organizations contributed to what Félix Padilla described as "a we-feeling or consciousness of ethnic solidarity and community" (1985, 67).

The experience of Puerto Ricans in Philadelphia offers another example of postwar labor migration and the US economy's need for cheap labor. Earlier studies of Puerto Rican migration to this city (Siegel, Orlans, and Grier 1975; Koss 1965) showed a bidirectional pattern of migration of contract laborers, with individuals coming to work for a good part of the year on Pennsylvania farms and then often returning to Puerto Rico during the winter months. A more detailed and well-documented history was provided by Carmen T. Whalen (2001), who noted that Puerto Ricans were recruited in large numbers to engage in "farm and railroad work for men, domestic and garment work for women" (5). As in Chicago, Puerto Ricans were faced with the racial tensions and struggles of the civil rights era and relegated to a subordinate status, being labeled "a culture of poverty" (Lewis 1963) or "an underclass" (Lemann 1991; Katz 1993). Whalen argued that these paradigms "ignore labor re-

Women workers in the garment industry. Archives of the Puerto Rican Diaspora, Centro de Estudios Puertorriqueños, Hunter College.

cruitment, the impact of structural changes, and migrants' motivation in seeking work and a better life" (15).

Just as Puerto Rican migrants chose large US cities for their place of settlement, they also came to smaller cities of the Northeast and Midwest. Agricultural areas in Vineland, New Jersey, and factory work in Camden, New Jersey, are representative of the contract labor that started in the late 1920s and continued through the 1950s. Other cities, like Lorain, Ohio, recruited workers for the US Steel plant, providing the foundation for the larger Puerto Rican community that exists today in that city.

Conceptualizing Puerto Rican Migration

In many respects, migration was at the heart of Puerto Rico's industrialization effort at the end of World War II. It proved to be the catalyst that enabled the island to rapidly grow its per capita income, due to the impact it had on reducing island population growth. But is there a way to adequately characterize the Puerto Rican migratory process and its variations over time? Are its salient features those of place-to-place migration, as experienced by the waves of European migrants that came to the United States at the beginning of the twentieth century? Or is it more reminiscent of a return-migration process, as identified during the first decade after the Great Migration began? Perhaps it is neither and best described by the circular, or commuter, phenomenon that seems to prevail today, as Puerto Rican migrants continue to move between the United States and the island.

The one constant that has characterized the Puerto Rican migratory experience in the postwar period has been the continual ties to the island and the fact that US Puerto Rican communities are fed by waves of newer migrants, albeit at rates that are lower today than they were in the past. Moreover, new areas of settlement seem to be arising, populated initially by migrants that already were residing in the United States and shortly afterward by migrants from the island.

Networks of family, friends, and acquaintances play a large role in the transmission of information across localities. Although these information networks have always been present in the Puerto Rican migratory experience, they have taken on an even larger role today than in the period of early migration, when the Commonwealth government was more directly involved in promoting migration to the United States. With the increased frequency of movement that characterizes commuter migration, it seems reasonable to expect that information flows have become more accurate over time. In the earlier days of large-scale migration, many more people were involved in making the trek north, and the points of destination were fewer than today. At the same time, the primary sources of information were the Commonwealth government or the Migration Division as well as family and acquaintances that first experienced the move.

Today, the dynamics of information flows are more complex, as more and more points of destination are identified throughout the country, involving a wide variety of communities and labor markets. The increased frequency with which migrants are moving across these communities, from areas of "older" settlement and to areas of newer settlement, and from the island to these Puerto Rican enclaves, is further evidence of the importance of information flows in the process of migration. No doubt, technological improvements in transportation and communication continue to fuel these interactions, leading to enhanced mobility and migration.

What do these new and complicated patterns of mobility mean for the transmission of cultural, social, political, and economic institutions across space and time? While one may argue that processes of assimilation into Anglo-American society and Puerto Rican cultural autonomy may conflict in very complicated ways here, the links and ties between the island and the colonial metropolis remain strong, transforming individuals and communities in both areas of origin and destination. The result is a hybridity that calls us to assess and reassess just what it means to be a Puerto Rican living in the United States (see Chapter 7).

Notes

1. Luis Muñoz Marín assumed the governorship of the island in 1948 with a strong mandate and a slogan calling for "bread, land, and liberty" for the island population. This was a significant rebuke to the absentee agricultural elite in the sugar industry. The hallmark of his administration was the deferral of discussions of political status until social and economic progress was well under way.

2. See Alex W. Maldonado (1997) for an in-depth view of Moscoso's role in Puerto Rico's industrialization process.

3. The minimum wage boards were abolished in the mid-1970s, and parity with the US minimum wage level was achieved by 1980. For additional information on this issue, see Santiago (1989, 1991, 1993).

4. The average annual growth rate of the population of Puerto Rico was 1.6 percent from 1899 to 1950 and 1.1 percent from 1950 to 2000.

5. In absolute terms, the largest population movements in recorded history include the African Slave Trade between 1500 and 1900, in which 18 million slaves were forcibly removed from the African continent; Asian emigration between 1820 and 1930, when 50 million emigrants (many indentured servants) moved from India, China, Japan, and the Pacific Islands; and the European emigration from 1820 to 1930, as upward of 60 million emigrants left for the United States, Canada, Australia, New Zealand, and South Africa. See "Labor Migrations, 1500–1930" at http://www.sscnet.ucla.edu/classes/cluster 22/lectures/lecture3/ts1d002.htm. (August 26, 2003).

6. One should keep in mind that population growth on the island of Puerto Rico primarily, but not entirely, reflects changes in the population born in Puerto Rico. How-

ever, the foreign-born population in Puerto Rico has increased considerably since 1960. Rivera-Batiz and Santiago (1996) wrote: "In 1990, the largest immigrant group in Puerto Rico was made up of those born in the Dominican Republic. The Dominican-born residing in Puerto Rico doubled during the 1980s, increasing from 20,558 in 1980, to 41,193 in 1990" (113).

7. Chapter 5 will take up the issue of the changing socioeconomic status of Puerto Ricans in the United States and the geographic dimensions of this topic.

8. Much of the discontent among Puerto Ricans in Hartford erupted in 1969 when rioting broke out in the city, as Puerto Ricans decried discrimination, police brutality, and the lack of representation. See Cruz (1998).

9. For a more detailed review of Puerto Rican migration to Orlando, see Duany and Matos-Rodríguez (2005).

5

A Demographic
Portrait

Multiple generations of Puerto Ricans have resided in the United States over the past century. These cohorts continue to reinforce each other through successive waves of migration from the island. Given the nature of the migratory processes described in Chapters 3 and 4, a certain dynamic emerges wherein Puerto Ricans residing in the United States as well as those living on the island are continuously transmitting their experiences and cultural practices from one location to another. There also have been significant transmissions of wealth—and poverty—across generations and across communities, both on the island and in the United States.

Among those included in the Hispanic/Latino umbrella designation, Puerto Ricans remain the second largest group in the United States, after Mexicans/Chicanos. The increased dispersion of Puerto Ricans across the US continent, the multiple points of destination for migrants who come directly from Puerto Rico, and the urban character of both older and emerging settlements in different localities have brought a special dimension to the Puerto Rican experience. Despite the relatively free mobility of people between the island and the continent because of the Puerto Ricans' unique citizenship status, there are lessons to be learned and shared about that population's integration into US society and its cultural milieu.

In this chapter we review the socioeconomic status of Puerto Ricans residing in the United States and how they have fared relative to other ethnic and racial groups, focusing on issues of income and poverty. The labor market characteristics of the Puerto Rican population that are related to socioeconomic status also are given some attention. Of particular interest is the changing income and poverty profile of the Puerto Rican population relative to that of other ethnic and racial groups in US society. Our question is, has the economic progress of the 1980s and 1990s, suggested by increases in household income, filtered down to the poorest Puerto Ricans? Or to what extent has a lack of uniform economic progress led to higher poverty rates among them?

As we will see, the demographic and household characteristics associated with poverty shed some light on these issues. The age structure of a population, for instance, makes a significant difference in terms of poverty levels: Except for the very old, as persons age, they generally tend to have higher income than when they were younger. As a result, if the average age of a population declines, its average income may go down. Moreover, a key variable associated with poverty is the proportion of all households headed by women without a spouse present. Economists Sheldon Danziger and Peter Gottschalk observed, "Since these [female-headed] households have much lower income than married-couple families, this demographic shift places more families in the lower tail of the distribution and is clearly poverty-increasing" (1993, 14). In addition, differences in poverty levels related to gender, educational attainment, migrant status, and marital status are considered. Finally, the chapter explores the geographic distribution of poverty rates for Metropolitan Statistical Areas (MSA) as well as the levels of public assistance benefits. The chapter ends by showing the consequences of poverty on the standard of living of Puerto Ricans, focusing on the characteristics of households as well as the impact of poverty among children.

The most commonly used measure of economic status is income. The determinants of income and income generation are many and often interact in significant and complex ways. However, there are different ways to look at income and how it is distributed. In some cases, the size distribution of income is used to study income inequality. In this approach, individuals are ranked by income level and then grouped, often in quintiles. Thus, the size distribution of income would show the total share of income going to the 20 percent of the population with the highest income and the bottom quintile showing the total share of income going to the 20 percent of the population with the lowest income levels. While this is a common approach in the study of income distributions, it is not useful for comparing relative income levels across time and among various ethnic and racial groups, as we want to do here.

Therefore, we take a different approach, using a measure of household income per capita to make the necessary comparisons. Because we rely on income levels as determined by the US Bureau of the Census, we use its definition of income, which is calculated in monetary units (dollars) and counts as income the amount of money earned before personal income taxes, social security, union dues, and other deductions are made. At the same time, it excludes noncash benefits, which may be quite substantial for certain groups. Noncash benefits include such things as health benefits, food stamps, rent-free housing, employers' contributions to retirement and medical programs, and others.

The largest component of household income is earnings, since it reflects employment in the labor market. But there certainly are many other important components of household income.[1] Wages and salaries are, by far, the largest source of earnings. We review some of the many factors that determine the level of earnings and income in this chapter. Age is one of the most important determinants of income and income growth. Since earnings reflect the degree of labor market involvement by an individual, the extent to which an individual and other family members participate in the labor force over their lifetimes is another important determinant of earnings and hence income. Clearly, both the industry and the occupation in which someone is employed will have an important effect on his or her income and one's level of education will influence the type of job skills that a labor force participant possesses.

To arrive at the appropriate income measure for our purposes—the mean, or average, household income per capita—we take average household income and divide it by the average household size.[2] When we examine the mean household income per capita for racial and ethnic groups in the United States from 1970 to 2000 (see Table 5.1), we can see the effect of household size, which varies considerably from group to group, on income. Hispanics have had significantly larger households than non-Hispanics, and their household size has increased over the past thirty years compared to the non-Hispanic population. This rise in Hispanic household size has been driven by the growth of the Mexican/Chicano population, particularly by the waves of more recent immigration.

Among Puerto Ricans, average household size surpasses that of non-Hispanic whites and blacks, but the thirty-year trend for Puerto Ricans has been toward smaller households. All other things being equal, this decline in the number of people in Puerto Rican households has led to an increase in mean household income per capita.[3]

Puerto Rican household income per capita, though lower than similar figures for the entire United States, has been increasing at a relatively rapid rate. In fact, incomes among Puerto Ricans grew at a faster rate than the national average for the decades of the 1980s and 1990s. In 1980, income levels among Puerto Ricans were among the lowest for any ethnic and racial group in the country and the prospects for a positive change were pessimistic. At that time, mean household income per capita among Puerto Ricans was only slightly over 50 percent of the US average. After reviewing the socioeconomic progress of Puerto Ricans in the United States in the 1970s, the US Commission on Civil Rights came to the following conclusion:

> The Commission's overall conclusion is that mainland Puerto Ricans generally continue mired in the poverty facing first generations of all immigrant or migrant groups. Expectations were that succeeding generations of mainland Puerto Ricans would have achieved upward mobility. One generation later, the essential fact of poverty remains little changed. Indeed, the economic situation of the mainland Puerto Ricans has worsened over the last decade. (1976, 145)

Table 5.1 Mean Household Income per Capita by Groups, 1980–2000 (in nominal dollars)

	1980			1990			2000		
	Mean Household Income ($)	Number in Household	Mean Household Income per Capita ($)	Mean Household Income ($)	Number in Household	Mean Household Income per Capita ($)	Mean Household Income ($)	Number in Household	Mean Household Income per Capita ($)
United States	19,684	2.75	7,163	37,035	2.63	14,082	56,651	2.59	21,865
Non-Hispanic white	20,602	2.65	7,771	39,037	2.50	15,615	60,364	2.43	24,876
Non-Hispanic black	13,936	3.08	4,530	25,319	2.88	8,797	39,618	2.73	14,534
Hispanic	16,023	3.50	4,582	29,677	3.58	8,295	43,671	3.61	12,096
Mexican	16,016	3.76	4,260	28,681	3.86	7,423	42,831	3.92	10,939
Puerto Rican	12,631	3.31	3,813	26,633	3.19	8,343	40,151	3.00	13,399
Cuban	18,956	2.98	6,357	35,470	2.81	12,638	52,254	2.75	18,995
Other Hispanic	17,330	3.14	5,511	32,178	3.33	9,656	45,158	3.44	13,144
Asian	22,853	3.26	7,004	45,174	3.35	13,485	67,055	3.09	21,667

Source: Integrated Public Use Microdata Series (IPUMS 5% sample files) 1980 and 1990. Census 2000, Public Use Microdata Sample (PUM) 5% Files.
Note: IPUMS 1970 file doesn't have total household income information.

By 1990 the mean income of Puerto Ricans was 59 percent of the US average, and in the year 2000, it reached 61 percent of US mean per capita household income. This upward trend in income among Puerto Ricans provides some evidence of a slowly emerging middle class. It also demonstrates that the dire appraisal of their socioeconomic progress in the mid-1970s was not entirely justified (Rivera-Batiz and Santiago 1994).

One important factor to keep in mind is that ethnic and racial groups in the US population vary considerably by age, which has an important effect on the household income of the group. For example, younger households generally have more children who do not earn an income, whereas older households are more likely to have multiple earners. The Puerto Rican population remains a relatively young one compared to the larger US population, although it has been aging. In part, this aging is due to the large number of people having grown up in the continental United States and the decline in arrivals of migrants from the island.

While 62 percent of the Puerto Rican population was under the age of 34 in 2000, only 49 percent of the total US population was under 34 (see Table 5.2). Moreover, only the Mexican/Chicano population has remained consistently younger than the Puerto Rican population, owing in large measure to the continued migration from Mexico to the United States. Migrant populations are by and large younger than the nonmigrant native population. The US Puerto Rican population has continued to age, and other Hispanic groups represented in the more recent waves of immigration have been augmenting their numbers with younger members.

Age is reflected in other ways on household income per capita. We know that age is related to the timing of both entry into and exit from the labor market and that earnings change over the life cycle. Potential workers look for their first job at an early age or after they have completed some degree of schooling, and they retire at an age when their skills are generally on the decline. This relationship between earnings and age is depicted in Figure 5.1. The curvilinear pattern of the age-earnings profile captures these life cycle effects.

It is particularly noteworthy that the age-earnings profile reflects significant differences by gender. Over their lifetimes, Puerto Rican men residing in the United States earn substantially less than other men. This age-earnings gap is much larger than the one between Puerto Rican women and other US women. Nonetheless, for both the total US and Puerto Rican populations, men earn more than women over their lives. It should be noted that the gender gap among Puerto Ricans is smaller than the gender gap within the total US population because Puerto Rican men earn so much less than other US men. These differences can also be accounted for by a number of factors that are discussed below. However, they do reflect some unknown level of discrimination, in terms of gender, race, and ethnicity.[4]

Table 5.2 Age Structure of the US Population and by Groups, 1970–2000 (percentages of age group in the population group)

Age Group	Total US Population	Non-Hispanic White	Non-Hispanic Black	Hispanic	Mexican	Puerto Rican	Cuban	Other Hispanic Subgroups	Asian
1970									
0–34	58.2	56.4	66.0	70.6	72.5	68.8	55.3	67.9	52.2
35–64	31.9	32.8	26.9	24.8	23.3	21.4	38.6	26.4	32.1
Over 64	10.0	10.7	7.2	4.6	4.3	2.7	6.2	5.7	6.7
1980									
0–34	57.8	55.2	66.4	71.6	74.8	73.7	57.2	67.7	64.5
35–64	30.9	32.3	25.8	23.8	21.3	23.2	41.1	26.7	29.7
Over 64	11.3	12.5	7.8	4.6	3.9	3.0	11.7	5.6	6.0
1990									
0–34	53.4	49.9	61.6	68.7	72.2	67.8	44.6	64.8	60.0
35–64	34.0	35.7	29.7	26.4	23.9	27.8	39.5	29.8	33.8
Over 64	12.7	14.5	8.7	5.0	4.0	4.4	15.9	5.4	6.3
2000									
0–34	49.3	44.6	57.5	66.4	70.1	62.4	39.5	63.4	56.2
35–64	38.3	40.6	34.5	28.8	26.0	31.5	41.8	31.7	36.7
Over 64	12.4	14.9	8.0	4.8	3.8	5.6	18.8	4.9	7.1

Source: Integrated Public Use Microdata Series (IPUMS 5% sample files) 1970, 1980, and 1990. Census 2000, Public Use Microdata Sample (PUMS) 5% Files.

Figure 5.1   Age-Earnings Profile for the Total US Population and the US Puerto Rican Population, by Gender, 2000

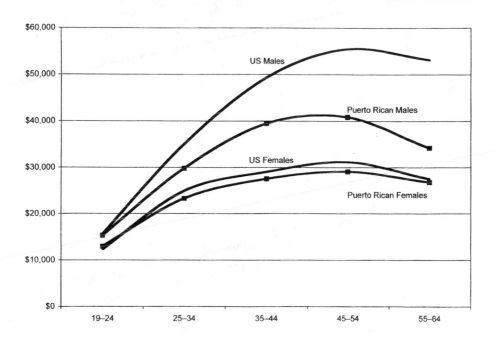

Since earnings, the major component of income, are determined by whether an individual is employed or not, it is clear that differences in labor force participation across ethnic and racial groups will influence the relative level of income. The higher the level of labor force participation, the greater the likelihood that an individual will either have a job or secure employment over a particular period of time. The labor force participation rate captures the fraction of the total working age population that is either currently employed or searching for work. Ironically, if an individual decides not to continue looking for work and drops out of the labor force, the labor force participation rate will fall—this is known as the "discouraged-worker" effect.

Over the past thirty years, the labor force participation rate among Puerto Ricans has remained below that of the total US population by approximately 5–6 percentage points, but it did trend upwards from 1970 to 2000 (see Table 5.3). Participation rates among Puerto Ricans have historically been among the lowest in the United States. But the aging of the Cuban population has led to significant declines in their labor force participation rate, so that by 2000 this group's labor force participation rate dropped below that of Puerto Ricans.

In addition to relatively low labor force participation among Puerto Ricans, unemployment among them has tended historically to be high. Since 1980, un-

Table 5.3   Labor Force Participation by Groups, 1970–2000 (in percentages)

	1970	1980	1990	2000
Total population	58.24	61.90	65.13	63.99
Non-Hispanic white	58.32	62.08	65.26	64.99
Non-Hispanic black	57.53	59.33	62.42	60.69
Hispanic	57.99	63.26	67.25	61.33
Mexican	56.36	64.45	68.08	62.17
Puerto Rican	53.50	54.58	60.27	58.62
Cuban	66.16	66.00	65.02	56.02
Other Hispanic	60.88	64.53	69.29	61.39
Asian	63.23	66.54	67.20	63.67

Source: Integrated Public Use Microdata Series (IPUMS 5% sample files) 1970, 1980, and 1990. Census 2000, Public Use Microdata Sample (PUMS) 5% Files.

employment among Puerto Ricans has stayed at double-digit levels, closely paralleling unemployment rates among the African-American population (see Table 5.4). In 2000, the non-Hispanic Black population experienced an 11.3 percent unemployment rate while Puerto Ricans had a 10.6 percent unemployment rate, and at the same time the national unemployment rate stood at 5.7 percent, approximately half of that of African Americans and Puerto Ricans.

High unemployment often reflects the inability to successfully match a worker's skills with a particular job or task, a mismatch between jobs and skills. This may be due to the lack of more general (schooling) or specific (on the job) training on the part of the worker. It can also reflect an inordinately long time for a person to find work. In some cases, a downturn in economic

Table 5.4   Unemployment Rate by Groups, 1970–2000 (in percentages)

	1970	1980	1990	2000
Total population	4.31	6.39	6.20	5.73
Non-Hispanic white	3.93	5.60	4.91	4.36
Non-Hispanic black	6.84	11.44	12.51	11.32
Hispanic	6.22	8.75	10.31	9.27
Mexican	6.97	8.96	10.54	9.21
Puerto Rican	7.07	11.19	12.22	10.62
Cuban	5.74	5.74	6.92	7.14
Other Hispanic	4.87	7.94	9.70	9.27
Asian	3.50	4.68	5.30	5.40

Source: Integrated Public Use Microdata Series (IPUMS 5% sample files) 1970, 1980, and 1990. Census 2000, Public Use Microdata Sample (PUMS) 5% Files.

activity over the business cycle will result in layoffs of the more recently hired workers—this is known as the "last hired, first fired" phenomenon.

No matter what causes might exist for high unemployment, it is true that Puerto Rican workers in the United States experience unemployment at disproportionately high rates. As we discuss below, the late arrival of the largest group of Puerto Ricans in the Northeast at a time when the manufacturing sector was in decline, and their concentration in New York City when the city faced its most severe fiscal crisis, explain much of the hardship Puerto Ricans have faced in the US labor market.

During the 1950s Great Migration period, most migrants had relatively low skills for the US economy, and they often entered the low-paid service sector or the labor-intensive manufacturing sector, such as the apparel industry. Many of the migrants came from rural backgrounds, which made it difficult for them to find manufacturing employment upon their arrival. In Table 5.5, we present the distribution of the US labor force by industrial classification from 1970 to 2000.

It is clear that in 1970, Puerto Ricans were disproportionately represented in the manufacturing sector, since 42 percent of them were employed in manufacturing compared to 25 percent for the population at large. They were underrepresented in the professional and related services sector, construction, and retail trade. By 1980, the manufacturing sector was in decline, particularly in the Northeast, but it affected Puerto Ricans in particular: The decline in their employment in manufacturing was approximately 10 percentage points, while the national decline was only about 3 percentage points. This trend continued throughout the 1990s, when manufacturing employment among Puerto Ricans reached the national average of approximately 15 percent of the labor force. Thus, between 1970 and 2000, employment of Puerto Ricans in manufacturing declined by 27 percentage points, whereas the national decline over that same time period was only 9 points.

There is no doubt that Puerto Ricans, more than any other group in the United States, suffered disproportionately from the deindustrialization of this country. What is just as remarkable is that Puerto Ricans increased their presence substantially in the personal, entertainment, and recreational services sector as well as the professional and related services sector. Although some Puerto Ricans who were left jobless in the manufacturing sector did eventually move to the lower-wage service sector, one can hardly make the case that they moved to professional services. What these patterns do suggest is a bifurcated labor market process where the loss of manufacturing employment among Puerto Ricans kept their unemployment rates high, at the same time that some degree of upward professional mobility was taking place among other, presumably younger, Puerto Ricans.

To verify these patterns it is useful to examine the occupational distribution of the US population from 1970 to 2000 (see Table 5.6). Once again, there

Table 5.5 Industrial Distribution of the US Labor Force by Groups, 1970–2000 (in percentages)

				1970					
	US	Non-Hispanic White	Non-Hispanic Black	Hispanic	Mexican	Puerto Rican	Cuban	Other Hispanic	Asian
Agriculture, forestry, and fisheries	4.09	3.82	5.18	6.88	1.72	1.80	0.94	3.33	5.68
Mining	0.77	0.82	0.31	0.77	0.98	0.07	0.34	0.88	0.16
Construction	5.77	5.83	5.32	5.58	6.81	2.70	3.39	5.51	4.07
Manufacturing	24.69	24.79	22.69	29.51	26.09	42.11	38.60	26.97	16.56
Transportation	3.34	3.34	3.31	3.39	3.11	4.04	3.02	3.62	2.91
Communication and public utilities	2.87	2.93	2.85	2.00	1.96	1.82	1.51	2.25	2.13
Wholesale trade	3.71	3.83	2.54	4.12	4.63	3.49	4.19	3.60	3.86
Retail trade	17.55	18.24	11.78	16.20	16.10	14.34	16.73	17.02	19.92
Finance, insurance, and real estate	4.90	5.21	2.69	3.82	2.46	5.50	5.80	4.62	4.68
Business and repair services	3.07	3.12	2.59	3.16	2.94	3.38	3.22	3.38	3.00
Personal, entertainment, and recreational services	6.52	5.37	16.33	7.65	7.59	5.68	8.08	8.48	8.33
Professional and related services	17.41	17.47	18.32	12.64	11.03	11.16	12.54	15.67	21.33
Public administration	5.31	5.23	6.09	4.29	4.58	3.90	1.65	4.67	7.38

continues

Table 5.5 Continued

	US	Non-Hispanic White	Non-Hispanic Black	Hispanic	Mexican	Puerto Rican	Cuban	Other Hispanic	Asian
				1980					
Agriculture, forestry, and fisheries	3.33	3.31	2.24	5.58	8.22	1.62	1.16	2.27	2.66
Mining	0.97	1.05	0.39	0.95	1.25	0.13	0.12	0.85	0.24
Construction	6.18	6.38	4.82	6.32	7.55	3.02	4.84	5.33	3.07
Manufacturing	21.82	21.46	22.52	26.80	26.16	32.70	27.51	25.27	20.27
Transportation	4.14	4.06	5.10	3.82	3.43	4.51	4.82	4.16	3.56
Communication and public utilities	2.55	2.58	2.76	2.00	2.13	1.73	1.71	1.89	1.80
Wholesale trade	4.02	4.19	2.67	4.06	4.09	3.65	5.59	3.71	3.67
Retail trade	17.54	18.17	12.73	16.42	16.40	14.72	16.75	17.23	19.89
Finance, insurance, and real estate	5.66	5.91	4.29	4.44	3.16	5.51	7.65	5.64	6.33
Business and repair services	4.14	4.16	3.90	4.30	3.89	4.49	4.88	5.04	3.97
Personal, entertainment, and recreational services	4.82	4.35	7.87	5.86	5.52	4.70	6.22	7.18	6.03
Professional and related services	19.68	19.51	23.29	14.82	13.55	17.03	15.99	16.57	23.07
Public administration	5.15	4.86	7.43	4.63	4.66	5.18	2.76	4.86	5.45

continues

Table 5.5 Continued

	1990								
	US	Non-Hispanic White	Non-Hispanic Black	Hispanic	Mexican	Puerto Rican	Cuban	Other Hispanic	Asian
Agriculture, forestry, and fisheries	2.96	2.89	1.73	5.71	8.33	1.52	1.37	2.21	1.65
Mining	0.61	0.69	0.26	0.49	0.67	0.12	0.09	0.33	0.16
Construction	6.40	6.60	4.85	7.53	8.51	4.51	6.26	6.80	2.93
Manufacturing	17.28	17.13	16.43	19.76	20.15	20.28	18.28	18.93	18.11
Transportation	4.24	4.09	5.67	3.96	3.38	5.18	5.60	4.43	3.82
Communication and public utilities	2.51	2.58	2.76	1.79	1.84	2.03	2.02	1.50	1.69
Wholesale trade	4.14	4.30	2.79	4.48	4.47	4.27	6.12	4.20	4.12
Retail trade	18.30	18.34	16.45	19.19	19.52	17.69	17.02	19.59	21.74
Finance, insurance, and real estate	6.48	6.83	5.15	4.73	3.61	6.92	8.44	5.59	7.02
Business and repair services	4.95	4.79	5.56	5.92	5.46	5.91	6.04	7.05	4.61
Personal, entertainment, and recreational services	4.05	3.60	5.55	5.93	5.30	4.81	5.32	8.15	5.74
Professional and related services	23.49	23.80	25.91	16.82	15.09	21.82	20.07	18.06	24.49
Public administration	4.59	4.37	6.88	3.67	3.68	4.94	3.36	3.17	3.95

continues

Table 5.5 Continued

	2000								
	US	Non-Hispanic White	Non-Hispanic Black	Hispanic	Mexican	Puerto Rican	Cuban	Other Hispanic	Asian
Agriculture, forestry, and fisheries	1.84	1.79	0.71	3.61	5.25	0.72	0.75	1.62	0.66
Mining	0.43	0.50	0.20	0.35	0.42	0.06	0.07	0.32	0.12
Construction	7.57	7.73	5.00	10.60	12.40	5.13	7.82	9.12	2.71
Manufacturing	15.24	14.91	13.93	17.59	19.11	15.27	13.29	15.85	18.20
Transportation	4.58	4.33	6.60	4.36	3.72	5.76	6.64	4.90	4.15
Communication and public utilities	0.92	1.01	0.84	0.55	0.57	0.52	0.69	0.49	0.50
Wholesale Trade	3.80	3.85	2.58	4.74	4.82	4.08	6.60	4.54	3.89
Retail Trade	13.54	14.02	11.70	12.46	11.70	14.17	13.39	13.33	13.71
Finance, insurance, and real estate	7.18	7.63	6.37	5.12	4.02	7.72	9.07	5.97	7.70
Business and repair services	1.55	1.53	1.22	2.15	2.24	1.70	2.16	2.10	1.03
Personal, entertainment, and recreational services	17.12	16.23	18.36	19.88	19.51	18.05	16.84	21.63	21.86
Professional and related services	21.26	21.52	25.57	15.20	13.17	21.45	18.82	16.78	21.92
Public administration	4.98	4.97	6.92	3.39	3.06	5.39	3.86	3.35	3.56

Source: Integrated Public Use Microdata Series (IPUMS 5% sample files) 1970, 1980, and 1990. Census 2000, Public Use Microdata Sample (PUMS) 5% Files.

120

Table 5.6 Occupational Distribution of the US Labor Force by Groups, 1970–2000 (in percent of group)

				1970					
	US	Non-Hispanic White	Non-Hispanic Black	Hispanic	Mexican	Puerto Rican	Cuban	Other Hispanic	Asian
Managerial and professional	14.79	15.90	7.34	7.24	5.01	5.33	10.47	10.58	20.70
Technical, sales, and administrative support	32.43	34.57	17.12	23.59	19.64	24.10	28.54	28.01	29.95
Service occupations	14.68	12.79	30.61	16.89	16.53	16.29	13.75	18.44	18.21
Farming, forestry, and fishing	3.41	3.16	4.51	5.87	10.20	1.42	0.57	2.67	3.88
Precision production, craft, and repair	12.28	12.78	8.23	11.84	12.45	10.19	9.99	12.09	8.36
Operators, fabricators, and laborers	22.41	20.80	32.19	34.56	36.17	42.68	36.68	28.21	18.90

continues

120

Table 5.6 Continued

		1980							
	US	Non-Hispanic White	Non-Hispanic Black	Hispanic	Mexican	Puerto Rican	Cuban	Other Hispanic	Asian
Managerial and professional	20.42	21.96	12.29	10.95	8.58	10.95	17.72	14.81	26.67
Technical, sales, and administrative support	30.29	31.46	24.27	24.36	21.52	27.68	31.56	27.63	30.90
Service occupations	14.62	13.09	25.13	17.34	17.30	17.56	13.25	18.62	16.71
Farming, forestry, and fishing	3.29	3.24	2.57	5.41	7.93	1.72	1.08	2.25	2.61
Precision production, craft, and repair	12.16	12.62	8.43	12.92	13.91	10.47	11.69	12.04	8.11
Operators, fabricators, and laborers	19.22	17.63	27.31	29.01	30.76	31.62	24.70	24.64	15.00

continues

Table 5.6 Continued

				1990					
	US	Non-Hispanic White	Non-Hispanic Black	Hispanic	Mexican	Puerto Rican	Cuban	Other Hispanic	Asian
Managerial and professional	24.07	26.27	15.59	12.62	10.34	14.86	20.73	15.26	28.23
Technical, sales, and administrative support	31.81	32.80	28.58	26.00	23.71	32.51	33.63	26.82	33.93
Service occupations	14.68	12.80	24.18	19.84	19.32	19.12	14.10	22.86	15.90
Farming, forestry, and fishing	2.75	2.63	1.90	5.50	7.97	1.57	1.36	2.20	1.48
Precision production, craft, and repair	11.10	11.42	8.30	12.59	13.44	10.06	12.03	11.78	7.88
Operators, fabricators, and laborers	15.59	14.09	21.44	23.45	25.21	21.88	18.15	21.09	12.58

continues

Table 5.6 Continued

				2000					
	US	Non-Hispanic White	Non-Hispanic Black	Hispanic	Mexican	Puerto Rican	Cuban	Other Hispanic	Asian
Managerial and professional	26.45	29.54	18.31	14.13	11.85	18.49	24.22	15.90	32.67
Technical, sales, and administrative support	31.60	32.65	31.20	25.13	22.40	32.43	32.35	27.25	33.40
Service occupations	16.40	14.30	23.65	22.70	22.73	21.25	16.15	24.00	15.52
Farming, forestry, and fishing	0.91	0.64	0.50	3.11	4.59	0.63	0.50	1.32	0.41
Precision production, craft, and repair	12.11	11.86	10.35	16.78	19.06	11.31	12.78	14.52	7.55
Operators, fabricators, and laborers	12.53	11.20	15.99	18.15	19.37	15.89	13.99	17.01	10.45

Source: Integrated Public Use Microdata Series (IPUMS 5% sample files) 1970, 1980, and 1990. Census 2000, Public Use Microdata Sample (PUMS) 5% Files.

was a disproportionate number of Puerto Ricans (42.7 percent) serving as operators, fabricators, and laborers in 1970. This percentage matches up with the 42 percent of the Puerto Rican labor force in the manufacturing industry at the time. Puerto Ricans were disproportionately underrepresented in the managerial, professional, technical sales, and administrative support occupations in 1970. By 2000 the occupational distribution profile had dramatically changed, mirroring the changes in the earlier table of the industrial distribution of the Puerto Rican labor force.

Again, the decline in manufacturing occupations (operators, fabricators, and laborers) gave way to significant growth in the service occupations, where Puerto Ricans were overrepresented in the year 2000 compared to the larger US population. But one should note that the representation of Puerto Ricans in technical, sales, and administrative-support occupations was equal to that of the rest of the population. Moreover, although they continued to be underrepresented in managerial and professional occupations, 18 percent of the Puerto Rican population were in these jobs, compared to just 5 percent thirty years earlier. Thus, the Puerto Rican labor force has exhibited dramatic changes in occupational structure compared to other groups in US society.

Rising educational attainment among Puerto Ricans, and their increased presence in managerial, professional, technical, sales, and administrative support positions, are the main reason for the improvements that have been noted in terms of household income over the last thirty years. In 1970 over three-quarters of the Puerto Rican population did not have a high school education, and only 2 percent had a college degree. The rates of educational attainment were significantly higher for the total US population in 1970 (see Table 5.7). There is no doubt that twenty years after large-scale migration from Puerto

Table 5.7   **Educational Attainment by Groups, 1970–2000 (in percent of group)**

	1970			
	Less than High School	High School	Some College	College or More
Total population	47.90	31.01	10.43	10.66
Non-Hispanic white	44.84	32.54	11.11	11.50
Non-Hispanic black	68.94	20.88	5.70	4.48
Hispanic	68.03	21.29	6.20	4.48
Mexican	76.23	16.69	4.78	2.31
Puerto Rican	76.28	18.21	3.35	2.16
Cuban	55.30	23.17	10.28	11.26
Other Hispanic	55.35	29.05	8.58	7.01
Asian	37.50	30.02	11.71	20.78

continues

Table 5.7   Continued

| | 1980 | | | |
	Less than High School	High School	Some College	College or More
Total population	33.53	34.58	15.67	16.23
Non-Hispanic, white	30.47	36.03	16.10	17.41
Non-Hispanic, black	48.77	29.30	13.58	8.35
Hispanic	55.95	24.44	11.95	7.67
Mexican	62.34	22.35	10.41	4.90
Puerto Rican	59.82	24.49	10.12	5.57
Cuban	44.53	25.33	13.83	16.32
Other Hispanic	42.61	29.01	15.97	12.41
Asian	25.18	24.64	17.21	32.97

| | 1990 | | | |
	Less than High School	High School	Some College	College or More
Total population	21.96	31.18	25.79	21.06
Non-Hispanic white	18.48	32.44	26.40	22.68
Non-Hispanic black	32.64	29.90	25.27	12.18
Hispanic	47.23	22.85	20.27	9.65
Mexican	53.37	21.69	18.36	6.51
Puerto Rican	43.69	25.52	20.74	10.04
Cuban	38.66	20.85	22.67	17.82
Other Hispanic	36.78	24.83	23.90	14.49
Asian	19.23	19.61	23.16	38.00

| | 2000 | | | |
	Less than High School	High School	Some College	College or More
Total population	19.52	28.60	27.41	24.47
Non-Hispanic white	14.50	29.96	28.58	26.96
Non-Hispanic black	27.12	29.63	28.62	14.63
Hispanic	47.60	22.05	19.89	10.46
Mexican	54.19	20.80	17.53	7.48
Puerto Rican	36.81	25.97	24.69	12.53
Cuban	36.66	20.17	21.90	21.27
Other Hispanic	40.65	23.41	22.40	13.54
Asian	19.34	16.47	21.44	42.74

Source: Integrated Public Use Microdata Series (IPUMS 5% sample files) 1970, 1980, and 1990. Census 2000, Public Use Microdata Sample (PUMS) 5% Files.

Rico began in 1950, Puerto Ricans remained among the least educated of all groups in US society. However, by the year 2000, the educational landscape for Puerto Ricans had improved dramatically. Sixty-three percent of the population indicated that they had a high school degree or higher. Over 12 percent had completed a college degree and almost a quarter have had some college education. Although Puerto Ricans continue to have levels of educational attainment below those of the general US population, they no longer constitute the least educated in the society, and the gains have been real. The improvements in educational attainment among Puerto Ricans in the United States are consistent with the general improvement in educational attainment across the country since the 1970s.

One can argue that Puerto Ricans are now a greater part of the educational landscape, and that the initial stages, where the profile of the migrant population was largely dominated by a gloomy socioeconomic status, have ended. This is not to suggest that Puerto Rican educational attainment has no challenges—high school dropout rates continue to be relatively high; thus, access to higher education is still limited. It has yet to be determined how rapidly the gap between Puerto Rican educational attainment and that of the broader US society will disappear.

Overcoming Poverty

Although this chapter suggests that there has been real socioeconomic progress among Puerto Ricans in the United States since 1980, the gains have not been uniformly spread across the population. In this section we take up the issue of Puerto Rican poverty and review the progress that has been made at the lower end of the income spectrum.

Puerto Rican poverty has been an issue of some interest among social scientists but, for the most part, remains under-studied (see Aponte 1990; Massey 1992; Meléndez 1993a). The research questions that have been addressed generally entailed just how much the Puerto Rican experience could be explained by prevailing theories of poverty. Some analyses have focused on the geographic dimension by highlighting the fact that Puerto Ricans often reside disproportionately in cities that continue to lose their manufacturing base (called the "mismatch thesis"). The concentration of Puerto Ricans in the Northeast and in rustbelt urban centers contributes further to this notion. Others highlight the "culture of poverty" (Lewis 1966), although Lewis's deterministic view of Puerto Rican poverty has been severely criticized by scholars of Puerto Rico and the US Puerto Rican experience. Still others focus on female single-headed households and welfare benefits, and proponents of the human capital approach tend to focus on individual's educational attainment and skills in elevating productivity and hence incomes. And finally, Puerto Ricans have been identified as part of the urban poor in discussions of the "underclass" (Lemann 1991).

The real deficiency of many of these approaches to explain Puerto Rican poverty is that they often lack a solid factual base and that the hypotheses that emanate from them are rarely subject to rigorous empirical testing. For the most part, they may explain a component or some aspect of the US Puerto Rican experience, but they simply do not comprehend the totality, or the majority, of this experience. Thus we are left with rather limited approaches that do not capture all of the changes that have been occurring in the US Puerto Rican community.

The one approach, although outdated, that seems to have received significant attention from academics and the media in the Puerto Rican context is that of the urban underclass. It is virtually impossible to reconcile the various notions that have become associated with this concept. Since the seminal work of Wilson (1987), numerous articles and books have appeared that attempted to bring coherence to the theoretical debates and consistency to the empirical evidence. To some, the urban underclass referred to the coexistence of concentrated and persistent poverty (Wilson 1987; Levy 1977). In this view, those in the underclass differed fundamentally from the working poor because the former had little labor force "attachment." Others used the term to describe the behavior of a particular group, often identified by race, age, and/or ethnicity, whose behavior lay outside that of common social mores (Auletta 1982). These include teenage unwed mothers, alcoholics, street criminals, urban gang youth, and those involved in illicit drug activities.

There appears to be consensus among researchers studying the Latino population in the United States that the notion of an underclass does *not* readily apply to Latinos (see Moore and Pinderhughes 1993; Meléndez 1993a). This is not because persistent poverty does not exist in some Latino communities, but rather because the Latino/Hispanic umbrella encompasses so many different nationalities. The designation "Latino" is less a description of a reality than it is a term incorporating the varied political aspirations of those who have come to the United States from Spanish-speaking Latin America, the Caribbean, and Spain or who have always resided in what was once Mexico's northernmost provinces. An obvious omission from the US Census official definition for the Hispanic category are other Latin American nationalities, such as Haitians and Brazilians.

In the 1970s, the US Census Bureau arrived at the designation "Hispanic" to characterize the people who increasingly refer to themselves as Latino. The panethnic Hispanic or Latino label includes groups that differ among themselves by nationality, race, age, geographic residence, educational attainment, family headship, occupation, industry, and, ultimately, income, labor force, poverty status, and migration history. This diversity is but one reason why the connotation of urban underclass does not readily apply to Latinos. The current reality of Latino communities in the United States and the sociohistorical forces that forged these communities vary greatly.

However, there is an influential body of literature in the United States suggesting that, in contrast to other Latino groups, Puerto Ricans have failed to achieve significant economic progress. It is further argued that Puerto Ricans are at risk of becoming an "underclass." This suggestion was first made early in the 1960s by Nathan Glazer and Daniel Moynihan in their book *Beyond the Melting Pot* (1963). The idea was picked up in studies that suggested that the economic situation of Puerto Ricans was deteriorating over time instead of improving. Tienda (1989) noted that "among Hispanics, between 1970 and 1985 Puerto Ricans experienced a sharp deterioration in economic well-being while Mexicans experienced modest, and Cubans substantial, improvement in economic status" (106).

The result, it has been argued, is that "Puerto Ricans are the worst-off ethnic group in the United States" (Lemann 1991). One of the most vocal proponents of this viewpoint was Chávez in her book *Out of the Barrio* (1991), in which she suggested that "Puerto Ricans occupy the lowest rung of the social and economic ladder among Hispanics" (140). These widespread pronouncements bring us to the following questions: What is it about the Puerto Rican experience in the United States that is so different from that of other Latino groups and that has led to the characterization of Puerto Ricans as an urban underclass? Is this an accurate or adequate description?

One must first remember that Puerto Rican migration to the United States began essentially as a process of "expulsion." As we have seen, Puerto Rican and US leaders in the postwar period defined population pressure on the island as the biggest deterrent to economic growth and development.[5] Operation Bootstrap was never equipped to create the number of jobs necessary to gainfully employ the mass of Puerto Rican workers (largely coming from agriculture) without significant reductions in the population and the labor force. This does not mean that all Puerto Ricans who left Puerto Rico would have been better off by staying, but certainly those who remained benefited economically from the migration of others. Emigration kept both population growth and unemployment rates on the island "artificially" low, as over 20 percent of the active labor force left the island between 1950 and 1960.[6] As a result, per capita income in Puerto Rico increased dramatically. Puerto Rican migration remains one of the largest in modern times as a percentage of the population of origin.

The sheer magnitude of Puerto Rican migration during the 1950s is a clear indication that emigration was actively promoted. The government of Puerto Rico encouraged migration by providing information about economic opportunities, allowing US companies to recruit workers for agricultural and industrial work in the mainland, and promoting an infrastructure to facilitate the ability of people to move (such as low-cost airfare). In the absence of these incentives it is unlikely that Puerto Rican migration would have resulted in so large an outflow as actually occurred. While conventional human capital–based migration models posit that the likelihood of migration is highest among the more skilled, compared to the less skilled, the Puerto Rican migration stream largely consisted of agricultural and low-skill labor during the early decades of mass migration. In this sense, the state actively promoted migration of "surplus labor" as a method to increase the standard of living on the island, and emigration became the "safety valve" that it was envisioned to be.

Despite the importance of Puerto Rican migration in the study of Puerto Rico and the US Puerto Rican population, we really have little knowledge of the links between the institutional and behavioral forces involved in their migration and the economic outcomes of the migrants themselves. In fact, much of the research on Puerto Rican migration has focused exclusively on its impact on the island economy. We do know that Puerto Ricans are a very mobile group and the diaspora has been variously referred to as commuter migration, back and forth migration, and circular migration—the same individual moves frequently throughout his or her lifetime between the United States and Puerto Rico. Others refer to it as the *"guagua aérea,"* or airbus. In this context, some studies described how, to the extent that Puerto Rican migration has been circular in nature, migration disrupted work and schooling, leading to lower earnings over the individual's life. This view was supported by Tienda and Díaz (1987):

> Puerto Ricans have suffered disproportionately with the decline of inner-city manufacturing in the Northeast. But what separates them from other inner-city minority groups is their circular migration between the Island and the United States, which severely disrupts families and schooling, leading inevitably to a loss of income. (A31)

Another factor that must be considered in the assessment of Puerto Rican poverty in the United States is English-language proficiency. This affects the migration experience, since the ability to use the English language is important for economic mobility in the United States. The dominant language spoken in Puerto Rico is Spanish, and even after more than a century of US presence, the island's population is far from being bilingual. According to the US census, in 1980, 58 percent of the island's population (over five years of age) spoke no English and another 28 percent indicated that they only spoke it with difficulty. In 2000 the fraction of the population that did not speak any English was down to approximately 45 percent, and 21 percent spoke English with difficulty. Perhaps this data can help us understand why English is popularly referred to in Puerto Rico as "El Difícil" (the Difficult One) (Sánchez 1994).

Recent immigrants do not perform as well as natives in the US labor market. There is generally a period of adjustment in which the immigrant ultimately adapts to conditions in the local labor market. Eventually, however, immigrant earnings tend to rise rapidly and often outpace those of natives. The

same phenomenon is present in the context of Puerto Rican migration. However, the gap in earnings, unemployment, and poverty is quite large between
recent Puerto Rican migrants and nonmigrants. In fact, even with higher average levels of educational attainment on the part of the migrants, their labor
market performance (that is, earnings, unemployment, and poverty) tends to
lag behind that of Puerto Rican nonmigrants. In this case, the fundamental difference between Puerto Rican migrants and nonmigrants residing in the
United States is English-language proficiency. Recent Puerto Rican migrants
indicate that they are considerably less proficient in the use of English compared to US-born Puerto Ricans.[7] Thus, the institutional features of Puerto
Rican migration, the expulsive character of early migration, the circularity of
recent migration, and the adherence to the Spanish dominant language of the
island all produce an experience and economic outcome unique to US Puerto
Ricans, an outcome that is not readily captured by conventional explanations
for the existence of an "urban underclass."

Poverty rates have come to represent important indicators of the lack of
economic well-being in the population of the United States. They are cited as
evidence of economic disadvantage among ethnic and racial groups in society;
they serve to justify a host of social programs; and they are also used to determine eligibility for as many as twenty-seven federal programs. Poverty rates
are computed by designating an income threshold and indicating the fraction
of the population with incomes below the threshold or poverty line. Poverty
thresholds are computed by size of family and the number of related children
under eighteen years old. A family "below the poverty level" is a family whose
income lies below a minimum poverty threshold representing the lowest nutritionally sufficient (according to the government) standard of living for a family in the United States. It is revised annually to incorporate changes in the cost
of living, as measured by the Consumer Price Index (CPI).

The average poverty threshold in the United States for a family of four
persons (two adults and two related children) was $13,254 in 1990 and rose to
$17,463 in 2000.[8] Use of the poverty threshold has come under criticism, but
the extent to which it understated or overstated actual poverty is not really
known.[9] The poverty rate generally understates the level of poverty by relying
on outmoded, static, and unchanged determinants of a nutritionally sufficient
living standard while simultaneously overstating poverty by relying on erro-
neous and underestimated levels of income.

For changes in the poverty rates of various ethnic and racial groups according to the decennial US census of population, see Table 5.8. Overall, the
poverty rate in the United States rose during the 1980s and declined in the
1990s. But in many respects poverty rates remained relatively unchanged between 1980 and 2000. In 1980, 12.5 percent of the population lived in households with income below the poverty level, and twenty years later that figure
had declined to 12.3 percent. This slight downward trend was replicated for all

Table 5.8   Poverty Levels of Non-Hispanic and Hispanic Groups, 1970–2000

	% Under Poverty Level, 1970	% Under Poverty Level, 1980	% Under Poverty Level, 1990	% Under Poverty Level, 2000
Total Population	13.85	12.51	13.05	12.32
Non-Hispanic white	10.28	8.93	8.97	8.24
Non-Hispanic black	35.77	29.96	29.26	24.45
Hispanic	25.33	23.61	25.13	22.65
Mexican	29.30	23.34	26.07	23.50
Puerto Rican	29.87	36.70	31.52	26.05
Cuban	13.13	12.82	14.44	14.49
Other Hispanic	18.51	18.78	21.35	20.69
Asian	11.07	12.83	13.73	12.60

Source: US Department of Commerce, *1970, 1980, 1990,* and *2000 United States Census of Population and Housing,* 5% Public Use Microdata Sample (PUMS).

major groups in the country, but important differences exist among Latino groups.

In 1980, the Puerto Rican poverty rate was among the highest in the nation at 36 percent—this contrasted with a lower poverty rate of not quite 30 percent just ten years earlier. In 2000 the Puerto Rican poverty rate had declined by ten percentage points, the largest absolute decline among the major ethnic and racial groups. This improvement over time ran contrary to notions of a lack of socioeconomic progress among Puerto Ricans in the United States in the second half of the twentieth century. Nevertheless, poverty rates for Puerto Ricans were still among the highest in the nation. There have also been few efforts among the academic and public policy community to document the improvement empirically and to provide suitable explanations for it. Moreover, in the competitive politics of poverty relief and in the struggles for ethnic representation in the United States as well as the promotion of income maintenance programs, there is little advantage to claiming real economic progress.

Undoubtedly, the 1970s was a decade of real disappointment for the US Puerto Rican population. Over 58 percent of the total migrant population lived in New York City at the beginning of the decade, and the economic downturn at the national and local level hit Puerto Ricans very hard. Cruz and Santiago (2000) described the turn of events in the following way:

> By 1980, the Puerto Rican population in the United States was viewed as the group for which the "American dream" was just that—a dream. All of the relevant socioeconomic indicators pointed to this reality. In the national context, Puerto Ricans had among the lowest income levels, highest poverty rates, low

labor force participation and high welfare dependency, significant numbers of single female-headed households, and low educational attainment. Yet, given their high concentration in New York City and the calamity that befell that city from 1974 on, could things have really been any different? (15)

New York City's fiscal crisis and the accompanying economic downturn in the larger metropolitan area proved to be extremely detrimental to economic progress among Puerto Ricans between 1970 and 1980. As relatively new immigrants to New York City, Puerto Ricans were subjected to "last hired, first fired" policies in both the public and the private sectors. They were also disproportionately represented in the manufacturing sector at a time when manufacturing employment was in decline. Additionally, they were overrepresented in the laborer and service occupations when technological innovation was changing the nature of these occupations and labor demand for them. The fact that job skills and educational attainment among Puerto Ricans were limited compared to other groups in society meant that they were extremely vulnerable to economic downturns. If timing is everything, the concurrence of Puerto Rican migration with economic and industrial structural change in the United States in the postwar period resulted in an environment that was not conducive to socioeconomic advancement among this sector of the population.

What is truly surprising in this context is that between 1980 and 1990 Puerto Ricans made real economic gains. Rivera-Batiz and Santiago (1994) wrote:

> Puerto Ricans exhibited substantial socioeconomic progress in the 1980s. . . . The median household income per capita of Puerto Ricans in the United States increased by close to 30 percent. The result was an upgrading in the relative economic status of Puerto Ricans vis-à-vis other Hispanic groups. . . . Poverty rates declined, welfare participation dropped, labor force participation increased—especially among women—and so did earnings and occupational advancement. (5)

The reversal of socioeconomic prospects for Puerto Ricans between 1980 and 1990 has been attributed to a number of factors, including increased educational attainment (particularly at the associate's degree level) and dispersion to other parts of the country where the economy was more robust. Rivera-Batiz and Santiago (1994) closed "by expressing awe at the resiliency and adaptability of change of the Puerto Rican population" (121). It can be concluded that the economic progress among Puerto Ricans in the 1980s did manage to show itself in lower poverty rates.[10] However, the impact was comparatively small, considering the fact that Puerto Ricans continue to have one of the highest poverty rates among all ethnic and racial groups.

In 2000, the poverty rate among Puerto Ricans still remained the highest among US Latinos. This occurred in spite of the fact that mean household income per capita of Puerto Ricans surpassed that of other Latinos. One implication is that there was greater income inequality among Puerto Ricans than among other Latino groups. The larger proportion of Puerto Ricans at the bottom of the income ladder explained the higher poverty rates. It also gave evidence of the continued emergence of a Puerto Rican middle class and persistent inequality, which Rivera-Batiz and Santiago (1994) had noted ten years earlier.

What variables are associated with higher poverty rates? The extensive literature on poverty in both the general population and the Latino population pointed to several demographic factors.[11] More recent migrants have had higher poverty rates than both older migrants and the general population partly because of the adjustment period required to find gainful employment once in the continental United States. Indeed, as immigrants increase their English-language proficiency, find more information about the local labor market, and cope with their new environment, their income rises substantially, which can be expected to reduce poverty rates (see Chiswick 1978; Borjas 1985; Rivera-Batiz 1991, 1992). This pattern is representative of the Puerto Rican experience in the United States.

In 2000 the highest poverty rates among Puerto Ricans occurred for the most recent migrants, those who migrated to the United States between 1991 and 2000 (see Table 5.9). The poverty rate of these migrants was equal to 31.3 percent, compared to a 25.9 percent poverty rate among Puerto Ricans who moved to the United States during the 1981–1989 period and 23.8 percent poverty among those migrating between 1970 and 1980. The poverty rate among US-born Puerto Ricans (19.4 percent) remained lower than that of migrants. This pattern held true substantially for 1980 and 1990.

Higher educational attainment is associated with lower unemployment, higher labor force participation, and, ultimately, higher earned income. Therefore, higher educational attainment should lead to a lower poverty rate. Thus, educational attainment and poverty rates are expected to be inversely related. Indeed, this seemed to have been the case for Puerto Ricans in the United States, as indicated in Table 5.9. But more important, the disparity in poverty levels was particularly acute between those who have completed a high school education and those who have not.

Individuals who had not completed high school education had almost twice the poverty level of those who had, irrespective of what time period is selected. The poverty rate of persons in 2000 with less than a high school diploma was equal to 40.2 percent, compared to a poverty rate of 21.0 percent for those with a high school education, 12.9 percent for those with some college, 6.4 percent for those completing college, and 4.9 percent among persons with educational attainment greater than a college degree. One of the changes in the Puerto Rican population during the 1980s was a notable increase in the number of people with some college education, but not a completed degree.

**Table 5.9   Percentage of Adult Puerto Ricans Under the Poverty
Level, by Migrant Status, Education, Gender, Marital Status,
and Age, 1980–2000**

	1980	1990	2000
Migrant status:			
US born	22.44	20.44	19.45
Migrated 1991–2000			31.30
Migrated 1981–1990		35.39	25.88
Migrated 1970–1980	33.46	30.98	23.83
Migrated before 1970	27.61	22.42	19.97
Educational attainment:			
Less than high school	37.74	38.50	40.22
High school	19.89	20.33	21.00
Some college	17.06	14.12	12.95
Finished college	8.31	7.44	6.42
More than college	11.13	5.52	4.93
Gender:			
Male	20.38	18.33	17.75
Female	35.52	30.44	26.26
Marital and headship status (ages 20–55 only):			
Never married	37.08	34.22	31.83
Married	18.10	13.11	12.10
Divorced	38.45	31.12	25.84
Separated	58.22	48.08	40.90
Widowed	45.60	40.51	39.54
Female-headed household	60.73	49.10	39.36
Age:			
20–29	30.86	28.08	25.60
30–39	29.59	24.38	21.67
40–49	24.60	21.20	19.50
50–54	23.56	21.00	20.50
55 and older	27.24	26.48	24.94

Source: US Department of Commerce, *1980, 1990,* and *2000 United States Census of Population and Housing,* 5% Public Use Microdata Sample (PUMS).

For those individuals with some college education, poverty rates decline substantially compared to those with only a high school education.

Poverty rates vary considerably by marital status. Married persons tend to have lower poverty rates, owing to the pooling of resources associated with marriage. Conversely, marital dissolution is associated with higher poverty rates. But there is some difference in poverty rates by marital status—poverty rates for those divorced are lower than for the widowed or separated. Previous research has also shown that two major trends have affected the demography of the Puerto Rican island population. Rivera-Batiz and Santiago (1996) pointed out: "The trend toward delayed marriage in Puerto Rico has been accompanied by another significant social trend: marriages on average are lasting shorter periods of time. This is reflected in a rapidly rising divorce rate" (37–38). Puerto Rico's divorce rate is the highest in Latin America and the Caribbean, rapidly approaching US levels (which are among the highest in the world). These trends have had an obvious impact on the Puerto Rican population residing in the United States.

Among US Puerto Ricans, those who were married in 2000 had sharply lower poverty rates than unmarried people. Among married persons in the 20 to 55 age range, the poverty rate was 12.1 percent, which contrasts with a 31.8 percent poverty rate among persons who had never married, 25.8 percent among divorced persons, 39.5 percent for widows, and 40.9 percent for the separated. The high incidence of marital dissolution among Puerto Ricans has resulted in significant numbers of female-headed households that are experiencing very high poverty rates. Although the 39.36 percent poverty rate of female-headed households (in 2000) shown in Table 5.9 is for women ages 20–55 years, the rate is substantially higher when younger cohorts are included.

The declining proportion of married-couple families among Puerto Ricans represents an important factor in explaining their resilient poverty rates. In New York City, for example, the proportion of all households consisting of married-couple families declined from 58.2 percent in 1970 to 33.5 percent in 1990. During this same time period, the proportion of all Puerto Rican households in New York City consisting of a female householder with no husband present rose from 25.4 percent in 1970 to 34.5 percent in 1990. It reached 37 percent in 2000 (City of New York 1993).

Except for the elderly (those over 65 years of age), older workers tend to have higher incomes and lower poverty rates—this is the typical life-cycle age-earnings pattern. The highest poverty rates occur among the younger populations (Table 5.9). For those in their twenties, the poverty rate in 2000 was 25.6 percent. Among persons in their thirties, the poverty rate was 21.7 percent, for those in their forties it was 19.5 percent, and for persons 50 to 55 the proportion was close to 20 percent. For those over 55 years of age, the poverty rate increased to 24.9 percent, considerably higher than the previous cohort.

Generally, women earn less income than men in the labor market and tend to have higher poverty rates. Poverty among women is especially high among households headed by one adult with no spouse present. This is particularly important because of the rising proportion of female-headed households in the United States. As sociologists William Julius Wilson and Kathryn Neckerman (1986) noted: "The rise of female headed families has had dire social and economic consequences because these families are far more vulnerable to poverty than other types of families. Indeed, sex and marital status of the head [of household] are the most important determinants of poverty status for families, especially in urban areas" (240).

Poverty rates among Puerto Rican women in 2000 were substantially higher than among men. Over 26 percent of Puerto Rican women aged 20 to 55 were below the poverty level in 2000, compared to 17.7 percent among men. This situation has been linked to the growing proportion of female-headed households among the Puerto Rican population. An interesting anomaly was that despite the growing number of female-headed households among Puerto Ricans, a declining percentage of female-headed households found themselves below the poverty level. Whereas 28 percent of all Puerto Rican female-headed households found themselves in poverty in 1980, that figure declined to 22 percent in 2000.

Changes in the percentage of female-headed households in the US population by race and ethnicity were significant. The proportion of female-headed households rose for all groups by about 10 percentage points (from 24.3 to 34.9) between 1970 and 2000, but among Puerto Ricans the rate rose from 31.7 percent in 1970 to 47.3 percent in 2000—almost 16 percentage points and the largest increase for any group (see Table 5.10).

In conjunction, the five variables discussed here encompass most of the dimensions of the poverty present within the Puerto Rican population. How is poverty distributed across Puerto Rican communities? Do benefit levels vary significantly across Metropolitan Statistical Areas (MSAs), generally considered extended cities? What consequences does the high rate of poverty among Puerto Ricans have for the present and future standard of living of the population? These questions are discussed in the next two sections.

Table 5.10   **Percentage of Female-Headed Households Among Non-Hispanic and Hispanic Groups, 1970–2000**

	1970	1980	1990	2000
Total population	24.30	27.74	32.50	34.87
Non-Hispanic white	21.55	25.83	30.26	32.54
Non-Hispanic black	39.69	44.35	51.98	54.17
Hispanic	29.20	26.48	30.75	32.84
Mexican	16.67	21.96	26.16	27.55
Puerto Rican	31.70	40.57	45.42	47.31
Cuban	19.93	23.05	28.56	32.54
Other Hispanic	26.52	29.30	33.96	37.07
Asian	14.29	21.01	23.52	27.65

Source: US Department of Commerce, *1970, 1980, 1990,* and *2000 United States Census of Population and Housing,* 5% Public Use Microdata Sample (PUMS).

Differences Among Communities

One of the crucial findings of this chapter is that geography matters. Where you reside influences your earnings and job prospects, housing, and the provision of educational services. We know that the Puerto Rican population is very mobile, both within the continental United States and between the island of Puerto Rico and the United States. Thus, it is not surprising that poverty is also spread across communities in a nonuniform manner.

If one looks at poverty rates in cities with the largest concentrations of Puerto Ricans, one can draw some conclusions (see Table 5.11). First, Puerto Rican poverty was quite high in specific urban areas of the Northeast. Of the top twenty-five metropolitan areas where Puerto Ricans reside, nine exhibited poverty rates of 30 percent or higher in the year 2000. For example, poverty

Table 5.11   Puerto Rican Poverty Rates in US Cities with Largest Concentrations of Puerto Ricans, 1980–2000

	1980	1990	2000
New York, NY PMSA	41.81	37.26	35.71
Philadelphia, PA–NJ PMSA	44.96	44.62	39.39
Chicago, IL PMSA	33.05	31.16	21.83
Orlando, FL MSA	18.82	15.43	15.25
Newark, NJ PMSA	38.84	31.93	26.69
Miami, FL PMSA	25.97	23.48	21.13
Nassau–Suffolk, NY PMSA	15.66	10.24	11.55
Tampa–St. Petersburg–Clearwater, FL MSA	20.37	20.37	18.77
Hartford, CT MSA	56.79	47.09	33.98
Springfield, MA MSA	60.28	56.11	45.41
Bergen–Passaic, NJ PMSA	n.d.	22.18	17.91
Boston, MA–NH PMSA	53.33	40.19	32.30
Jersey City, NJ PMSA	39.16	29.84	26.39
Fort Lauderdale, FL PMSA	10.07	12.07	13.29
Cleveland–Lorain–Elyria, OH PMSA	31.45	40.63	29.00
Middlesex–Somerset–Hunterdon, NJ PMSA	n.d.	13.87	12.23
Los Angeles–Long Beach, CA PMSA	19.58	18.77	20.47
Bridgeport, CT PMSA	38.15	34.79	23.09
Allentown–Bethlehem–Easton, PA MSA	48.50	40.66	35.61
Rochester, NY MSA	35.05	42.46	39.64
Washington, DC–MD–VA–WV PMSA	10.19	6.08	7.53
New Haven–Meriden, CT PMSA	49.90	38.92	36.87
Providence–Fall River–Warwick, RI–MA MSA	50.65	49.22	51.24
Monmouth–Ocean, NJ PMSA	n.d.	16.72	14.44
West Palm Beach–Boca Raton, FL MSA	22.90	25.57	17.09

Source: US Department of Commerce, *1980, 1990,* and *2000 United States Census of Population and Housing,* 5% Public Use Microdata Sample (PUMS).

rates in Providence, Rhode Island, and Springfield, Massachusetts, were 51 percent and 45 percent, respectively, among Puerto Ricans. Second, Puerto Rican poverty was very low in other areas, such as the extended Washington, DC, area or Long Island, New York. From a public policy perspective, the varying concentration of poverty in these communities means that interventions might be more effective when applied within specific geographic areas. In addition, there were very large drops in poverty in one-third of these areas, such as Hartford, Connecticut; Springfield, Massachusetts; and Chicago. Many cities that had large concentrations of Puerto Ricans and high rates of poverty in 1980 saw significant declines in their poverty rates just twenty years later.

The public assistance beneficiary rate is the proportion of the population receiving some public assistance income. For Puerto Ricans there has been considerable correspondence between poverty rates and beneficiary rates in PMSAs (Primary Metropolitan Statistical Areas) and MSAs. Metropolitan areas with high poverty rates (Table 5.11) also had high beneficiary rates (see Table 5.12). The correlation coefficient between poverty and beneficiary rates in metropolitan areas remained quite high but has been declining over the past twenty years.[12] Nevertheless, on average, beneficiary rates were significantly less than poverty rates. In other words, a substantial portion of the Puerto Rican population with incomes below the poverty line did not receive income from public assistance. Given the significantly lower beneficiary levels than poverty rates, it is unlikely that relative mean public assistance income was a major determinant of Puerto Rican mobility.

Poverty is also directly related to the inability of a family to sustain minimum nutritional standards. However, it is also associated with the failure to sustain other basic needs, such as housing, health, and children's welfare. This failure, in turn, negatively affects the ability of current and future generations to attain productive lives, perpetuating a vicious cycle of poverty.

The comparatively high poverty rates among the Puerto Rican population also potentially affected the economic welfare of the children. In 2000, over 44 percent of all school-age Puerto Rican children resided in households living below the poverty level (see Table 5.13). This represented a drop relative to the poverty levels of children in 1990, when the proportion of Puerto Rican school-age children living in poor households was 49 percent. Although progress has been slow, it is important to note that in 1980 almost 55 percent of Puerto Rican school-age children resided in households below the poverty threshold.

The decline in the poverty rate of school-age children for the Puerto Rican population replicated the trend among the general population. For the United States overall, the proportion of school-age children living in poor households fell from 39 percent in 1980 to 36 percent in 2000. Still, of all groups in the population considered in Table 5.13, Puerto Ricans ranked second in percent-

Table 5.12 Distribution of Public Assistance Benefits Among Puerto Ricans in Cities with Largest Puerto Rican Populations, 1980–2000

	1980		1990		2000	
	% of PR Population Receiving Benefits	Mean Public Assistance Income Among Puerto Ricans	% of PR Population Receiving Benefits	Mean Public Assistance Income Among Puerto Ricans	% of PR Population Receiving Benefits	Mean Public Assistance Income Among Puerto Ricans
New York, NY PMSA	14.70	3,051.39	14.06	3,961.75	7.13	3,527.87
Philadelphia, PA–NJ PMSA	13.15	3,234.67	12.87	3,750.98	6.16	3,120.12
Chicago, IL PMSA	8.83	2,961.87	9.86	3,423.39	3.08	2,450.68
Orlando, FL MSA	1.14	2,251.00	2.95	3,341.93	1.91	1,720.83
Newark, NJ PMSA	10.28	3,307.98	8.54	4,212.05	4.08	3,271.77
Miami, FL PMSA	4.82	2,415.49	4.34	3,331.10	3.61	2,511.47
Nassau–Suffolk, NY PMSA	4.34	3,635.71	3.39	5,474.95	1.15	3,789.49
Tampa–St. Petersburg–Clearwater, FL MSA	1.98	1,791.36	3.35	3,066.60	2.61	1,894.62
Hartford, CT MSA	13.68	3,461.06	14.62	4,664.09	7.96	3,463.58
Springfield, MA MSA	15.87	3,401.50	18.59	5,777.30	7.90	4,236.27
Bergen–Passaic, NJ PMSA	n.d.	n.d.	4.72	3,919.99	3.11	3,088.83
Boston, MA–NH PMSA	14.08	3,569.11	13.61	4,787.45	3.87	3,611.14
Jersey City, NJ PMSA	9.62	2,858.73	9.42	3,927.55	3.74	3,067.90

continues

Table 5.12 Continued

	1980		1990		2000	
	% of PR Population Receiving Benefits	Mean Public Assistance Income Among Puerto Ricans	% of PR Population Receiving Benefits	Mean Public Assistance Income Among Puerto Ricans	% of PR Population Receiving Benefits	Mean Public Assistance Income Among Puerto Ricans
Fort Lauderdale, FL PMSA	2.55	2,520.00	2.35	3,242.14	1.37	2,234.04
Cleveland–Lorain–Elyria, OH PMSA	10.12	2,373.46	13.08	3,350.66	4.60	2,077.81
Middlesex–Somerset–Hunterdon, NJ PMSA	n.d.	n.d.	3.72	3,056.95	1.89	2,161.29
Los Angeles–Long Beach, CA PMSA	8.05	2,897.67	8.00	5,493.57	3.28	3,628.33
Bridgeport, CT PMSA	11.80	3,464.14	10.10	4,604.95	4.62	4,215.95
Allentown–Bethlehem–Easton, PA MSA	12.92	2,846.38	10.46	4,116.08	4.83	4,033.74
Rochester, NY MSA	8.23	3,086.74	13.02	4,393.01	8.40	3,515.76
Washington, DC–MD–VA–WV PMSA	1.09	2,440.00	1.39	3,840.47	0.66	2,807.09
New Haven–Meriden, CT PMSA	11.75	3,897.28	12.26	5,457.21	6.48	3,273.06
Providence–Fall River–Warwick, RI–MA MSA	12.66	2,819.50	11.23	5,604.63	9.37	4,285.67
Monmouth–Ocean, NJ PMSA	n.d.	n.d.	5.77	2,970.55	2.22	4,294.96
West Palm Beach–Boca Raton, FL MSA	1.31	605.00	3.37	3,113.39	1.38	3,077.40

Source: US Department of Commerce, *1980, 1990, and 2000 United States Census of Population and Housing, 5% Public Use Microdata Sample (PUMS)*.

Table 5.13   Percentage of Children Among Non-Hispanic and Hispanic Groups Living in Poor Households, 1980–2000

	1980	1990	2000
Total population	39.17	37.62	36.45
Non-Hispanic white	32.17	30.36	28.61
Non-Hispanic black	47.53	45.26	44.64
Hispanic	50.94	46.95	44.94
Mexican	52.59	49.15	46.88
Puerto Rican	54.84	49.05	44.48
Cuban	25.40	23.63	20.99
Other Hispanic	44.63	40.84	42.47
Asian	38.99	36.00	31.10

Source: US Department of Commerce, *1980, 1990,* and *2000 United States Census of Population and Housing,* 5% Public Use Microdata Sample (PUMS).

age of children living in poor households, with only Mexicans having higher rates.

The issue of adequate housing and home ownership is a very important consideration in discussions of poverty. As of 2000, Puerto Ricans had the lowest rate of home ownership in the United States when compared to other groups (see Table 5.14). Only slightly more than one-third of the US Puerto Rican population lives in housing that they own, far less than the two-thirds home-ownership rate in the total population.

A major element driving the lower home-ownership rates among Puerto Ricans is the dearth of single-family housing in New York City, where a quarter of the population resides. Home ownership among Puerto Ricans residing in the New York City MSA is 15 percent, and 35 percent for the total MSA population. But home ownership among all Hispanics in New York City is extremely low. In addition, there is some evidence that the number of persons who reside in a Puerto Rican household is quite high compared to the population at large (Rivera-Batiz and Santiago 1994, 52). Although home ownership has been rising among Puerto Ricans, it remains quite low.

If one were to evaluate the socioeconomic progress of the Puerto Rican population in the United States over the second half of the twentieth century, one would probably reach a mixed conclusion. On the one hand, there is no doubt that the Puerto Rican population has faced, and continues to face, significant economic hardship, obstacles, and challenges. The fact that Puerto Ricans came to the United States in ever-increasing numbers just as the US economy was in the early stages of transforming itself from an industrial economy based on manufacturing to one where high-skill and high-paying jobs in the technology sector were becoming dominant certainly worked against the full integration of Puerto Ricans in the US economy. The extent of Puerto Rican

Table 5.14   Percentage of Owner-Occupied Living Quarters Among Non-Hispanic and Hispanic Groups, US and New York City, 1980–2000

	United States		
	1980	1990	2000
Total population	65.00	64.22	66.09
Non-Hispanic white	69.00	69.05	72.07
Non-Hispanic black	45.37	43.77	45.95
Hispanic	44.16	42.25	45.68
Mexican	49.82	46.92	48.44
Puerto Rican	21.10	25.85	34.36
Cuban	44.32	50.93	57.63
Other Hispanic	45.40	37.99	42.86
Asian	52.01	52.63	52.59

	New York City (MSA)		
	1980	1990	2000
Total population	31.55	32.89	34.73
Non-Hispanic white	39.54	43.60	46.59
Non-Hispanic black	19.64	21.87	26.34
Hispanic	11.89	12.41	14.93
Mexican	16.55	9.05	8.41
Puerto Rican	9.19	11.32	15.26
Cuban	19.93	21.58	25.84
Other Hispanic	15.05	12.87	14.78
Asian	25.81	32.62	35.65

Source: US Department of Commerce, *1980, 1990,* and *2000 United States Census of Population and Housing,* 5% Public Use Microdata Sample (PUMS).

poverty and its many dimensions—female-headed households, job insecurity, geographic and urban concentration, circular migration, youth in their formative years, and inadequate housing—have all posed serious obstacles to those with the task of alleviating poverty in these communities.

Yet, on the other hand, real progress has been made. Household income has increased, poverty rates continued to decline, educational attainment has risen, and a middle class has slowly emerged. Academics and policymakers need to come to grips with this reality. To some it may seem new, but it has been emerging since the 1980s. As long as opportunities are available to augment education and labor market skills and to move to regions and parts of the country where jobs are available and these skills and training are appropriately compensated, the US Puerto Rican population will continue to make noticeable economic gains. The economic hardship of the 1970s should never be repeated, since Puerto Ricans took the brunt of New York City's fiscal crisis.[13] Recovery has been slow but sustained.

The consequences of continually high poverty rates, for both current and future generations of Puerto Ricans, are serious. Low standards of living, reflected in such essential ways as inadequate housing conditions and high rates of children living in poor households, permeate the daily lives of a large portion of the US Puerto Rican population. That so many Puerto Rican children find themselves in circumstances of significant poverty should be a major concern to politicians, policymakers, and others, as we may be leaving a generation behind if steps are not taken to address these conditions. There is a need to focus on crucial support structures, such as local schools, in ensuring a secure future for this sector of the population.

The reasons for the increase in Puerto Rican income per capita during the 1980s and 1990s provide some guide as to how Puerto Ricans are attempting to overcome poverty in the medium- to long-term range. One answer is mobility and the second is educational attainment. Those Puerto Ricans who did leave areas of economic distress and located in more favorable labor markets benefited from their move. The loss of manufacturing employment in the Northeast during the 1970s and 1980s represented a particularly difficult challenge to Puerto Ricans. Approximately 40 percent of the Puerto Rican population in the United States was engaged in manufacturing then. In 2000 only 15 percent of the population was in that line of activity. Given this severe sectoral dislocation, those able to find jobs in expanding labor markets, often far from their original residence, managed to improve their economic lot.

The second key, not unrelated to the first, is educational attainment. The increase in educational attainment among Puerto Ricans during the 1980s and 1990s was most pronounced among those completing two-year and associate's degrees. Individuals acquiring these skills managed to find employment in the expanding service and technical fields (for example, nursing). Nevertheless, it is easy to identify the individuals most at risk among the population. Clearly, those with less than a high school education experienced a dramatic decline in their incomes from 1980 to 2000, as manufacturing employment dried up and the lack of skills made it impossible for them to compete effectively in the areas of emerging employment growth. To many, the alternative continues to be precarious low-wage service sector employment.

A major concern is the extent to which the changes since the 1980s have resulted in greater inequality within the Puerto Rican community. The concentration of Puerto Ricans in midsize cities of the Northeast—cities with a declining employment and tax base—is leading to pockets of extreme poverty surrounded by an infrastructure in decline. It is ironic that despite difficult economic times in these cities, Puerto Ricans continue to gravitate to these places.[14] The economic challenges facing Puerto Rican communities in the

Northeast present a serious threat to the ability of these communities to maintain themselves as viable agents of social and economic progress.

Notes

1. Among the components of income designated by the Census Bureau outside of earnings are "unemployment compensation, worker's compensation, social security, supplemental security income, public assistance or welfare payments, veteran's payments, survivor benefits, disability benefits, pension or retirement income, interest income, dividends, rents, royalties, and estates and trusts, educational assistance, alimony, child support, financial assistance from outside of the household, other income, and government transfers." See the US Bureau of the Census (http://www.census.gov/) for complete definitions of these items.

2. According to the Census Bureau: "A household consists of all the people who occupy a housing unit. A house, an apartment or other group of rooms, or a single room, is regarded as a housing unit when it is occupied or intended for occupancy as separate living quarters; that is, when the occupants do not live and eat with any other persons in the structure and there is direct access from the outside or through a common hall. A household includes the related family members and all the unrelated people, if any, such as lodgers, foster children, wards, or employees who share the housing unit. A person living alone in a housing unit, or a group of unrelated people sharing a housing unit such as partners or roomers, is also counted as a household. The count of households excludes group quarters." See http://www.census.gov/population/www/cps/cpsdef.html.

3. The decline in household size can reflect a decline in family size (fewer children) or fewer adult members of the household. Although in purely mathematical terms, the decline in average household size would reduce mean household income per capita, the underlying nature of household size will impact average (mean) household income.

4. Puerto Ricans identify themselves along various racial classifications, including white and black. See Rodríguez (2000) for an informative discussion of race and the census in the Puerto Rican context.

5. See A. W. Maldonado (1997) for a detailed description of the protagonists, their policies, and the debates during Operation Bootstrap.

6. In comparing post–World War II population growth among export-oriented open economies, Santiago (1992) found that Puerto Rican population growth was extremely low, due entirely to migration rather than the natural increase in the population. For example, Puerto Rico exhibited a population growth rate of 0.6 percent in 1950–1960, compared to Hong Kong (4.4 percent), Israel (5.2 percent), Singapore (4.7 percent), and Taiwan (3.4 percent).

7. Santiago-Rivera and Santiago (1999) found a complex relationship between migrant status, English-language proficiency, and educational attainment among Puerto Ricans in the United States. They concluded: "Both English-language proficiency and educational attainment influence decisions regarding the frequency of migration and a migrant's length of stay in complex ways. It appears that educational attainment alone is not sufficient to assure a Puerto Rican migrant's success in the US labor market if the person's English-language skills are inadequate. While English-language proficiency may compensate for low educational attainment among Puerto Rican migrants, one cannot say that the reverse is true" (241).

8. For more details on the determination of poverty thresholds as used by the 2000 census, see "How the Census Bureau Measures Poverty," US Census Bureau (2002).

9. A 1995 report by the National Academy of Sciences recommended that modifications be made to the definition of poverty in the United States. The proposal suggested making additions to an individual's income by including transfer payments such as food stamps, school lunches, and public housing, while simultaneously subtracting taxes, child-support payments, medical costs, health insurance premiums, and a number of other work-related expenses. See Galvin (1995).

10. A legitimate question is whether the decline in poverty rates for Puerto Ricans from 1980 to 1990 might have been reversed during the early 1990s, coinciding with the economic slowdown in the United States. Information from the Current Population Survey indicates that the poverty rate among Puerto Ricans did rise somewhat after 1990 but did not reach its 1980 level. This demonstrates the cyclical sensitivity of poverty rates to the business cycle and also reinforces the notion that Puerto Ricans did make real economic gains during the 1980s.

11. For surveys on the determinants of poverty, see Tienda and Jensen (1988), Lynn and McGeary (1990), and Meléndez (1993).

12. The coefficient of correlation between beneficiary and poverty rates was 0.68, 0.53, and 0.48 for 1980, 1990, and 2000, respectively.

13. To this date, New York City continues to carry a debt burden from the 1970s. In 2004 the city's debt was around fifty billion dollars, the highest in the country.

14. One reason for the continued migration of Puerto Ricans to these midsize cities is that housing rental rates are relatively low in these communities and for a renter population such as Puerto Ricans, this proves a real alternative to the high housing costs of a metropolis like New York City.

6

Social and
Civil Rights Struggles

In the mid-1970s, a study about Puerto Ricans in the United States sponsored by the US Commission on Civil Rights made reference in its subtitle to their "uncertain future" (1976). This assessment of their overall status was based on the analysis of all the available census data, which showed that Puerto Ricans remained at the bottom of the socioeconomic ladder, part of that unprivileged "other America" (Harrington 1962), still afflicted by socioeconomic and racial inequalities and segregation. All official indicators made it evident that Puerto Ricans were far from reaping the benefits of many of the reforms that came out of the 1960s Great Society. The data called into question the traditional "melting pot" model of immigrant assimilation that ostensibly led to social mobility and integration into mainstream society, since it did not seem to apply to Puerto Ricans or other ethnoracial minorities (Glazer and Moynihan 1963; Torres 1995).

The fact that the civil rights achievements and social transformations of the 1960s and 1970s did not have a significant impact on improving the underprivileged status of US Puerto Ricans led some policymakers to simplistic generalizations about "the Puerto Rican problem," "the Puerto Rican underclass" (Tienda 1989; Lemann 1991), or "the Puerto Rican exception" (Chávez 1991). The combined effect of these characterizations is a portrait of a group lagging behind other nationalities that are part of a growing Latino population ostensibly on its way to joining the US mainstream. The unfavorable socioeconomic status of Puerto Ricans only reinforced the argument that the advantage of being the holders of US citizenship, whether they were born in Puerto Rico or in the United States, did not necessarily make Puerto Ricans better off than other Latinos or, for that matter, non-Latino ethnoracial groups. It also allowed some policymakers and scholars to continue putting forward debasing explanations regarding the subordinate status of Puerto Ricans by blaming the victim or by arguing that their condition was largely "self-inflicted" (Chávez 1991, 161).

What is usually lacking from the many disparaging past assessments of the US Puerto Rican population is a more discerning sociohistorical analysis of ways in which the colonial relationship between Puerto Rico and the United States perpetuates most of the conditions that produce migration. The long-term consequences on Puerto Ricans living in a racially segregated and socially stratified environment and the structural factors that limit their social mobility and keep them as part of an underprivileged working class are also missing from those analyses.

When scholars and policymakers refer to the status of Puerto Ricans and other ethnoracial groups, they generally focus on the discouraging picture that comes out of official socioeconomic data without giving enough attention to the notion that those groups that remain marginalized because of their lower socioeconomic indicators are far from resigning themselves to a life of deprivation and hardship and do not passively accept their poverty status. Closer to reality are the many ways in which working-class Puerto Rican migrants have fought for social justice and a better life for their families and communities, and how their limited representation in the ruling structures of US society remains a major obstacle in achieving any dramatic improvements in their socioeconomic conditions. Against unfavorable odds, Puerto Ricans as well as other minorities have a long history of challenging the power structures around specific issues, pursuing social change, and striving to overcome many of the class and racial inequalities that impair their social progress. But despite some encouraging new patterns of empowerment and socioeconomic progress visible since the 1990s, the existing disparities and overall widening gap between the wealthy and the poor in US society still continue to curtail the possibilities for significant change for Puerto Ricans and other minorities.

In general, Latino struggles for social justice are a neglected component of the civil rights movement and of the North American nation's entire history of social and political struggles. There is a tendency to see the civil rights movement as largely the result of African American concerns and activism, minimizing the participation of Latinos from various national origins, including Puerto Ricans, in these struggles. Few studies have focused on the experiences of specific Latino groups (Acuña 1972; Cockcroft 1995; Torres and Velázquez 1998; Cruz 1998). Nonetheless, as the history of the Puerto Rican diaspora and its various communities continues to be documented through the efforts of some researchers, a different portrait begins to unfold; one that is far from the widely held stereotypes of a docile or apathetic Puerto Rican community, and that transcends catchy but demeaning stereotypical concepts or the many sweeping generalizations found in a substantial portion of the previous scholarship. As we have stated, these include being branded as part of "the culture of poverty" (Lewis 1966) or of "public welfare" (Horwitz 1960), being categorized as part of "an underclass" (Tienda 1989), or bogged down by oversimplified arguments about a population suffering from "self-inflicted wounds" (Chávez 1991) or from a "lack of community organization" (Glazer and Moynihan 1963). New research has contradicted some of these old notions; nevertheless, for the wider US mainstream society, Puerto Ricans, like African Americans, still embody the portrait of a largely apathetic and disenfranchised community, beleaguered by unemployment and welfare dependency, with its youth derailed into a world of gang violence, drug abuse, dropping out of school, and all the other social ills associated with poverty. These problem-oriented characterizations, which have tended to dominate the social science literature on Puerto Ricans for many decades, share a common thread: denying agency to the efforts and struggles of working-class migrants arriving in the US colonial metropolis with the same hopes and dreams of socioeconomic prosperity and a better future that many other groups of immigrants held before them, and enduring the racial prejudices and segregation also experienced by African Americans and Native Americans.

Some of the reasons for the disadvantaged status of Puerto Ricans, especially before the 1990s, already have been analyzed in detail in earlier chapters. A good portion of the traditional scholarship displayed a tendency to overemphasize the most pressing problems affecting Puerto Ricans without giving due attention to their collective struggles and numerous contributions both to the development of their own communities and to the wider US society. By examining concrete examples of collective action, in this chapter we attempt to provide a more balanced portrait by drawing attention to the different forms of activism that have engaged Puerto Ricans in the United States.

There were several forms of social and political engagement bourgeoning in the various US Puerto Rican communities during the civil rights era. However, it is also important to point out that Puerto Ricans, like other Latino groups, waged many battles during earlier periods in defense of their rights or around specific issues related to the welfare of their respective communities. Their activism in the civil rights movement represents a visible continuation of a long history of fighting back against the injustices or indifference of the power structures. Earlier efforts, however, took place in a society torn by racial strife, one with fewer opportunities and legal protections for those groups considered nonwhite. For many decades the "invisibility" of these groups in the Anglo-American mainstream was obvious. Prior to the 1960s, it was rare for the established mainstream organizations to be responsive to minority concerns or agendas. These groups were therefore compelled to create their own professional and grassroots organizations and media outlets to voice their specific issues and needs. Those organizations focusing on Puerto Rican or pan-Latino affairs range from mutual aid societies, social and cultural clubs, churches, business associations, advocacy groups, and community service agencies, to outright political organizations.

Political and Educational Activism

Of all the areas of community activism, political organizations were the most radical, particularly during the decades of the 1960s and 1970s. Racism and related issues of inequality and social justice were central to the Puerto Rican agenda, as they were for other minority groups. Nevertheless, most of the Puerto Rican political organizations established during the civil rights struggles reflected concerns that were very specific to that population, including the island's colonial relationship with the United States. Within the various Puerto Rican communities, political organizations worked for increased representation in city governments and the Democratic Party in order to address some of the most critical problems and issues, but Puerto Rico's political status was an issue that often linked some US-based political organizations to those on the island. That being the case, there was an expectation that a shared concern about Puerto Rico's colonial condition would bring the communities of the island and the diaspora closer to one another in the pursuit of common political goals.

But ironically, Puerto Rican political organizations in the United States were far from reflecting the political preferences of island residents. Since the late 1960s the majority of Puerto Rico's electorate has been almost evenly divided between support for the Commonwealth status quo and for future statehood for the island, with less than 4 percent of the voters supporting independence.[1] In contrast, a large number of US-based Puerto Rican political organizations supported independence, even when they were concentrating on specific concerns of their local communities.[2] This political stance, along with their socialist orientation, limited their appeal to only a small sector of the migrant population. One of the few issues that resonated with Puerto Ricans from both shores was seeking the release of Nationalist political prisoners, some incarcerated in federal prisons since the 1950s. This particular cause was dramatized when the Puerto Rican flag was hung on the forehead of the Statue of Liberty in 1977 by a group of activists seeking the freedom of Puerto Rican political prisoners.

A number of the political organizations that emerged in major US cities with large concentrations of Puerto Ricans during the civil rights period reflected the left-wing radicalism of those years, both ideologically and in their practices. Socialism proved to be a useful tool in denouncing the exploitation and socioeconomic disparities perpetuated by the capitalist system and US colonialism and imperialist domination over Puerto Rico and other Third World countries. The Vietnam antiwar movement and the rejection of compulsory military service by many Puerto Ricans, along with the demands for new civil rights protections, equality of economic and educational opportunities, and the overall plight of the poor in the richest country in the world provided a broader context for these particular struggles to be carried out. Massive demonstrations, strikes, and other forms of mobilization mirrored the wider political unrest in North American society.

Torres (1998, 5) identified eight core groups that represented the radical political spectrum within the Puerto Rican diaspora during this period: The Young Lords Party (YLP, later to change its name to the Puerto Rican Workers' Organization), El Comité-MINP (Movimiento de Izquierda Nacional Puertorriqueña; Puerto Rican National Leftist Movement), the Puerto Rican Student Union (PRSU), the Movimiento de Liberación Nacional (MLN, Movement for National Liberation), the Frente Armado de Liberación Nacional (FALN, Armed National Liberation Front), the Partido Socialista Puertorriqueño (PSP, Puerto Rican Socialist Party), the Partido Nacionalista Puertorriqueño (PN, Puerto Rican Nationalist Party), and the Partido Independentista Puertorriqueño (PIP, Puerto Rican Independence Party). Several of these organizations originated in the United States, but a few others, such as the PSP, the PN, and the PIP, were branches of political parties originally founded in Puerto Rico, all of them calling for the island's independence.

Of the different range of organizations listed above, the Young Lords is the one that best represents the concerns of Puerto Rican urban youth and their commitment to make a difference in dealing with the everyday problems of the inner city barrios. The group originated in Chicago in 1969; its founders had been part of a Latino youth gang encouraged by members of the city's Black Panthers to channel their activities into the more constructive path of social and political activism aimed at improving conditions in their poor neighborhoods. Several Puerto Rican college students from New York had come together to form the Sociedad Albizu Campos (Albizu Campos Society), an organization that defended Puerto Rico's right to self-determination. They heard about Chicago's Young Lords and went to that city to meet Cha Cha Jiménez, the group's leader. During the visit they were inspired by the grassroots activist agenda of Chicago's Young Lords and secured their consent to start their own chapter in New York (Guzmán 1998). Eventually, the New York chapter of the Young Lords ended up being the most visible and active, although branches also were established in Philadelphia, Newark-Hoboken, Bridgeport, and Puerto Rico. In their organizing efforts, the Young Lords tried to reach out not only to those living in the urban barrios but also to students on college campuses, community professionals, and other activists who could help them advance the organization's social and political goals.

The Young Lords were most effective in mobilizing youth for their campaigns to create breakfast programs for needy children and people's health clinics for the detection of lead-poisoning, tuberculosis, diabetes, and other illnesses. Additionally, they fought for the improvement of hospital services and prison conditions, and pressed on to make inner-city schools more responsive to the educational needs of migrant children with limited English proficiency. They supported bilingual education and curricular reforms that incorporated a student's cultural heritage. The Young Lords even engaged in more mundane undertakings, such as mobilizing the community to help out in cleaning up the garbage on the streets of the barrios and forcing the city's municipal government to improve its garbage collection practices.

The Young Lords' newspaper *Pa'lante* (Moving Forward) was an important vehicle for denouncing injustices against the Puerto Rican and Latino communities, as much as it was a consciousness-raising tool.[3] The group's popular slogan, "Tengo Puerto Rico en mi corazón" [sic] (I carry Puerto Rico in my heart),[4] was more than a reflection of their pride in their cultural roots. It translated into a political agenda against US imperialism and its colonial domination of Puerto Rico, and in support of the island's independence.

The radicalism of most of the organizations mentioned stemmed from seeing capitalism and racism as major sources of workers' oppression and from their endorsement of socialism. Their commitment to Puerto Rico's self-determination had been invigorated by the United Nations in 1972, when this international organization called for an end to the colonial relationship between Puerto Rico and the United States (see Gautier Mayoral and Argüelles 1978). Another related issue was the demand for freedom for Puerto Rican political prisoners, mainly former members of the Nationalist Party and the FALN.

As described in Chapter 3, the repressive measures against Puerto Rican Nationalists were part of a more concerted effort that had begun in the mid-1930s. It was aimed at discouraging support for Puerto Rico's independence among the island's population and within the diaspora. These coordinated measures involved the FBI, CIA, and the island's police and government agencies. Most notorious for its domestic covert operations was the FBI's counter-intelligence program (COINTELPRO), which carried out a war against political dissent in the United States during the 1960s and 1970s (see Churchill and Wall 1990). For more than half a century, imprisonment, blacklisting, surveillance, and other forms of political persecution were systematically used by public officials to suppress political dissent toward leftist or proindependence groups, or any groups labeled as "subversive" because of their opposition to US colonial rule in Puerto Rico (see Acosta 1987; Churchill and Ward 1990; Bosque Pérez and Colón Morera 1997). *Carpetas* (files) were created by the police for any individual suspected of being a dissident. Files or cards for over 150,000 individuals were kept by the Intelligence Division of the Puerto Rican police (Bosque-Pérez and Colón Morera 1997, 303). Along with these repressive measures, island institutions, the school system in particular, was used to "Americanize" Puerto Ricans and create a consensus to justify US control over the island (see Negrón de Montilla 1971; Silva Gotay 1997). The result of these sometimes overt, sometimes less evident, policies was to deflect the perception that Puerto Rico was under the yoke of US imperialism and substitute the more agreeable notion that at best, the relationship between the two countries is the result of "a compact" or "mutual consent" and, at worst, a reflection of "colonialism by consent."

In the continental United States, the 1950s was a decade characterized by the numerous civil rights struggles and the anti-Communist hysteria and witch-hunt tactics fostered by the hearings of the House of Representatives' Committee on Un-American Activities (HUAC) and those instigated by Senator Joseph McCarthy. Notorious investigations and intimidation tactics were directed against numerous groups and individuals. Conducted under the guise of protecting the country against the threat of communism, they created an environment that violated basic civil liberties.

While the focus of US society shifted toward the Communist threat, racial violence and segregation continued to affect the lives of nonwhite groups. This was seen more vividly in the southern states, although it also was a problem in inner cities with large concentrations of ethnoracial minorities. For Puerto Rican migrants and other minorities living in this environment, being the holders of US citizenship did not prove to be advantageous, since being considered nonwhite meant that they would be excluded from having the same rights and opportunities shared by the white majority.

A large number of Puerto Rican political organizations of the civil rights period were consistent in denouncing the abuses of capitalism and the virtues of socialism, although frequently they ventured out of this broader ideological agenda. Their solidarity with grassroots efforts to deal with specific community issues is well known, and they were most effective when they collaborated with local groups in these efforts. Puerto Ricans came together to denounce situations that involved issues such as abuses by the police and slumlords, inadequate schools and health services, institutional discrimination, and segregation and violence in the urban barrios.

It is fair to say that the radical positions espoused by some of the political organizations, mainly those issues related to the island's independence and to socialist revolution, had limited appeal to the majority of the migrant population. Since the mid-twentieth century, independence has not been the preferred status choice of Puerto Rico's electorate, and even less so after the coming into power of the PPD and the subsequent inauguration of the current Commonwealth in 1952. The downturn in support for Puerto Rico's independence during the second half of the twentieth century was due in part to the success of Muñoz Marín's populist movement, since his party discarded this political alternative in favor of a permanent, albeit subordinate, relationship with the United States (see Chapter 3). Other important factors in the decline of political support for independence were the fear that the violent methods advocated by Nationalists and other radical groups instilled among the Puerto Rican population and the Commonwealth government's collaboration in the systematic persecution of these groups and other independence supporters (see Bosque Pérez and Colón Morera 1997).

Two of the most radical Puerto Rican political groups during the 1970s were the MLN and FALN. Functioning underground, they resorted to clandestine activities and the use of violence to draw attention to Puerto Rico's colonial condition. The FALN claimed responsibility for several bombings of naval bases and tourist hotels in Puerto Rico, and some of its members were held responsible for the 1985 robbery of millions of dollars from a Wells Fargo armored truck in Hartford, Connecticut. Another radical group, the Puerto Rican People's Army, or Los Macheteros (the machete wavers; see Fernández 1987), was mostly active in the United States. Several of its leaders were on a long list of Puerto Rican political prisoners in the United States found guilty of conspiracy and sedition with cases often built around questionable evidence. Some of these radical organizations justified the use of violence as an adequate response to the aggression and persecution exerted by the colonial power structures against independence advocates, but from the perspective of the ruling authorities, they were simply terrorists and a threat to the established order. Thus their appeal to the general population was limited, and by the 1990s most of these groups had faded away.

Trying to usurp or tear down the Establishment's oppressive social and political structures was not, by any means, the only course of action taken by Puerto Rican organizations. Challenging the legality of segregation and discrimination in the courts was a path that yielded some landmark results in the struggles for civil rights reforms. Chicanos and Puerto Ricans, following the model of the National Association for the Advancement of Colored People (NAACP) in its advocacy for improving the status of African Americans, established their own legal institutions to seek social justice and challenge the constitutionality of segregation. With a seed grant from the Ford Foundation, the Mexican American Legal Defense and Education Fund (MALDEF) was founded in 1968 and the Puerto Rican Legal Defense and Education Fund (PRLDEF) in 1972. With a main focus on litigation, public policy, and education, the PRLDEF has initiated landmark class action suits, the most notable being the successful ASPIRA consent decree, discussed below; the Proyecto Ayuda (Project Aide), aimed at securing benefits for the families of the victims of the September 11 terrorist attacks; legal support for the people of Vieques in their efforts to force the US Navy to discontinue military target practices that were having negative consequences on the population's health and environment; and challenges to politically influenced redistricting in Latino communities.[5]

The National Congress for Puerto Rican Rights (NCPRR), founded in the South Bronx in 1981, with chapters later established in Boston, Philadelphia, and San Francisco, is another advocate for the human and civil rights of Puerto Ricans. The NCPRR favors rallies and demonstrations to try to influence policy (Cruz 2000) and prides itself on being an independent entity. It does not rely on government funds for its local or national campaigns "against environmental racism, police abuse, racially-motivated violence, and other forms of discrimination" (www.columbia.edu/~rmg36/NCPRR.html).

Political representation of Puerto Ricans in the ranks of state and national electoral politics has been limited. Only a handful of Puerto Ricans have been elected to Congress, all to the House of Representatives. This in part reflects the low rate of Puerto Rican participation in US electoral politics, despite the fact that over 80 percent of the voters in Puerto Rico cast their vote on any local elections. It is also a reflection of how slow the Democratic and Republican Parties have been in engaging Latino voters. The majority of US Puerto Ricans serving in Congress in 2006 are representing New York City districts, with one representative from Chicago. Herman Badillo was the first Puerto Rican elected to the US Congress and the only one for most of the 1970s. Robert García, a former assemblyman and senator in the New York State legislature, replaced Badillo when he gave up his congressional seat in the 1980s to join New York City's Koch administration and pursue his still unrealized aspirations to become the city's first Puerto Rican mayor. An investment scandal prompted García's resignation from Congress; he was replaced in 1990 by José Serrano, also a former member of the New York State legislature. Three years later, Serrano was no longer the only voting representative of Puerto Ricans in Congress when he was joined in the House by Nydia Velázquez from New York and Luis Gutiérrez from Chicago.

Many US Puerto Rican community organizations have been making voter registration a priority issue and frequently sponsoring voter registration campaigns. The result is that Puerto Ricans have been doing better than before at being elected in state and municipal legislative posts. According to the National Puerto Rican Coalition, in 1999 there were 95 Puerto Rican elected officials in legislative positions around the country (1999).

Only a few Puerto Ricans have been elected mayors of large cities: Maurice Ferré, who served in the early 1970s in Miami; Eddie Pérez, elected in 2000 in Hartford, Connecticut, a city where Puerto Ricans represent almost a third of the total population; and George Pabey, elected in 2004 in East Chicago, Indiana. Appointments to high-level government posts have not fared any better. Teodoro Moscoso, the main architect of Puerto Rico's Operation Bootstrap, was appointed by President John Kennedy as US ambassador to Venezuela and, later on, as head of the Alliance for Progress, a major Kennedy administration US foreign policy initiative to promote economic development and democracy throughout Latin America. Gabriel Guerra Mondragón, a prominent lobbyist in Washington, DC, served as ambassador to Chile during President Bill Clinton's administration. Another high-level administrative post was occupied by Antonia Novello, appointed surgeon general during George W. H. Bush's administration; she was subsequently selected by Governor George Pataki to head the New York State Department of Health. Novello is a fervent advocate of HIV/AIDS prevention among minority populations. Attorney José Cabranes was first appointed federal district judge in Connecticut by President Jimmy Carter and later received an appointment to the Second Circuit US Court of Appeals by President Clinton. A noted legal scholar, his name is frequently mentioned as a potential candidate for the Supreme Court. Back in the 1970s, Cabranes was a founding member and chair of the PRLDEF and also headed ASPIRA's Board of Directors.

In summarizing the political accomplishments and challenges of US Puerto Ricans, Cruz (2000) offered a sobering assessment. He noted that elected officials tended to focus on "amelioration and the short term" (56) without a good balance with longer-term objectives. He pointed to a lack of "a two-pronged policy agenda, seeking both economic growth and equality" (57), and argued that for the diaspora "the political system has failed most of its members" (56). There were a few examples of what Cruz described as "convergence," where radical agendas were subsumed by political compromise and electoral mobilization in order to get more representation in the city councils and state legislatures, as happened in cities like Hartford and Philadelphia (50). Finally, Cruz made a discouraging, but realistic, statement about the general attitude of the US Congress by stating that it had a long history of treating island Puerto Ricans with "selective inattention" and US Puerto Ricans with "oblivious disregard" (57).

In 2005, of twenty-five Latinos serving in the US Congress, only the aforementioned three were Puerto Rican. Occasionally, Latino elected officials have come around in support of some common issues that transcend individual nationalities, but it cannot be said that at this time there is a unified Latino political force in Washington, DC. The rapid growth of the US Latino population, however, is forcing the major political parties to increasingly seek their vote, and it is reasonable to assume that eventually this will translate into more political power for Puerto Ricans and other groups.

The most obvious accomplishments of the Puerto Rican civil rights movement were in the educational arena. The many persistent problems faced by students in New York City's public schools and those of other large cities where the majority of Puerto Ricans resided, made it relatively easy to define an agenda for change. Among the most pressing educational problems were high dropout rates at the secondary school and college levels, the lack of bilingual education and instruction in English as a second language for new migrants and their children, the underrepresentation of Puerto Rican and Latino teachers and other professions, and the large number of inadequate and quasi-segregated schools in minority communities. Community involvement in denouncing these conditions and their demands for better schools and a more effective education were major catalysts in promoting reforms.

Grassroots organizations stood out in the struggle for better schooling and against school segregation. Worthy of mention is the United Bronx Parents,

A 1960s mass demonstration against New York City's Board of Education advocating school desegregation and better quality schools and education. Archives of the Puerto Rican Diaspora, Centro de Estudios Puertorriqueños, Hunter College.

Inc., founded in 1964 under the leadership of Evelina López Antonetty. A dedicated grassroots activist, López Antonetty rallied Puerto Rican parents to form an alliance with African American parents in order to advocate more effectively for school desegregation, the improvement of schools, and more effective preparation for students to go on to higher education. For many decades, the licensing of Puerto Rican and Latino teachers in general was curtailed by the practices of the New York City Board of Education and powerful teacher unions—the United Federation of Teachers (UFT) and the American Federation of Teachers (AFT)—which were controlled by the white majority. It was common practice for a Puerto Rican teacher with a Spanish accent to be denied a license by the board and relegated to the corps of auxiliary teachers with limited possibilities for advancing their careers. (This practice was applied to other teachers with foreign accents as well.) The parents demanded the hiring of more minority teachers and administrators and the establishment of bilingual education and a multicultural curriculum as a way of improving student-retention rates and academic achievement. They also denounced the common practice of "tracking" minority students into vocational areas, rather than encouraging them to go to college, and the overall disregard for their cultural heritage and Spanish language. Other demands included administrative decentralization and more community control over the schools.

No agency has influenced Puerto Rican and other Latino youth educational goals more than ASPIRA (to aspire or strive in Spanish; see www.aspira.org). Established in New York City in 1961 under the leadership of Antonia Pantoja, this organization reached out to high school students to increase their motivation and preparation for completing their secondary schooling, develop leadership skills, and pursue a college education.

In the 1950s, Pantoja had been a founder and president of the Hispanic Young Adult Association (HYAA), an organization that strove to make the New York City government more responsive to the needs of the expanding Puerto Rican migrant population. During its early years the HYAA held voter registration drives and worked toward improving conditions in shelters for the homeless and fostering educational and leadership development among youth. Pantoja was joined in these efforts by other Puerto Rican professionals, Alice Cardona, Louis Núñez, and Josephine Nieves, among them. As the organization expanded, the leaders of the HYAA decided to shift its focus to the specific needs of the Puerto Rican migrant community and, in 1954, changed its name to the Puerto Rican Association for Community Affairs (PRACA). Three years later, Pantoja and other leaders founded the Puerto Rican Forum (PRF, later to become the National Puerto Rican Forum, or NPRF). The PRF was originally conceived as "a launching-pad" for the establishment of new community organizations or service programs (Pantoja 2002, 92). The organization's original goals were to assess the community's main problems and priorities and to facilitate the creation of new institutions to deal more appropriately with specific areas of need. The PRF strove "to conceive ways of ensuring self-sufficiency and effective citizenship for the new wave of Puerto Ricans emigrating to the United States."[6] Under the directorship of Frank Bonilla, during its early years the PRF concentrated on developing leadership and increasing educational opportunities for Puerto Rican youth, and planted the seeds for the subsequent creation of ASPIRA. The PRF also provided services in adult literacy, English as a second language, and job placement. Another important accomplishment of the PRF was the creation of Boricua College in 1972, the first Latino bilingual higher education institution in New York City. With offices in New York, Chicago, and Río Piedras, Puerto Rico, the current NPRF still tends to the educational and employment needs of low-income Latinos. Every year the NPRF recognizes individuals whose work has made a difference to the Puerto Rican and Latino communities with their "¡Sí, Se Puede!" (Yes, We Can!) awards.

The War on Poverty, launched by the Johnson administration in the mid-1960s, provided the resources for a new wave of antipoverty programs. These new opportunities led to what was perhaps the best-funded endeavor aimed at alleviating the poverty of most Puerto Rican New Yorkers: the Puerto Rican Community Development Project (PRCDP). With the involvement of Pantoja and other PRF members, the PRCDP brought together the various professional agencies and grassroots organizations serving the community to develop "a model for comprehensive community development and advocacy" (Pantoja 2002, 114) aimed at reducing Puerto Rican poverty. But the project fell short of fulfilling its major goal. Stiff competition for controlling federal funding and other power struggles between members of the PRF and the Commonwealth's Migration Division provoked the resignation of Pantoja and many others from the PRCDP board. A few of the barrio leaders administering antipoverty programs used them for political patronage, intensifying rivalries and divisions within the community and the competitive undermining of one another's efforts. Like many of the antipoverty programs of this period, their positive effects were short-term; they gradually disappeared when the US Congress reduced and eventually eliminated federal funding for them.

Antonia Pantoja's multiple contributions to the US Puerto Rican community were recognized nationally when she was awarded the Medal of Freedom by President Bill Clinton in 1996. The former factory worker, schoolteacher, social worker, and activist dedicated over half a century to the various community-building activities described above, playing a leadership role in the creation of several of the most prominent organizations that continue to serve the Puerto Rican and Latino population of New York City.

As the leading advocacy agency for New York Puerto Ricans and other Latinos, ASPIRA joined forces in 1972 with the then newly created organization PRLDEF and filed a legal case against New York City's Board of Education demanding the implementation of bilingual education programs for students with limited English proficiency. The outcome of *ASPIRA vs. Board of Education* was a consent decree that mandated bilingual instruction in certain New York City schools. The most visible advocates of bilingual education throughout the state included educators such as Hernán La Fontaine, Luis Fuentes, Carmen

Pérez, María Ramírez, and Awilda Orta. La Fontaine and Pérez were among the founders and former presidents of the National Association for Bilingual Education (NABE), also established in 1972. Pérez and Ramírez played a leadership role in promoting bilingual and international education in New York State. For more than three decades, Pérez headed the Bilingual Education Bureau of the New York State Education Department, which monitors the implementation and effectiveness of these programs.

Several other founders of the HYAA have occupied leadership positions in organizations that promote the welfare of their communities. A notable figure was Alice Cardona, the program coordinator of the United Bronx Parents and cofounder of the Hispanic Women's Center (HACER [*hacer* means to do, make, or build]). This latter organization focused on the particular educational needs of women. Another HYAA founding member, Louis Núñez, was later among the founders and directors of the National Puerto Rican Coalition (NPRC; see www.bateylink.org) in Washington, DC. Since 1977 the NPRC has concentrated on advocacy and public policy issues, has been instrumental in drawing attention to the concerns of the US Puerto Rican community, and has tried to influence Congressional legislation.

Influencing legislation and formulating public policy at municipal and state levels were among the original goals of the Institute for Puerto Rican Policy (IPRP), established in New York in 1982 by Angelo Falcón. Since its early years, the IPRP has concentrated on the analysis of the patterns of Puerto Rican and Latino participation in New York's electoral politics and on redistricting issues. The IPRP has also tracked demographic changes in the state population. In 2000, the PRLDEF and the IPRP combined their legal and public policy expertise and merged into one organization. This alliance was dissolved in 2005, when they became separate organizations again. For several years, the IPRP served as the policy and advocacy division of the PRLDEF, coordinating projects on a variety of issues, such as Latino municipal priorities, voting rights and electoral reform, bilingual education, and advocacy training (see www.prldef.org).

The emergence of Puerto Rican Studies programs at various US universities, in particular those affiliated with the City University of New York (CUNY), State University of New York (SUNY), and Rutgers University systems, paved the way for dispelling many of the myths about Puerto Ricans perpetuated in the scholarly literature. New research and teaching endeavors exposed some of the shortcomings of the traditional scholarship and inspired new approaches to the study of Puerto Ricans. Foremost among the efforts of this generation of Puerto Rican scholars was to document the multifaceted experiences of a working-class diaspora, in relation to the island's colonial condition and as a marginalized ethnoracial minority within the United States. Researchers began to establish the link between Puerto Rico's colonial experience and the "internal colonialism" (Blauner 1972) being experienced by Puerto Ricans and other disenfranchised groups in US society. Unquestionably, Puerto Rican Studies scholars and activists in the United States continue to play a central role in the efforts to "decolonize" traditional interpretations of Puerto Rican migrant experiences, which often replicated the negative views and prejudices of the wider society. Puerto Rican Studies scholars concentrated their efforts on documenting and recovering a collective presence and heritage that had been largely distorted or excluded from conventional histories of the United States. They also drew attention to the power relations and structural dynamics that contribute to perpetuating social and racial inequalities within US society.

Puerto Rican Studies and other ethnic studies programs were the result of the activism from students, community members, and professionals, directed toward making higher education more responsive to the needs of Puerto Ricans and other minority students. These programs not only provided students with new knowledge about their historical and cultural roots but also promoted important paradigm shifts within the academic disciplines in their study of ethnic, racial, and gender differences and raised awareness about the conditions afflicting minority communities. Researchers also concentrated their efforts in documenting the many different ways in which Puerto Ricans have contributed to the development of US society. Their critical view of the shortcomings, biases, and exclusions of the traditional disciplines with respect to ethnoracial groups often made it difficult for these programs to be institutionalized or be accepted as a legitimate part of the academic enterprise. Among the pioneering wave of scholars involved in the administrative leadership of Puerto Rican Studies are Josephine Nieves, María Sánchez, and Virginia Sánchez Korrol at Brooklyn College; María Canino and Pedro Cabán at Rutgers University; Rafael Rodríguez and Jesse Vázquez at Queens College; Federico Aquino and Eduardo Seda Bonilla at City College; Antonio Pérez, Edna Acosta-Belén and Elia H. Christensen at the University at Albany, SUNY; and Alfredo Matilla and Francisco Pagán at the University at Buffalo, SUNY. By and large, Puerto Rican Studies scholars tend to be representative of the "organic intellectual," combining a commitment to the advancement of knowledge and scholarship about Puerto Ricans with meaningful pedagogical and mentoring experiences for students, and striving to change the biases and exclusionary practices of the traditional disciplines, their respective institutions, and the profession. Community activism is also an important component of these programs, since it provides internships and field experiences to students, along with opportunities for applied or basic research and for promoting social change.

The lack of institutional support and adequate resources caused the demise of many of the early Puerto Rican Studies programs, but a respectable number survived and became more established. Some of the initial Puerto

Rican Studies programs later joined forces with the more institutionalized Latin American and Caribbean area studies, or expanded into the broader panethnic field of Latino Studies, as the overall US Latino population has continued to grow in many different cities and becomes more diversified because of the influx of new migrants from other Latin American and Caribbean national origins. Some programs are promoting transnational hemispheric approaches for studying the interactions between the realities and conditions of US Latinos with those of their counterparts in the countries of origin.

The creation of the Centro de Estudios Puertorriqueños (Center for Puerto Rican Studies) in 1974 was an important outcome of the overall Puerto Rican ethnic revitalization movement. With the initial support of the Ford Foundation and under the visionary leadership of Frank Bonilla, the Centro sponsored new research and publications in neglected areas and began the long process of documenting the history of the Puerto Rican diaspora by engaging the community in this challenging endeavor. A vital aspect of these initial efforts was the development of the Centro Library and Archives, presently located at Hunter College. Through the years the Centro Library and Archives have turned into the leading repository of information about the Puerto Rican presence in the United States. The indefatigable efforts of archivists Nélida Pérez, Nelly Cruz, Amílcar Tirado, Pedro Juan Hernández, and others has made the Centro Library's special archival collections an indispensable institution for Puerto Rican Studies researchers and students from all over the world.

The emergence of Puerto Rican Studies as a legitimate academic field of inquiry brought about a debunking of the old myths and stereotypes about Puerto Ricans and new opportunities for scholarly research. The impact of these programs is far reaching, as they opened up new venues for the training of future generations of professionals with an increased knowledge and a more positive view of their cultural heritage, and better preparation to work for the socioeconomic and political empowerment of their communities. For white students, Puerto Rican and other ethnic studies programs introduced them to important issues of racial relations and cultural diversity and to a more accurate conception of the United States as a nation built with the labor and survival spirit of many different immigrant nationalities.

The Puerto Rican Studies Association (PRSA) was created in 1992 as a professional organization that brings together scholars, community activists, and students to discuss their research and other endeavors. The PRSA also promotes linkages between island and US scholars and organizations and holds a major conference every two years.

Puerto Ricans and other minorities were at the forefront of the battles for open admissions in the City University of New York system. Open admissions was a way of providing access to a higher education to those groups that had been underrepresented in public and private colleges throughout the United States. Educational activism brought about the establishment of minority recruitment programs, such as SEEK (Search for Education, Elevation, and Knowledge) and Educational Opportunity Programs (EOP) for students, and Affirmative Action programs to recruit more faculty, professional staff, and students in fields where they were not generally represented.

Other Community Organizations

For more than four decades the Oficina de Puerto Rico en Nueva York, also known as the Migration Division or the Commonwealth Office, which was established in 1951 during the administration of Luis Muñoz Marín (see Chapter 3), tried to facilitate Puerto Rican migrants' introduction to the New York environment. Additional branches were established subsequently in other major cities with large concentrations of Puerto Ricans. The office provided orientation and employment services, housing information, and promoted cultural activities. According to Cabán (2005), the Migration Division was an important component of the island's industrialization program by making it easier for relocated workers to find employment and housing, thus reducing the number of unemployed workers in Puerto Rico. The overall policies and control of Puerto Rico's government over this office did not always reflect the specific needs of the various migrant communities. But through the years, changes in the Migration Division's leadership and the emergence of new grassroots organizations that understood better the day-to-day problems and struggles of a migrant population and the issues of racism and marginality to which they were exposed made this office an important presence within the various communities of the diaspora. The Migration Division was also subject to the political changes in Puerto Rico: The office tended to receive more attention when the PPD was in power and less when the PNP took control of the island's government. In 1991, the division became the Department of Community Affairs, which was abolished in 1994 when PNP candidate Pedro Roselló was elected governor. It was replaced by the Puerto Rican Federal Affairs Administration (PRFAA; see www.prfaa.com), with its main headquarters in Washington, DC. This organization maintains only a few of the functions of the former Migration Division. The PRFAA does not offer employment and housing services, nor does it focus on migrants' needs or their transition into US society. Instead, the office pursues a broad legislative agenda on bills and programs that affect both island and US Puerto Ricans and that maintain the flow of federal assistance to Puerto Rico. Describing itself as "the mainland presence of the Commonwealth of Puerto Rico," the PRFAA promotes economic and public policy initiatives. But more important, the PRFAA coordinates Puerto Rico's lobbying efforts with the US Congress, the White House, and other federal agencies. During its early years, the agency was accused of using government funds to promote the pro-statehood agenda of the PNP.

There are more than a dozen PRFAA regional offices located in most parts of the country with large concentrations of Puerto Ricans. The regional offices work with state and city officials and with community leaders on a diversity of issues related to improving the condition of the Puerto Rican and Latino populations. One of their most notable efforts has been the massive Latino voter registration campaigns aimed at increasing political representation and engaging more Latino voters in the US political process.

On another front, the Puerto Rican Family Institute (PRFI; see www. prfi.org), founded in 1960 as a health and human service agency, focuses on services to Puerto Rican and other Latino families. Its services include crisis intervention, mental health, home care needs, and education. The PRFI strives to avoid the disintegration of poor families because of socioeconomic or health-related hardships, and other problems migrants experience in their transition to a culturally and linguistically different environment.

Grassroots activism has led through the years to the emergence of numerous Puerto Rican–focused community organizations in New York and other cities, but only a handful have had the opportunity to carry on and grow. A good example is provided by La Casa de Don Pedro (named after Pedro Albizu Campos) in Newark, which was started by ten migrant families striving "to achieve self-sufficiency and empowerment" (www.lacasanwk.org). Initially founding New Jersey's first bilingual day-care center, La Casa now runs about twenty different programs and has turned into a community-based development corporation. La Casa fosters economic development and educational attainment, provides important social services and employment opportunities, and supports a vast array of other community outreach activities.

Bringing together the combined strength and expertise of several established US-based Puerto Rican organizations to promote cultural enrichment, El Comité Noviembre (the November Committee), a nonprofit volunteer entity, was established in New York City in 1987. November has been designated as Puerto Rican Heritage Month, since it marks the arrival of the Spanish to the island on November 19, 1493. Organizations such as ASPIRA, the Center for Puerto Rican Studies, El Museo del Barrio, the PRLDEF, the NCPRR, and the PRFAA all support a wide range of cultural events under the umbrella of El Comité Noviembre. The organization sponsors a scholarship program and was instrumental in mobilizing the community around issues such as a solidarity campaign on behalf of the people of Vieques and the release of political prisoners. It also promotes social responsibility and community service among Puerto Rican youth.

Professional Puerto Rican women in the United States came together to form the National Conference of Puerto Rican Women (NACOPRW) in 1972 in Washington, DC, to deal with the "dual discrimination" they experienced because of their ethnicity and gender. The notion of women "organizing for change" was at the core of the NACOPRW's goals (NACOPRW 1977). Additional chapters were established in New York City, Chicago, and Hartford. The NACOPRW was an early advocate of the equal rights amendment (ERA) to the US Constitution. Additionally, it promoted women's leadership training, fought for equal representation of women in government agencies, and tackled neglected issues related to women's poverty, family planning, and health. The organization's visibility reached its peak during the United Nation's International Women's Year in 1975 and its subsequent Decade for Women (1975–1985), since it was the only women's group with a national reach voicing the concerns and needs of Latinas. Some of the Puerto Rican leaders involved in the early years of the NACOPRW were Aída Berio, Lourdes Miranda King, Paquita Vivó, Carmen Delgado Votaw, and Alice Cardona. Although not so visible as in the past, the NACOPRW continues to hold annual conferences, and the regional chapters now concentrate on issues that are specific to their particular local communities.

Cultural Citizenship

The concept of cultural citizenship, developed by Chicano anthropologist Renato Rosaldo (1987), refers to the process by which Latinos "claim and establish a distinct social space" within US society (Flores and Benmayor 1997, 1). Defining this "distinct social space" involves Latinos' asserting their rights, defining their different cultural domains, and contesting and renegotiating power relations with the wider society. These activities are all part of an empowering process that is taking place within the various Latino communities. This process allows Puerto Ricans and other groups to challenge racism and prevailing inequalities, dispel some of the negative images of their communities, and develop awareness of their presence and contributions to US society.

Some island politicians have argued that Puerto Ricans are the holders of "a second class" US citizenship because of their inability to be fully represented in Congress or vote in presidential or congressional elections, and because of the differential treatment given to Puerto Rico when compared to the states. They seem oblivious to the contradiction that, at least in theory, Puerto Ricans are entitled to full citizenship rights if they reside in any of the fifty states. That does not change in any significant way the fact that collectively US Puerto Ricans still face socioeconomic disadvantage, political disenfranchisement, and discrimination and have to continuously struggle to uphold their civil rights. In many ways, island politicians, notably statehood supporters, fail to grasp the historical weight of racism and segregation upon the lives of Puerto Ricans and other ethnoracial minorities within US society.

In almost every locality in the United States with a large concentration of Puerto Ricans or Latinos there are cultural centers or social clubs aimed at fostering their cultural heritage and a sense of community. These organizations promote cultural enrichment and provide entertainment and recreation in the form of musical and theater performances, art exhibits, dancing, and the consumption of typical foods.

The most prominent celebration for US Puerto Ricans is the Puerto Rican Day Parade in New York City. Originally known in Spanish as "el Desfile Puertorriqueño," this tradition started in 1959 as a symbol of the unity and strength of a growing community. According to Estades (1980), this event was inspired by the proliferation of Puerto Rican hometown clubs throughout the city. Town mayors back in Puerto Rico would bring delegations to New York City to participate in the parade, and many government officials and other celebrities started to join the cultural and social gatherings related to what is now an institutionalized annual summer event. Similar parades or festivals are held in Chicago, Hartford, Orlando, Philadelphia, and several other cities but none have yet attracted the large crowds and media coverage of the New York event.

The importance of hometown clubs in fostering solidarity and coalescing a sense of community has been underscored by Sánchez Korrol ([1983] 1994). Each club was created for the migrants coming from the same town in Puerto Rico. Sánchez Korrol noted that these clubs "provided a home away from home predominantly oriented toward sociocultural and political affairs" (1994, 12). Hometown clubs came together under the umbrella of El Congreso de Pueblos (Council of Hometown Clubs), led by community activist Gilberto Gerena Valentín.

Another tradition within the diaspora is the building of *casitas* (small wooden houses). These wooden houses bring aspects of the Puerto Rican countryside and the popular folklore to the inner city. Often located in empty or abandoned lots of devastated urban areas, the *casitas* are built on stilts and painted in bright colors by members of the community, like country houses back in Puerto Rico. They are used for community celebrations, meetings, social gatherings, and political rallies. The *casitas* recreate the visual images and cultural practices of the homeland, remembrances of Puerto Rican life relocated into the urban environments of New York City and Chicago. They are given names that reflect the nostalgia of the displaced migrant: Villa Puerto Rico (Puerto Rican Village), Rincón Criollo (Creole Safe Haven), Añoranzas de mi Patria (Yearning for my Homeland). The *casitas* are considered "a true architecture of resistance subverting the traditional city" (Aponte-Parés 1995, 14). In recent years, many of the New York *casitas* have been torn down by the city government.

There are a few well-established institutions that play a leading role in promoting Puerto Rican arts and the overall cultural enrichment of the various US Puerto Rican communities. These are discussed in more detail in Chapter 7.

In a newspaper article published in 1948, community activist and journalist Jesús Colón posed the following questions: "Why have the reactionary newspapers unleashed a concerted campaign against the Puerto Ricans coming to New York? Why do they describe the Puerto Ricans in the worst light they can imagine?" (1982). Colón's questions, which were articulated during the years of highest migration of Puerto Ricans to New York City, came as a reaction to the frequently biased reporting and sensationalist media that depicted Puerto Ricans largely as a social problem, depriving them of their human dignity and denying their capacity to improve their individual and collective lives. A man with a strong social consciousness, Colón understood the racial and social conditions that surrounded him and the historical invisibility endured by the working class, ethnic immigrants in particular. He foresaw the need to document Puerto Rican migrant struggles for social justice and to recognize their efforts in building their communities. He considered these struggles essential components of the process of forging a legacy for the younger generations. In this regard, Jesús Colón, along with his brother Joaquín Colón, Bernardo Vega, and many others, were early contributors to these endeavors (see Chapter 7). These pioneers offer an alternative view of migrant life, with all its problems and challenges, but centered around people working hard to make a living, engaging individually and collectively to claim their rights and foster social change, and reclaiming and defining their own historical and cultural legacies within US society.

Notes

1. For detailed data of Puerto Rico's election results by each political party from the 1920s to the present, see the website http://eleccionespuertorico.org.

2. Although most Puerto Rican political organizations in the United States advocated Puerto Rico's independence, among the migrant population there was little support for this political status alternative. The Institute for Puerto Rican Policy conducted the National Puerto Rican Opinion Survey in 1989, asking 615 Puerto Rican respondents their preference among the various status options: statehood, independence, and the current Commonwealth. The majority of the respondents chose the Commonwealth status quo.

3. The motto "Palante, siempre, palante," used by the Young Lords, means "forging ahead, always forging ahead." The Puerto Rican popular colloquial expression "siempre pa'lante, nunca pa' atrás" (always forge ahead, never go backwards) inspired the slogan. See Iris Morales, "Palante, Siempre, Palante: The Young Lords," in Andrés Torres, ed., *The Puerto Rican Movement: Voices from the Diaspora* (Philadelphia: Temple University Press, 1998), 210–227; and Young Lords Party and Michael Abramson, *Palante: The Young Lords Party* (New York: McGraw-Hill, 1971).

4. The Spanish slogan coined by the Young Lords was not grammatically correct. The correct expression in Spanish would be "Tengo a Puerto Rico en mi corazón." The missing preposition was in itself indicative of the differences between Puerto Ricans on the island and the diaspora in their command of the Spanish language.

5. Some of this information appears in the PRLDEF website at www.prldef.org.

6. For a more detailed description of this organization's activities, see the official website of the National Puerto Rican Forum at www.nprf.org.

7

Voices and Images of the Diaspora

I was not born in Puerto Rico
Puerto Rico was born in me.
—*Mariposa Hernández,*
"Ode to the Diasporican"

In Chapter 1, we documented the Puerto Rican presence in US society dating back to the second half of the nineteenth century. There are numerous examples to support the assertion that for many Puerto Rican migrants coming to the United States since then—whether for a brief stay or for a longer and more permanent residence—the experiences of migration and displacement have influenced and continue to be central to their cultural expressions and artistic creativity. For most of these migrants, the journey from the island to the continent meant dealing with a different cultural and linguistic milieu, nostalgia for their homeland, a more inclement climate, and, above all, a society beleaguered by racial discrimination and social inequalities. As a racially mixed population, Puerto Ricans are quickly racialized into a subordinate homogenizing nonwhite category, similar to African Americans and Native Americans.

As mentioned in Chapter 6, the "melting pot" Anglocentric ideology that for a long time served as the model of immigrant assimilation and social mobility within US society proved to be elusive for Puerto Ricans and other ethnoracial minorities. Easily labeled as nonwhite, Puerto Ricans and other Latinos are confronted with deeply rooted prejudices and exclusion, factors that impair their social progress and contribute to their unprivileged status. Like previous groups of immigrants, Puerto Ricans and other Latinos share the "American dream," hoping to forge a more prosperous life for themselves and their families in their new home. However, racial and cultural differences, along with prevailing structural inequalities, are barriers that have not been easy to overcome, especially before the civil rights reforms of the 1960s. The social and political changes that came out of the civil rights era banned discrimination and segregation, and promoted a more equitable North American society. But even the new US-born generations of Puerto Ricans, which now constitute 58 percent of this group's total population, have not yet been able to overpower the realities and consequences of decades of poverty, racism, and socioeconomic disadvantage.

The working-class origins and low socioeconomic status shared by a significant portion of the Puerto Rican migrant population, especially before the 1990s, explains the undermining of their cultural expressions and contributions to US society. Easily labeled as part of "an underclass" (Tienda 1989) or "a culture of poverty" (Lewis 1966), Puerto Ricans had to deal with the stigma of their unprivileged status. The generalized assumption that living in poverty also means experiencing a "poverty of culture," or the elitist notion that the working class has little to offer as producers of worthy cultural expressions, explain the neglect by scholars or critics for this particular aspect of their lives. Hence it is mostly since the 1970s that researchers and critics have been paying more attention to documenting and analyzing the historical and cultural legacies of the Puerto Rican diaspora. This chapter provides a sociohistorical context for the various forms of cultural activity that have engaged and continue to engage Puerto Ricans in the United States.

The Spanish-Language Press

Since the second half of the nineteenth century, Puerto Rican migrant and sojourner writers, artists, and other intellectuals have been coming to the United States and actively participating in the cultural life of New York and other US communities with large concentrations of Puerto Ricans and/or other Latinos (see Chapter 2). Thus, their work represents a valuable source for a deeper understanding of the different stages in the evolution of these communities. Puerto Rico's literary canon, for instance, recognizes the writings of a few of these individuals, especially the works written in Spanish, and the views of many island Puerto Ricans about their countrymen and women in the United States have been shaped to a large extent by what has been portrayed in this creative literature and the media.

Among the most valuable sources of information on the development of Puerto Rican and other Latino communities in the United States is the Spanish-language press. Since colonial times, it has provided important outlets for journalistic and creative endeavors and has discussed multiple issues that influenced the collective and individual lives of the various US Latino communities, their interactions with Anglo-American society, and their connections with the countries of origin. Initially, Spanish-language newspapers in the pioneer communities were part of an immigrant press that kept the population informed of local events as well as what was happening back in their native countries. These newspapers also represented the voice of a marginalized population facing some of the same civil rights and socioeconomic problems and challenges that other racially mixed groups have endured during different historical periods. The earliest Spanish-language newspaper that has been identified to date is *El Misisipí* (The Mississippian), published in New Orleans and dating back to 1808 (Kanellos and Martell 2000, 4).

By the late 1820s most of the former Spanish New World colonies had achieved their independence, with the exception of the Hispanic Caribbean islands of Cuba and Puerto Rico. In Chapter 2 we explained in more detail how the repressive measures of Spanish authorities on both islands forced many independence supporters into exile, turning US cities such as New York, Philadelphia, New Orleans, Tampa, and Key West into important sites of activity for an expatriate Antillean separatist movement. The presence in the United States of leading separatist intellectuals and political leaders was a catalyst for the emergence of Spanish-language newspapers aimed at promoting the liberation of Cuba and Puerto Rico from Spanish rule and envisioning their future as independent republics. These publications were also important outlets for creative writing. Many key ideas about the future of the islands after their sovereignty was secured, including their future relationship with the United States, were first discussed in these newspapers.

Several Puerto Rican émigrés who were among the most respected and fervent voices of the separatist cause—Ramón Emeterio Betances, Eugenio María de Hostos, Francisco "Pachín" Marín, Lola Rodríguez de Tió, Sotero Figueroa, and Arturo A. Schomburg, among others—spent some time in New York during this early period. Besides their political and cultural activities, discussed in more detail in Chapter 2, they were among the most prominent frequent contributors to the Spanish-language newspapers in New York and other cities where Latinos were concentrated. In newspapers such as *La Revolución* (Revolution) and *Patria* (Motherland) Betances, Hostos, and Rodríguez de Tió promoted solidarity and unity among Puerto Ricans and Cubans in the common struggle for freedom and expressed their patriotic sentiments.

The idea of the annexation of both islands by the United States was anathema to Hostos's vision of a federation of sovereign Antillean republics that would include Cuba, Puerto Rico, and other non-Hispanic Caribbean islands. Some of Hostos's writings on these issues appeared in *La Revolución* and his *Diario* (Diary).

Betances was even more adamant about the possibility of a US intervention to put an end to the Spanish-Cuban War. His slogan "The Antilles for the Antilleans," promoting a sense of a unified Antillean struggle, was important not only for achieving the sovereignty of both islands but also for keeping them out of the hands of the United States. There were many social, racial, and political divisions within the Antillean separatist movement, but several of its most ardent supporters worked ceaselessly to promote unity. Cuban leader José Martí proclaimed, "With all, and for the good of all," while Puerto Rican poet Lola Rodríguez de Tió called for a unified struggle and Antillean solidarity in the verses of her memorable poem "A Cuba" (To Cuba):

> Cuba y Puerto Rico son
> de un pájaro las dos alas
> reciben flores o balas
> sobre el mismo corazón.
> [Cuba and Puerto Rico are
> the two wings of one bird.
> They receive flowers or blows
> on the very same heart.]
> (Rodriguez de Tió 1968, 321)

In Chapter 3, we discussed the presence and activities of Puerto Rican "pilgrims of freedom" like Rodríguez de Tió and others in the formation of the early settlements. Their writings in the Spanish-language press during this period are particularly important from a nation-building perspective, since living in exile allowed them to freely articulate their vision of a sovereign Puerto Rico and reaffirm a sense of national identity separate from the Spanish colonial metropolis. In the poem "Autógrafo" (Autograph), Rodríguez de Tió fervently repeats the verse "Porque la Patria llevo conmigo" (Because I carry the Motherland within me), which represented her life of exile in the name of freedom.[1]

Artisans Sotero Figueroa and Arturo Alfonso Schomburg, who had arrived in New York in the early 1880s, were among the most active and dependable supporters of the separatist movement. An experienced typographer, Figueroa ran his own printing press and undertook the role of administrative editor of *Patria,* which had been founded by Cuban patriot José Martí in 1892. In this capacity, Figueroa wrote many of the newspaper's editorials and other articles, especially when Martí went on his fund-raising campaign trips to the émigré communities in Florida and other parts of the United States. Worthy of mention is a series of six articles Figueroa published under the title "La verdad de la historia" (The Truth About History), in which he traced the long struggle of Puerto Ricans to liberate their country from Spanish tyrannical rule. He was the first to underscore the historical importance of the Grito de Lares revolt and the heroic activities of the revolutionaries who risked or gave their lives fighting for freedom. Figueroa also tried to dispel the autonomists' claim that there were no separatists in Puerto Rico:

> Los pueblos conquistados jamás aceptan pasivamente el yugo de sus conquistadores, y pugnan siempre por romper la cadena de la esclavitud hasta que al cabo lo logran.
> Puerto Rico, al igual que Cuba, no ha podido sustraerse a esa sugestión de la dignidad; y aunque por una táctica pueril, o por desviar la sospecha de que se les tenga por cómplices o simpatizadores, han dicho y repetido los corifeos de las agrupaciones liberales puertorriqueñas que en la menor de las Antillas españolas no hay ni ha habido separatistas, esto es, según vulgar expresión, querer tapar el sol con la mano, porque esa rotunda negación tiende a desmentir la verdad histórica, y hacer de los puertorriqueños que tienen conciencia de su futuro destino y que han pugnado y pugnan por ser libres,

ilotas degradados sin fe y sin aspiraciones regionalistas, que soportan el agravio y no vuelven altivos por la reparación; y que reciben el castigo y besan sumisos las manos que los maltratan. (1892, 1)

[The conquered people never accept passively the yoke imposed by their conquerors, and battle for breaking away from the chains of slavery until finally they do so.

Puerto Rico like Cuba has not been able to extract itself from that violation of its dignity, and even if it is just a childish tactical strategy or to divert suspicion from being considered accomplices or sympathizers, the coryphaeus of the liberal organizations in Puerto Rico has said repeatedly that there are not and never had been separatists there, which is, according to a vulgar expression, wanting to cover the sun with one hand. This categorical denial tends to refute what is historical truth, and makes those Puerto Ricans who are aware of their future destiny and who have and are fighting to be free, degraded slaves without faith or regional aspirations who tolerate insults and do not have the pride to ask for satisfaction, and who accept their punishment and submissively kiss the hand of those who mistreat them.]

Martí's death in 1895 brought out old ideological and social divisions within the Antillean separatist movement, giving an upper hand to the separatists favoring US intervention in the Spanish-Cuban War and the annexation of the islands. Figueroa kept the newspaper *Patria* going for several more years and remained active in the Sección de Puerto Rico of the PRC, which founded the newspaper *Borinquen* in 1898. The year after the US invasion of the islands, he left New York for Cuba, where he held administrative posts in the new Cuban government and continued his journalistic activities.

When Arturo A. Schomburg lived in Puerto Rico, like Sotero Figueroa, he developed close friendships with other artisans, especially with the *tabaqueros* and typographers. Schomburg did some typographic work at a San Juan stationery shop before departing for New York. When he arrived in New York, he immediately connected with other artisans residing in the city. Through the club Dos Antillas (The Two Antilles), Schomburg collaborated with labor activist Flor Baerga and others in seeking financial assistance to secure weapons and medical supplies for the fighting rebels in Cuba. After the War of 1898 and US takeover of Cuba and Puerto Rico, Schomburg remained in the United States and shifted his intellectual and political energies to collecting and documenting the experiences of African peoples around the world. An avid bibliophile, Schomburg was able to amass a valuable collection of books, maps, and other materials, which he sold to the New York Public Library in 1926. Schomburg was not a prolific writer, but in the handful of articles he published during his lifetime, he emphasized the importance of blacks learning about their past, and advocated the establishment of a Chair for Negro Studies, foreshadowing the African American Studies programs that emerged at US universities during the late 1960s and 1970s. He also wrote a few biographical profiles highlighting the contributions of previously ignored black personalities from different parts of the world. The Schomburg Collection for Black Culture is now internationally known among researchers of the African experience.

The journalistic activities of separatist poet and typographer Francisco Gonzalo "Pachín" Marín were mostly devoted to his own revolutionary newspaper, *El postillón* (The Conductor), which had been the main cause for his exile from Puerto Rico, but his poems and articles occasionally appeared in *Patria*. His article "La bofetada" (A Slap in the Face, 1892) was quick to condemn the political compromises being made by Puerto Rican liberal autonomists back on the island in their pursuit for reforms from the Spanish government, rather than choosing the path of revolution to secure independence. He also wrote a series of *crónicas* (personal vignettes) for *La Gaceta del Pueblo* (The People's Gazette) that reflected his views of different cultural and linguistic aspects of being an exile in the large US metropolis. The *crónica* "Nueva York por dentro" (New York from Within, 1892) offered the ironic perspective of a newcomer overwhelmed by an environment where wealth and poverty went hand in hand:

> To attain an intimate knowledge of this elephant of modern civilization, you will need to set foot to the ground without a quarter to your name, though you may bring a world of hope in your heart.
>
> Indeed! To arrive in New York, check into a comfortable hotel, go out in an elegant carriage pulled by monumental horses every time an occasion presents itself, visit the theaters, museums, *cafés*, chantants, cruise the fast-flowing East River, . . . visit Brooklyn Bridge—that frenzy of North American initiative—and the Statue of Liberty—that tour de force of French pride—, . . . frequent, in short, the places where elegant people of good taste gather, people who can afford to spend three or four hundred dollars in one evening for the pleasure of looking at a dancer's legs, oh!, all that is very agreeable, very delicious, and very . . . singular; but it doesn't give you the exact measure of this city which is, at one and the same time, an emporium of sweeping riches and rendezvous-point for all the penniless souls of America. (Kanellos 2002, 342)

The US takeover of Cuba and Puerto Rico put an end to the political activities of Antillean separatist émigrés but opened the gates to increased migration. With the new colonial regime in Puerto Rico, the flow of businessmen and well-known political and intellectual figures to the United States intensified. Puerto Ricans from the more privileged sectors came to the United States to advance their education, for professional and leisure activities, or to distance themselves from the unfavorable political environment in Puerto Rico. Working-class Puerto Ricans were recruited by US industries, and contract labor was heavily promoted by the colonial government in order to deal with the high levels of poverty and unemployment on the island, and to provide these industries with a steady source of low-wage labor.

In 1901, autonomist political leader and journalist Luis Muñoz Rivera settled in New York during a period when the supporters of US annexation for Puerto Rico had the upper hand in influencing the policies implemented on the island by the new colonial administration. Muñoz Rivera's concern about how little US citizens knew about Puerto Rico and his opposition to the misguided policies of North American officials inspired him to start the bilingual newspaper *The Puerto Rico Herald* (1901–1904). He remained in New York only a few years before returning to his former political life in Puerto Rico. There he joined the Partido Unión Puertorriqueña (Unionistas, or Unionist Party), a political organization fighting to increase Puerto Rican representation in the colonial government and seeking new measures for self-government. With the Unionists' support, Muñoz Rivera was elected resident commissioner, a nonvoting representative of the island to the US Congress, a post he occupied from 1908 until his death in 1916.

Many Puerto Ricans from the most privileged social sectors saw in the island's relationship with the United States opportunities for expanding their educational and professional careers and those of their offspring. Muñoz Rivera's tenure in Washington, DC, for instance, allowed his son, Luis Muñoz Marín, to attend Georgetown University, and it was in the United States where the young Muñoz Marín developed his journalistic and creative writing skills. His formative years in the United States were crucial in setting the course of his future political life. Muñoz Marín shuttled back and forth between Puerto Rico, Washington, and New York from his childhood until the early 1930s, when he finally settled in Puerto Rico and became more involved in island politics. A good number of the articles and poems reflecting his early social and political views were written in English and published in well-established journals, such as the *American Mercury, New Republic, Nation,* and *Poetry,* or widely read newspapers such as the *New York Tribune* and the *Baltimore Sun.* It has been noted that during the years he lived in New York City's Greenwich Village in the 1920s, Muñoz Marín and his North American wife, poet Muna Lee, befriended many liberal and socialist thinkers and artists who helped shape the populist ideology that was to guide his political career and actions in Puerto Rico in subsequent decades (Acosta-Belén et al. 2000). As mentioned in Chapter 4, Muñoz Marín was to become the first elected Puerto Rican governor of the island and the mastermind of the political, social, and economic transformation of Puerto Rico during the 1940s and 1950s.

An important publication in New York during the 1930s was the *Revista de Artes y Letras* (Review of Arts and Letters; 1933–1939), founded by Puerto Rican feminist activist Josefina "Pepiña" Silva de Cintrón. This monthly magazine circulated widely in the professional sector of New York's Spanish-speaking community and in several Spanish-speaking countries. The *Revista* fostered a panethnic sense of *hispanismo* or *latinismo* (consciousness of being Hispanic or Latino) within the United States by calling for the maintenance of the Spanish language and Hispanic heritage. Its intellectual and literary focus attracted the collaboration of many well-known writers from various Spanish-speaking countries and the New York community. Some frequent contributors to the journal were writers Pedro Juan Labarthe, Clotilde Betances Jaeger, and Pedro Caballero. Labarthe was the author of the novel *Son of Two Nations: The Private Life of a Columbia Student* (1931), the first published narrative written in English by a Puerto Rican migrant. The *Revista* paid special attention to women's issues and community concerns, and Clotilde Betances Jaeger, the niece of patrician leader Ramón Emeterio Betances, was a frequent contributor to this publication. She wrote about women's rights and the historical significance of the Lares insurrection and the expatriate Antillean separatist movement.

Promoting Puerto Rican–focused issues, as well as a panethnic sense of *hispanismo,* was at the core of *Alma Boricua* (Boricua Soul; 1934–1935), which called itself an "órgano defensor de la integridad boricua" (an instrument to defend Boricua integrity). One of its founders was Joaquín Colón, Jesús Colón's brother. The magazine started publication in 1934 during the years of increased political activity by Puerto Rican Nationalists and of their persecution by colonial authorities.

In the 1940s, Spanish-language newspapers continued to play an important role for Spanish Civil War exiles in New York City and for the increasing number of Puerto Ricans coming to the city during the early years of the Great Migration. Two of the best-known newspapers were *Pueblos Hispanos* (Hispanic Peoples, 1943–1944), founded by Puerto Rican Nationalist poet Juan Antonio Corretjer, and *Liberación* (Liberation, 1946–1949), started by Spanish exiles. These publications fostered a panethnic sense of *hispanismo* and solidarity based on what were perceived at the time to be common political causes: condemning fascism in Spain and other parts of Europe and US colonial domination in Puerto Rico and denouncing racism against Hispanics and the exploitation of their labor in US society. The writings of Latinos and Latinas from many different nationalities were also promoted in these publications. Bernardo Vega, for instance, wrote a few pioneering articles about Puerto Rican migration to the United States for *Liberación.*[2]

There is no doubt that the Spanish-language press in the United States represents one of the most valuable sources to understand the evolution of the Puerto Rican and other Latino communities, the issues of interest to particular localities and groups, and how these groups saw themselves in relation to the Spanish metropolitan power, their countries of origin, and the United States. Newspapers kept US Puerto Rican and other Latino communities abreast of what was happening in their native countries as much as they contributed to their adaptation process into Anglo-American society. They were important outlets for community businesses and organizations to advertise their services and events, and they played a key role in the publication of creative literature.

Although some Spanish-language newspapers are still published in the US Latino communities, by the mid-twentieth century they had stopped being an important source for the publication of creative writing. Authors wanting to publish their works had to rely on publishing houses, and for the most part, mainstream publishers did not have any interest in the US Latino experience or Latino writers. Self-publishing was another option used by some authors to get their writings out to the reading public.

New York was an important refuge for Puerto Rican Nationalists between the 1930s and the 1950s. In coming to New York many nationalists distanced themselves from the relentless persecution and blacklisting that US and Puerto Rican colonial authorities had been practicing in Puerto Rico for more than half a century (see Bosque Pérez and Colón Morera, 1997; Acosta 1987). Initially, the large metropolis provided a much needed sanctuary and opened opportunities for Nationalists to establish bonds of solidarity with fellow migrants or with political exiles from Spain and other Latin American countries living in the city.

Among the most prominent Puerto Rican Nationalists living in New York during this period were Corretjer; his wife, Consuelo Lee Tapia, who helped administer and occasionally wrote for *Pueblos Hispanos*; feminist poet Julia de Burgos, a regular columnist for the newspaper; and avant-guard poet Clemente Soto Vélez, a regular contributor to many New York Spanish-language newspapers.

Some of these authors were already well known in Puerto Rico and a good portion of their work was tied to the island, but often their writings also reflected aspects of their lives in the New York metropolis. Julia de Burgos, for instance, who left a rich legacy of poems of loneliness and abandonment and of unrequited love, also wrote poems that address the social, racial, and gender inequalities and political issues that affected the lives of Puerto Ricans. In addition, de Burgos wrote a cultural column for *Pueblos Hispanos*. Nevertheless, she is best remembered for her feminist and socially oriented poems, such as "Yo misma fui mi ruta" (I was my own route):

> Yo quise ser como los hombres quisieron que yo fuese:
> un intento de vida,
> un juego al escondite con mi ser.
> Pero yo estaba hecha de presentes
> Y mis pies planos bajo la tierra promisora
> No resistían caminar hacia atrás,
> Y seguían adelante, adelante...
> Burlando las cenizas para alcanzar el beso
> De los senderos nuevos.
> [I wanted to be like men wanted me to be:
> an attempt at life;
> a game of hide and seek with my being.
> But I was made of nows;
> and my feet leveled upon the promised land

would not accept walking backwards,
and went forward, forward,
mocking the ashes to reach the kiss
of the new paths.]
(de Burgos 1997, 56–57)

De Burgos suffered from severe alcoholism, an ailment that contributed to
an early death; she collapsed in the streets of New York at the age of forty-four.
Although the large majority of her poems were written in Spanish, it is ironic
that her last poem, "Farewell in Welfare Island," was written in English while
she was convalescing at the city's Goldwater Memorial Hospital. This particular poem reflects the loneliness and despair that overwhelmed the last months
of de Burgos's life and foreshadows her death:

Where is the voice of freedom,
freedom to laugh,
to move
without the heavy phantom of despair?
My cry that is no more mine,
but her and his forever,
the comrades of my silence,
the phantoms of my grave
It has to be from here,
forgotten but unshaken
among comrades of silence
deep into Welfare Island
my farewell to the world.
(de Burgos 1997, 357)

Another Nationalist poet, Clemente Soto Vélez, had been incarcerated in
a federal prison for several years along with Juan Antonio Corretjer and party
leader Pedro Albizu Campos. Soto Vélez, after his release, set roots in New
York during the early 1940s and remained there until his death in 1993. His
collection of poems *La tierra prometida* (The Promised Land, 1979) is a stead-
fast denunciation of US imperialist domination over Puerto Rico:

la tierra prometida
no
es
argumento
irguiéndose
de orgullo degollado
donde no
parpadea
el imperio de la persecución
donde
el empíreo del imperio
donde

el imperio del empíreo
no imperarán
sino transformados por la vanguardia
de la clase obrera
sca
la transformadora
la intérprete
de su propia realidad revolucionaria
o
sea
la moldeadora
en esencia
de su propio ser
[the promised land
is
not
an argument
that rises from
a truncated pride
where
the empire of persecution
does not blink
where
the highest sphere of the empire
and the empire of the highest sphere
will not prevail
but will be transformed by the avant-garde
of the working class
which will be
the transforming force
the interpreter
of its own revolutionary reality
or will be
the sculptor
of its own being.]
(Soto Vélez 1979, 79)

The negative experiences endured by working-class migrants in US society were central to the Puerto Ricans' literary and artistic production. One of the best-known and most powerful early depictions of the effects of migration on a Puerto Rican family is the classic drama *La carreta* (The Oxcart, 1951–1952) by René Marqués, a well-recognized author in Puerto Rico and throughout the Spanish-speaking world. Marqués, also a supporter of Puerto Rico's independence, lived in New York in 1949 while he was studying theater at Columbia University. It was there that he began to write *La carreta*, a play that for many years was used by island Puerto Ricans as a point of reference for portraying the migrant experience.

La carreta focuses on the migratory journey of a peasant family forced by poverty and the lack of work opportunities to move from the Puerto Rican countryside to an urban slum in San Juan and later to New York's Spanish Harlem. The play illustrates how the uprooted peasant family members deal with the individual and collective effects of their difficult and alienating life, first in the island's capital, and then in the US metropolis. The family's experiences are filled with tragedy. They lose the oldest son in a factory accident, an event that forces the remaining family members to return to the abandoned Puerto Rican homeland. Marqués's unrealistic and tragic view of migrant life tends to downplay the social and political dynamics of migration by focusing on the wrong personal choices made by individual family members, even when they are forced to do so by prevailing social and political conditions. In the end, the surviving characters of *La carreta* come to the realization that they have "betrayed" the Puerto Rican homeland by abandoning it, and that their only "redemption" is to return to the island. In reality, that was not the choice made by the large majority of migrants who settled in the United States, regardless of the many hardships they had to confront. *La carreta* was first performed in New York in 1953 and in Puerto Rico's major theater festival a few years later. The play was well received by critics, and its popularity as a work representative of the migrant experience would last for many decades.

Other island writers of Marqués's generation, such as José Luis González, also spent brief periods in New York. González's stay in the city inspired his short novel *Paisa* (Fellow Countryman, 1950) and the collection of short stories *En Nueva York y otras desgracias* (In New York and Other Tragedies, 1973). In these narratives, the author denounced the exploitation of working-class Puerto Ricans by the US capitalist system, but also shared Marqués's tragic view of migrant life. Both Marqués and González were perceptive in their portrayal of the distressing socioeconomic and racial realities faced by Puerto Ricans in New York, but their writings reflected more an observer's or outsider's point of view than the experiences of those Puerto Ricans leading productive lives in the United States who chose not to return to Puerto Rico.

The despairing or tragic view of migrant life was also replicated in the writings of other island authors of the same generation. The poignant short stories of Pedro Juan Soto's acclaimed collection, *Spiks* (a pejorative term for Spanish-speaking people, 1957), his novel *Ardiente suelo, fría estación* (Hot Land, Cold Season, 1962), and Emilio Díaz Valcárcel's novel *Harlem todos los días* (Daily Life in Harlem, 1978) are among the best-known narratives. All these narratives share a pessimistic undertone, but manage to capture some of the cultural and social conflicts, sense of displacement, and marginality experienced by many Puerto Rican migrants during the mid-twentieth-century Great Migration years.

The creativity of Puerto Ricans in the United States spans a broad range of genres and themes, reflecting long-standing literary, musical, and artistic traditions, as well as the influences that come out of the dislocations, cultural conflicts, and adjustments that are part of the overarching migrant experience. The literary legacy of the diaspora started with the contributions of the so- journers, those who lived in the United States for a time, and other working- class migrant pioneers whose writings, for the most part, still remain scattered in Spanish-language newspapers and other periodical publications.

There are two significant works that bear testimony to the working-class ex- periences of early Puerto Rican migrants to the United States. These are *Memo- rias de Bernardo Vega* (Memoirs of Bernardo Vega; written in the 1940s and published in 1977), and *A Puerto Rican in New York and Other Sketches* (1961) by Jesús Colón. Both Bernardo Vega (1885–1965) and Jesús Colón (1901–1974) were of working-class origin and came to New York from the mountain town of Cayey, Puerto Rico. They emigrated to the United States as young men: Vega in 1916 and Colón in 1918. Back in Cayey, then a tobacco-growing area, both men were exposed during their formative years to the culture of the socialist *tabaque- ros*. The *tabaqueros* represented an enlightened sector of the Puerto Rican work- ing class, since it was common for them to hire *lectores* (lectors, or readers) to read to the workers from raised platforms at the tobacco factories and work- shops. Having *lectores* allowed these workers to become familiar with many of the classics of world literature and social and political writings, as well as with the daily news. Thus the *tabaqueros* were well versed about local and interna- tional issues and events. The *lectores* tradition was replicated in the late nine- teenth century and early twentieth century by cigar industry workers in the United States, most of them of Cuban, Puerto Rican, Spanish, and Italian origin (see Mormino and Pozzetta 1987; Ingalls and Pérez 2003).

A large portion of Vega's and Colón's writings is autobiographical; in these texts they gave testimony to the hardships and struggles faced by early migrants trying to make a living in US society. Although these two committed community activists occasionally returned to Puerto Rico to visit their rela- tives and friends, they each resided in the United States for about half a cen- tury. Thus their personal accounts of the migration experience shed light on an important period in the evolution of New York's Puerto Rican community, a period that had not been well documented in previous studies of the diaspora. Vega's and Colón's narratives go back in time to the second half of the nine- teenth century, the years when Cuban and Puerto Rican political émigrés started coming to the United States and established *colonias* in several major US cities. They provide detailed information about many of the expatriates forced into exile because of their involvement in the struggle to liberate Cuba and Puerto Rico, Spain's last two colonies in the Americas. They also ac- knowledge the contributions of blue-collar workers, including those seeking employment in manufacturing or in the tobacco industry. This latter sector of the US economy was booming, especially after the 1880s, and relied to a large measure on immigrant labor (see Mormino and Pozzetta 1987; Ingalls and Pérez 2003).

In their respective writings, Bernardo Vega and Jesús Colón offered an engaging composite of the struggles, challenges, and contributions of working-class migrants during the formative stages of New York's Puerto Rican community. These authors emphasized the interethnic and class solidarity among workers, the importance of informal networks, and they described a community where social and political activism often went together with intellectual and other cultural pursuits. In this community, workers frequently stood side by side with members of the intellectual and political elites, defending the cause of Antillean independence or their civil rights. Vega and Colón also drew attention to the numerous grassroots organizations, newspapers, and individuals contributing to these endeavors. Their socialist formation and their active involvement in the cultural, social, and political life of the community provided the insights that were missing from mainstream accounts of Puerto Rican migrant life.

In his *Memorias*, Vega offered abundant details about important events, the emergence of all kinds of community organizations, the names of the people involved in these endeavors, along with a critical view of the social and racial ills of US society. The author, aware of the importance of creating a historical record of the community's early years, clearly understood the significance of documenting his experiences and those of other working-class migrants.

Vega also was drawn into journalistic endeavors. He bought the Spanish-language newspaper *Gráfico* (Illustrated, 1927–1931), originally founded by Afro-Cuban actor and writer Alberto O'Farrill, and turned it into an important forum for informing New York's Latino community about events and issues that had a bearing on their daily lives. In addition, the newspaper was an effective tool for consciousness-raising and a source of entertainment. The December 2, 1928, issue of *Gráfico* compared Harlem's Lenox Avenue to the Latin Quarter of Paris, with Harlem's bohemian nights reminiscent of nightlife in other cosmopolitan cities such as Madrid, Rio de Janeiro, or Buenos Aires. This was in part a spilling over of the cultural vitality that characterized the pan-African and Harlem Renaissance movements during the 1920s and 1930s, but the contributions of the Puerto Rican and wider Latino community added to this environment.

Colón was a regular columnist for *Gráfico*, along with several other labor activists, journalists, and creative writers from New York and Puerto Rico. Besides his writings in *Gráfico*, Colón left a rich legacy of articles published in various other New York newspapers, including *Pueblos hispanos, Liberación,* the *Daily Worker, Mainstream,* the *Worker,* and the *Daily World* (see Acosta-Belén and Sánchez Korrol 1993; Padilla 2001). Colón's weekly columns "Lo que el pueblo me dice" (What I Am Hearing from the People) and "As I See It from Here" for the *Daily Worker* (later to become the *Worker;* 1955–1968) are excellent examples of how the working-class perspective dominated his writings.

In some of Colón's newspaper columns and short narratives, which he called "sketches," the author deplored the lack of bibliographic sources on labor organizations and trade unions, even though at the time the majority of New York City's Puerto Rican population was working class. Thus, like his countryman Bernardo Vega, Jesús Colón was aware of the need to forge a historical record for posterity about the building of a Puerto Rican community from the labor and survival struggles of the working class. Both writers offered a male working-class perspective of migrant life, but they also tried to acknowledge the contributions of women to community life. Despite the fact that the great majority of the female population identified themselves as housewives, they were often engaged in home-based piecework for the needle industry and other activities such as child care and taking in boarders (Sánchez Korrol 1983). Around one-fourth of all the migrant women worked outside the home in the garment and tobacco industries, and there also were a few writers among them.

Two Puerto Rican feminist tobacco workers' union activists, Luisa Capetillo and Franca de Armiño, migrated to the United States in the early decades of the twentieth century. These two women were involved at different times in the activities of Puerto Rico's Federación Libre de los Trabajadores (Free Federation of Workers, FLT). Capetillo arrived in the United States in 1912 and spent a couple of years working in the tobacco factories of Ybor City, Florida, and those of New York, where she was employed as a reader. She then lived in Cuba and Puerto Rico and returned to New York again in 1919. As she did when she was living in Puerto Rico, Capetillo was a frequent contributor to workers' newspapers. Her experiences working in the United States shaped some of the writings in her book *Influencia de las ideas modernas* (Influence of Modern Ideas, 1916). These writings illustrate Capetillo's anarcho-feminist ideology and a revolutionary utopian vision that challenged social conventions and denounced prevailing inequalities among the various social sectors and between men and women.[3]

While still living in Puerto Rico during the early 1920s. Franca De Armiño had been the leader of a tobacco stripper's union and president of the Asociación Feminista Popular (Popular Feminist Association), a suffragist workers' organization. There is some evidence that she lived in New York in the late 1920s and 1930s, since she published a few articles about the need for workers to organize in Bernardo Vega's newspaper, *Gráfico*. Her little-known revolutionary play, *Los hipócritas* (The Hypocrites, 1937), was also published in New York. This play denounces the abuses of capitalist employers during the years of the Great Depression and reaffirms the author's socialist ideals.

Sharing the activist spirit of his brother Jesús Colón, Joaquín Colón also felt the need to give recognition to those Puerto Ricans migrating to the United States in the early decades of the twentieth century. His *Pioneros en Nueva York 1917–1947* (Pioneers in New York 1917–1947; 2002) was not published until almost four decades after his death, but its importance is indisputable, since it documented in detail the activities of various grassroots organizations and the different areas of activism within the early Puerto Rican community. The book confirmed the difficulties faced by early migrants and how they struggled to improve their conditions. There is a clear sense in Joaquín Colón's writings that the trials and tribulations that migrants had to endure only increased their social consciousness and activism, a view far from the stereotypical portrayal of the apathetic or despairing poor migrant:

> En aquel ambiente arduo, insólito, anticívico tenía que florecer la efervescencia. . . . Aquella vida agudizólos sentidos de nuestros compueblanos y se fundieron allí hombres y mujeres aguerridos en las luchas cívicas. Paradas, manifestaciones, piquetes, hojas sueltas y mítines tuvieron entre aquella multitud el más cálido respaldo. Y mucha de la legislación progresista que hoy disfrutamos emanó de allí. Muchos de nuestros compatriotas se hicieron expertos en las leyes de inquinilato, de sanidad, y sobre la importancia de los derechos civiles. (Colón 2002, 43)
> [From that harsh, strange, anticivic environment some action had to flourish. . . . That life sharpened the senses of our fellow compatriots and defiant men and women ready to engage in civic struggles were molded there. Parades, demonstrations, picketing, leaflets, and political rallies garnered the warmest support from a multitude of people and a great deal of the progressive legislation that we enjoy today came from there. Many of our compatriots became experts in housing and health regulations, and the importance of civil rights.]

Bringing Puerto Rican folklore and oral traditions to the New York Puerto Rican community was the life endeavor of librarian Purá Belpré. She was the first Puerto Rican librarian in the New York Public Library system; her early experiences in the 1920s working at the branch that later became the Schomburg Center solidified her lifelong commitment of exposing the children of a working-class diaspora to their Spanish, Taino, and African cultural roots through storytelling. Belpré's folklorist interests, civil rights concerns, and pride in her Puerto Rican cultural heritage are best represented in her books for children *Pérez and Martina* (1932), *The Tiger and the Rabbit and Other Tales* (1946), and *Once in Puerto Rico* (1973). This devoted advocate of children worked as a librarian for more than half a century. As a black Puerto Rican, Belpré had to deal with the blatant racism and class marginality endured by her community during the pre–civil rights years. These concerns often surfaced in her allegorical tales.[4]

A New Cultural Discourse

As the vicissitudes of migrant life were not central issues to Puerto Ricans living in Puerto Rico, for many decades the separation between island and mainland communities was more than a matter of geography. Island Puerto Ricans could not conceive of engaging in a discussion about Puerto Ricans in the United States without making emphatic points about cultural, linguistic, or class differences. There was the prevailing view that Puerto Ricans born or raised in the United States were not only beleaguered by poverty and discrimination but also culturally and linguistically deficient when compared to Puerto Ricans on the island. In some ways islanders regarded the diaspora as a distorted mirror of what it meant to be Puerto Rican. Their counterparts in the United States were frequently depicted as too assimilated into Anglo-American values and unable to speak Spanish well or at all, believed to be indicators of their disregard for their own cultural heritage. In sum, US Puerto Ricans incarnated some of the worst apprehensions about the Americanization process that island Puerto Ricans had so much resisted in their own country since the US takeover; they were, therefore, quickly dismissed for not being "true" Puerto Ricans or were even regarded as "pseudo–Puerto Ricans" (see Seda Bonilla 1972). The words "Nuyorican" and "Neorican" were coined to separate those in the diaspora from the ostensibly "real" or "authentic" Puerto Ricans back on the island.[5] It was not until a group of Puerto Rican poets born or raised in New York decided to adopt the term "Nuyorican" to differentiate themselves from island Puerto Ricans that the original negative connotations were stripped from this label and it became more acceptable.

As objectionable as the separation was to many Puerto Ricans, the widespread tendency to make the distinction between the populations of the island and the diaspora was deeply rooted in history. After the US invasion of Puerto Rico, the ill-advised Americanization policies implemented by the colonial government during the first four decades of occupation had left a bitter taste among island Puerto Ricans. These policies included the imposition of English as the official language of Puerto Rico and of its public school system and the concomitant undermining of Spanish, the native language of island Puerto Ricans. Public education was aimed at indoctrinating Puerto Ricans into Anglo-Saxon values and ways of life with an overall disregard for local historical and cultural traditions. Protestant religious proselytizing was another tool used to convert a primarily Catholic island population. Of great importance to the new rulers was Puerto Rico's strategic value for the geopolitical designs of the United States in the hemisphere, which gradually transformed the island into a US military bastion in the Caribbean region. This militarization was carried out through the expropriation of lands and the proliferation of bases established by the US Navy and other branches of the North American armed forces.

All these policies and actions contributed to making island Puerto Ricans extremely sensitive and defensive about cultural and language issues vis-à-vis US influence and domination. Needless to say, these issues have and continue to generate frequent and heated debates. Over the years there have been numerous writings and discussions regarding the preservation and erosion of

Puerto Rican national identity and cultural traditions, the strong US influence in Puerto Rico, and their inexorable connection with the island's political status. These discussions, however, often fail to transcend the political context of the status question or tend to lead to a fervent protectionism of an immutable set of Puerto Rican cultural traditions and the Spanish vernacular. Sometimes they result in the denunciation of a professed transculturation in which all cultural and linguistic changes taking place in Puerto Rico are erroneously attributed to an unrestrained Americanization process. This defensive stance is part of a deep-rooted Puerto Rican cultural nationalism that historically has overpowered any forms of political nationalism aimed at extricating the island from the US colonial grip.

One aspect of this national debate is the question of the cultural identity of those Puerto Ricans living in the United States or, as it has been described more accurately, "the identity in question" (Sandoval-Sánchez 1992). An obvious shortcoming of these identity discussions is that they tend to be dominated by essentialist and monolithic conceptions of identity. For island Puerto Ricans, the identity of those in the diaspora represents another layer of complexity in an already sensitive and controversial national debate.

Unquestionably, discussions of Puerto Rican national identity now transcend island borders, drawing more attention to a diaspora that keeps growing in leaps and bounds and that is projected to equal or surpass Puerto Rico's population within the next few years. The demographic reality and the transnational commuting nature of Puerto Rican migration have helped lessen the sense of separation between island and US Puerto Ricans, but there has been a propensity to focus on their differences rather than on the issues that might bring both communities closer together.

One of the first sectors to point to the separation between these communities was the writers. Island intellectuals were often predisposed to ignore or be critical about those US Puerto Rican authors who identified themselves as Puerto Rican but did not necessarily speak or write Spanish fluently, which was perceived to be a clear indication of their assimilation into Anglo-American culture. With few exceptions, the work of US Puerto Rican authors—who write primarily (although not exclusively) in English or bilingually—was regarded as a mere extension of North American literature. There was a generalized reluctance to acknowledge any considerable relationship of the diaspora's literary and cultural experiences with those of the island. Other times, appreciation of the diaspora's cultural expressions did not transcend the simplistic notion that they were evidence of a "Nuyorican identity crisis," suggesting that this particular identity issue was totally disconnected from the island and its colonial relationship with the United States (see Acosta-Belén 1992).

Since the early 1970s, Puerto Rican scholars at North American universities and colleges have concentrated their efforts in recovering and documenting the historical roots and evolution of the Puerto Rican presence in the

United States, especially the different ways in which Puerto Ricans construct and reaffirm a collective sense of identity within the various communities of the diaspora. The significance of the overall process of historical recovery and affirmation of cultural identity for diasporic populations was aptly captured by Stuart Hall (1990) when he stated: "Cultural identity . . . is a matter of 'becoming' as well as of 'being.' But, like everything which is historical, [identities] undergo constant transformation. . . . identities are the names we give to the *different ways* we are positioned by, and position ourselves within the narratives of the past" (22, emphasis added).

Hall stressed the importance for migrant populations of constructing a historical memory of their experiences in the host society as a way of validating who they are, and where they came from. This process involves an interplay between the cultural traditions of the country of origin and the host society. In the case of Puerto Ricans and other Latinos, they share a heritage that has been slighted in mainstream historical narratives. Thus, recovering this heritage provides present and future generations with an empowering knowledge about their place in and contributions to US society. Doing so has been as important to Puerto Ricans as it has been for many other (im)migrant groups.

Adding another layer of complexity to the heated Puerto Rican national identity debate has been difficult at best, but never before have the communities of the island and diaspora been so interested in discovering the issues and conditions that both separate and bring them together. And never before has the US Puerto Rican community tried to understand itself not solely in reference to Puerto Rico, but as part of the larger configuration that is the United States. Within the US context, Puerto Ricans are part of a rapidly growing and diverse Latino population and share many of the ethnic barrios with other Latin American and Caribbean nationalities as well as non-Latino minority groups. It is quite ironic that because of its association with the United States, Puerto Rico has had a long struggle being accepted as a "legitimate" Latin American or Caribbean nation, but in the United States, Puerto Ricans are not only given back a reconstituted Latino identity, but whether they are white, black, or of mixed complexion, they are racialized and placed in the ambiguous "people of color," or nonwhite, category. The racialization and placement of Puerto Ricans and other Latinos under this label tends to homogenize these populations and obscure their multiracial background and the long history of racial mixture that exists within the diverse Latino groups.

The cultural expressions of Puerto Ricans and other US ethnoracial minorities demonstrate the creative ways in which writers and artists deal with the inequalities and conflicts that arise from their collective interactions with the white Anglo-American mainstream society. They also show how individuals and particular ethnic groups address these conditions from their subaltern position. Serving a variety of functions, these cultural expressions create a link with the past and the countries of ancestry while, at the same time, in Hobsbawm's terms "a tradition is invented" (Hobsbawm and Ranger 1983). Within the diaspora new cultural configurations emerge that play a fundamental social, political, and psychological role in the process of constructing more positive identities and in building a historical record of each group's presence in and contributions to US society. US Puerto Rican writers and artists view their cultural straddling as a sign of resistance to assimilation into Anglo-American society and a way of denouncing its racial and social problems through their personal experiences and of reaffirming their sense of Puerto Rican identity.

For Puerto Ricans and other Latinos, defining their place and respective legacies represents both a challenge and an endeavor that does not fit old assimilation models. Instead, these groups are introducing new forms of cultural affiliation and citizenship that do not rely entirely on "giving up" one's ethnic heritage in order to be embraced as "a true and loyal American." As historian David W. Noble has pointed out, "By the 1970s . . . Anglo-Protestants had lost their claim to represent the universal national and to monopolize agency within the history of the English colonies and the United States" (2002, 260). This statement implies that the historical authority of Anglo-American exceptionalism has been subjected to the same intellectual challenges that questioned the ethnocentric assumption that only certain privileged elites in Western societies could be the main historical agents and producers of culture. These major paradigm shifts have validated the many different cultures and (im)migrant groups that have participated in the historical development of US society.

A factor that contributes to a strong sense of Puerto Rican identity within the diaspora is the geographic proximity between Puerto Rico and the United States and the commuter nature of Puerto Rican migration. The continuous migratory flow reinforces meaningful transnational connections between the island and the metropolis and also fosters a cultural straddling and hybridity that better reflects the conditions and reciprocal influences between both contexts. This pattern is now shared by most US Latino groups.

Only 42 percent of the Puerto Ricans in the United States are first-generation migrants, meaning that more than half of the total population is US-born. As a result, it can be expected that cultural continuity from one generation to another will be accompanied by substantial changes and transformations. These generational differences define a Puerto Rican cultural context in which there is a constant influx of new arrivals joining those generations of Puerto Ricans born or raised in the United States.

Literary expression is an area where these differences are quite evident. For instance, there are Puerto Rican writers currently living or who have lived in the United States and whose works are studied as an extension of the island's literature because they write primarily in Spanish and were born and raised in Puerto Rico. But those born or raised in the metropolis, whose primary language is usually English, are often ignored by the island's literary establishment. This snobbishness has provoked critical reactions in the past from some writers. In the words of renowned US Puerto Rican author Nicholasa Mohr:

> The separation between myself and the majority of Puerto Rican writers in Puerto Rico goes far beyond a question of language. The jet age and the accessibility of Puerto Rico brought an end to a time of innocence for the children of the former migrants. There is no pretense that going back will solve problems, bring equality and happiness. This is home. This is where we were born, raised, and where most of us will stay. Notwithstanding, it is my affection and concern for the people and the land of my parents and grandparents which is my right and my legacy.
>
> Who we are and how our culture will continue to blossom and develop is being recorded right here, by our writers, painters, and composers; here, where our voices respond and resound loud and clear. (Mohr 1989, 116)

Mohr echoed the voices of the generations of Puerto Ricans feeling "at home in the USA" (Turner 1991), but who were replacing the myth of assimilation with a sense of identity that straddled two different cultures and languages (Flores [1988] 1993; Acosta-Belén 1992). It is evident that these writers have carved out new hybrid cultural spaces to interpret their experiences and legacies.

Puerto Rican literature in the United States has tended to be critical of Anglo-American mainstream society, its values, and social and racial disparities. Writers have not necessarily been more benevolent in their views of their ancestral island and culture. Tato Laviera's poetry is a case in point. The title of his book *La Carreta Made a U-Turn* (1979) demythified the inevitability of René Marqués's tragic view of migration in the play *La carreta*. Instead, Laviera affirmed the resilience of the Puerto Rican spirit and the migrant community's capacity to find creative responses to the obstacles they confront in their daily lives.[6] Laviera, in the poem "nuyorican," decried the rejection he felt from his island compatriots because of his "American ways," but also took the opportunity to denounce the Americanization of Puerto Rico:

> yo peleo por ti, puerto rico, ¿sabes?
> yo me defiendo por tu nombre, ¿sabes?
> entro a tu isla, me siento extraño, ¿sabes?
> pero tu con tus calumnias, me niegas tu sonrisa..
> me desprecias, me miras mal, me atacas mi hablar,
> mientras comes mcdonalds en las discotecas americanas.
> (Laviera 1985, 53)
> [I fight for you, Puerto Rico, you know?
> I defend your name, you know?
> I come to your island, I feel a stranger, you know?
> but you with your slanderous accusations, deny me a smile. . .
> you despise me, your look is demeaning, you attack my speech,
> while you eat McDonald's in American discoteques.]

The perceived rejection described in Laviera's verses has impelled US Puerto Rican writers to define a different identity that validated the cultural and linguistic back-and-forth movement and hybrid nature of the migrant experience and, at the same time, dismissed the widespread ethnocentric and elitist views of both Anglo-Americans and island Puerto Ricans. The Anglocentric characterization of US society was replaced by a validation of cultural and linguistic diversity that celebrated popular expressions and the working-class experiences of most of these writers. This reconstituted identity that in this case was both North American and Puerto Rican—or to use Laviera's coined term, *"AmeRícan"*—reaffirmed a populist sense of individual and collective liberation rather than embracing the mythical "melting pot" model that strives to erase all cultural differences (see Flores 1988; Acosta-Belén 1992). Also included in *AmeRícan* is Laviera's poem "asimilao":

> assimilated? qué assimilated,
> brother, yo soy asimilao,
> asi mi la o sí es verdad
> tengo un lado asimilao.
> (Laviera 1985, 54)[7]
> [assimilated? no way assimilated,
> brother, I am "asimilao"
> asi mi la o that's the truth
> a part of me is asimilao.]

Nuyorican poet Miguel Piñero called Puerto Rico "the slave-blessed land / where nuyoricans come in search of spiritual identity / and are greeted with profanity" ("This is Not the Place Where I Was Born," *La Bodega Sold Dreams*, 1990, 14). Piñero's verses offered another illustration of how the generations of Puerto Ricans born or raised in the US metropolis and wishing to drink from the ancestral fountain of "spiritual identity" often felt some degree of cultural rejection and were exposed to the prevailing prejudices that continued to separate the diaspora and the island communities. This particular feeling of uprootedness was exacerbated by the prejudice and marginality Puerto Rican migrants also experienced in US society.

Another prominent Nuyorican poet, the late Pedro Pietri, in his "Love Poem for My People," included in his much-acclaimed collection *Puerto Rican Obituary* (1973), called upon his people to trade the trappings of a materialistic society for pride and self-reliance:

> turn off the stereo
> this country gave you
> it is out of order
> your breath
> is your promised land
> if you want

to feel very rich
look at your hands
that is where the definition of magic is located at.
(Pietri 1973, 78)

Sandra María Esteves was among the few women that were part of the early years of the Nuyorican poetic movement. Some of her poems also reflected the identity fragmentation and straddling that has been so intrinsic to the Puerto Rican and Latino cultural experience in the United States, for example, "Not Neither," from *Tropical Rain: A Bilingual Downpour:*

> Being Puertorriqueña Dominicana, Borinqueña Quisqueyana,
>   Taíno Africana
> Born in the Bronx, not really jíbara
> Not really hablando bien
> But yet, not gringa either
> Pero no, portorra. Pero si portorra too
> Pero ni qué, what am I? . . .
> (Esteves 1984, 26)

Early studies of the diaspora's cultural expressions (Acosta-Belén 1978; Barradas and Rodríguez 1980; Flores 1988; Aparicio 1988) viewed this artistic production as a source for validating and affirming a collective sense of Puerto Rican identity, which served to counteract the detrimental effects of the socioeconomic and racial marginality experienced by US Puerto Ricans and the pressures to assimilate into a society that rendered them almost invisible or that minimized their presence and contributions. The cultural effervescence taking place in the metropolis, especially from the 1960s on, was also part of a wider burgeoning consciousness among ethnoracial minorities in the United States (see Chapter 1).

As we have seen, the terms "Nuyorican" and "Neorican" began to be used in the early 1970s to identify those Puerto Ricans born and raised in the United States and to differentiate them from those on the island. Besides its initial negative connotations, the label also implied some obvious geographic limitations, since not all US Puerto Ricans live in New York and, therefore, do not identify with the term. The origin of the term is not clear, but as early as 1964, island artist and writer Jaime Carrero used the word "Neorican" in the title of his collection of poems, *Neorican Jetliner/Jet neorriqueño.* The Nuyorican variation first appeared in the literature in an essay by anthropologist Eduardo Seda Bonilla included in his book *Requiem por una cultura* (1972), but this scholar claimed that the term was already "in the air."

In the early 1970s a group of New York–raised Puerto Rican writers came together to share their work. Frequent gatherings of many of these writers at Miguel Algarín's home evolved into the Nuyorican Poets' Cafe, which opened in 1974 (Turner 1991). Most of the Nuyorican poets got their first public exposure and support from their readings at the cafe. Located in the Lower East Side (renamed Loisaida by these poets), the cafe is now a New York cultural icon that provides a stage for performers from many nationalities who dare to participate in their notorious poetry slams (see Algarín and Holman 1994).

Less than a year after the opening of the cafe, in 1975, Miguel Algarín and Miguel Piñero published the anthology *Nuyorican Poetry: An Anthology of Puerto Rican Words and Feelings,* introducing a more positive ideological context for using the term "Nuyorican." For these authors, adopting this label was an affirmation of their culturally and linguistically hybrid experience; it reflected their new sense of Puerto Rican identity grounded in shared working-class realities and experiences of poverty and racism. "Nuyorican" was meant to differentiate those Puerto Ricans born or raised in the United States from those living in Puerto Rico. The Nuyorican experience was said to include a new language based on the mixing of English and Spanish linguistic codes (technically known as code switching), and the morphological adaptation of words from both languages, commonly described as "Spanglish" (Acosta-Belén 1977; Aparicio 1988; Stavans 2003). Nuyorican reality was deeply rooted in the streets of the urban barrios, where Puerto Ricans faced the consequences and challenges resulting from the social and racial ills of US society. Nuyorican artistic expression frequently underscored African and indigenous cultural influences, as well as those from other Latino groups with whom Puerto Ricans shared the urban barrios.

The *Nuyorican Poetry* anthology featured the writings of Pedro Pietri, Sandra María Esteves, José Angel Figueroa, Jesús Papoleto Meléndez, and a few others and included poems by Algarín and Piñero. Since then Algarín has published several books of poetry, with *Mongo Affair* (1978) being among the most prominent. His work as a cultural activist had been key to the establishment of the Nuyorican Poets' Cafe. He also directed the Nuyorican Playwrights/Actors workshop and the Nuyorican Theater Festival (Algurín and Griffith 1997). Piñero became an acclaimed playwright when his play *Short Eyes* (written in 1974), a depiction of the harshness of the prison life he had experienced at a young age, received a New York Critics' Circle Award and the Obie for best off-Broadway play and was made into a film. In 1980, Piñero published the collection of poetry *La Bodega Sold Dreams* as well as a few short plays. He became a TV actor and played a recurrent role in the *Miami Vice* (1984–1989) action series. A few years after his death, his life and writings were featured in the major motion picture *Piñero,* which came out in 2001.

After the publication of *Nuyorican Poetry,* some of these poets began to produce their own single-author collections and emerged among the most recognized literary voices of the diaspora. Pedro Pietri received critical acclaim for his volume *Puerto Rican Obituary* (1973), and his recordings and dramatic readings of his own poems demonstrated that oral communication and interaction with an audience were an essential part of the Nuyorican creative experience. The publication of Sandra María Esteves's collection *Yerba Buena* in 1980 demonstrated that in the early days of this literary movement women writers were also carving their own spaces and exploring not only similar cultural, racial, and class issues but also those related to the subordination of women within Puerto Rican culture. José Angel Figueroa's *Noo Jork* (which came out in 1981) was one of the first poetry collections translated into Spanish and published in Puerto Rico. Figueroa has been quite active in promoting poetry programs in the public schools.

There were other poets not affiliated with the Nuyorican poetic movement publishing their work during those years. One of the first to publish a single-author collection was Víctor Hernández Cruz, author of *Papo Got His Gun* (1966) and *Snaps* (1969). Many of Hernández Cruz's poems emphasize Afro Caribbean cultural imagery, musical rhythms, and the magical realism that is so characteristic of the contemporary Latin American literary tradition. Subsequent poetry collections, such as *Mainland* (1973), *Tropicalization* (1976), and *Rhythm, Content & Flavor* (1989), have made Hernández Cruz one of the most prolific and widely anthologized US Puerto Rican poets. His poem "Borinkins in Hawaii" captures the historical circumstances that account for the Puerto Rican presence in those islands and the cultural hybridity that comes out of this contact between cultures:

> Off the boat Borinkin . . .
> A ship which left San Juan
> Turn of the century
> Transported workers music
> And song
> They thought they were
> California bound
> But were hijacked by
> Corporate agriculture
> Once they got to land
> They folded over
> They grew and mixed
> Like Hawaii can mix. . . .
>
> You hear the shouts
> You hear the groans
> You feel the wind of the
> Cane workers' machete
> And in the eyes you see
> The waves of oceans
> You see beads
> Which form a necklace
> Of islands
> Which have emerged
> Out of the tears
> (Hernández Cruz 1989, 100–101)

New generations of poets continue to enrich the US Puerto Rican literary experience. Worthy of mention are María Teresa (Mariposa) Hernández and Willie Perdomo. Hernández's "Ode to the Diasporican" (1985) is a powerful affirmation of a Puerto Rican identity shared by those Boricuas born or raised in the United States:

> Some people say that I am not the real thing
> Boricua, that is
> Cause I wasn't born on the enchanted island
> Cause I was born on the mainland
> North of Spanish Harlem
> Cause I was born in the Bronx. . . .
> What does it mean to live in between
> What does it take to realize
> That being Boricua
> Is a state of mind
> A state of heart
> A state of the soul
> No nací en Puerto Rico
> Puerto Rico nació en mi.
> (Hernández 1995, 78)

But New York is not the exclusive location for Puerto Rican creativity. This is confirmed by the work of many other prominent authors. Included among them are Boston-based poet, Rosario Morales, and her California-based daughter, Aurora Levins Morales. Their joint collection of poetry and personal narratives, *Getting Home Alive* (1986), introduced a radical feminist perspective into Puerto Rican literary expression. Moreover, this particular volume captured the experiences of two Puerto Rican women from different generations as they acknowledged their multiple oppressions and defined and brought together the different components of their identity into a new cultural and racial synthesis, as in "Ending Poem":

> I am what I am.
> *A child of the Americas.*
> A light-skinned mestiza of the Caribbean.
> *A child of many diaspora, born into this continent at a crossroads,*
> I am Puerto Rican. I am US American. . . .
> We are new . . .
> *History made us . . .*
> *And we are whole.*
> (Levins Morales and Morales 1986, 213)

Aurora Levins Morales has continued a productive literary career with collections such as *Remedios* (Remedies, 1998) and *Medicine Stories: History, Culture and the Politics of Integrity* (1998). A mixture of testimony, historical account, and storytelling, these books revisit the author's feminist outlook and reveal her keen sense of the history of the Americas viewed through the oppressive experiences of women and of colonized indigenous and African cultures.

Another critically acclaimed Puerto Rican poet is Martín Espada. Espada combined his literary writing with a law practice and the teaching of creative writing at the University of Massachusetts, Amherst. His first collection of poems, *The Immigrant Iceboy's Bolero* (1982), included photographs of barrio life taken by his father, Frank Espada, which provided visual images of the social milieu that inspired the poems. The poet is also the author of *Rebellion Is the Circle of a Lover's Hand* (1990), a bilingual collection that focuses on the exploitative lives of immigrants and workers. Subsequent volumes include *Imagine the Angels of Bread* (1996), winner of an American Book Award, and *A Mayan Astronomer in Hell's Kitchen* (2000). As a whole, Espada's body of work combines an intense political and social consciousness with his commitment as an advocate of the downtrodden. He sees poetry as a form of revolutionary practice:

> Poetry of the political imagination is a matter of both vision and language. Any progressive social change must be imagined first, and that vision must find its most eloquent possible expression to move from vision to reality. . . .
> Political imagination goes beyond protest to articulate an *artistry* of dissent. The question is not whether poetry and politics can mix. The question is a luxury for those who can afford it. The question is how *best* to combine poetry and politics, craft and commitment, how to find the artistic imagination equal to the intensity of the experience and the quality of the ideas. (Espada 1998, 100)

A handful of US Latina writers have been instrumental in bringing sexuality issues out of the literary closet. Among them is Puerto Rican poet Luz María Umpierre, author of *The Margarita Poems* (1987). Umpierre was born and raised in Puerto Rico but has been living in the United States for several decades. She is a well-known literary critic and has taught Latin American literature at various US universities. *The Margarita Poems* is a courageous and moving bilingual collection of poems about love between women; it draws attention to a frequently slighted dimension in the lives of Latinas(os).

Growing-Up Narratives

An important tradition in Puerto Rican literature in the United States is the bildungsroman, or the coming of age narrative, which relates the events and experiences that shape the protagonist's personality from childhood through adulthood. The long list of writings by Puerto Rican authors that portray the adventures, challenges, and risks of trying to make it in or out of the barrios includes pioneering works, such as Piri Thomas's *Down These Mean Streets* (1967) and its sequel *Savior, Savior, Hold My Hand* (1972). Thomas's poignant autobiographical accounts of surviving racism, drugs, and imprisonment were among the first testimonies by a US Puerto Rican to expose the harsh realities of life on the streets of the inner city. For Piri Thomas, the vicissitudes of being a Puerto Rican mulatto growing up in the racially charged environment of the 1940s and 1950s made his story even more compelling. The author related his often self-destructive actions, but his narratives were also a tribute to his ability to overcome these conditions, turn his life around, and lead a productive and successful career as a free-lance writer and in the lecture circuit.

The great majority of the narratives that fall within the bildungsroman genre introduce readers to the lives of working-class migrant families. The late New York–based author Edward Rivera offered a different perspective of his own formative years in the stories of *Family Installments* (1982). Although he was a white, middle-class Puerto Rican, Rivera's more privileged background did not deter him from skillfully showing an awareness of the conflictive and sometimes degrading multiethnic environment of New York City. The author did not dwell on the crude and bleak realism of many earlier testimonial accounts, but rather relied on satiric humor to relate some of his thorny experiences in school, at home, or in his community and his relationship with the wider North American society.

Ed Vega (more recently publishing under the name Edgardo Vega Yunqué) is an author who tried to break away from the prescribed ethnic narratives. Vega relied on the use of satire to combat ethnic stereotypes and challenge the conventions of "ghetto literature." He published the novel *The Comeback* (1985) and the short story collections *Mendoza's Dreams* (1987) and *Casualty Report* (1991). His recent novel, *The Lamentable Journey of Omaha Bigelow into the Impenetrable Loisaida Jungle* (2004), continued to show his disdain for formulaic narratives and displayed his talent as one of the most powerful, complex, and original US Puerto Rican writers. Male novels of inner-city life also include those of Edwin Torres. A writer and a justice of the New York State Supreme Court, Torres has published a series of city crime–focused novels about the clashes between members of minority groups and the police. These novels, which appeal to popular audiences, also tend to reinforce some common stereotypes. Torres's novels *Carlito's Way* (1975) and *Q&A* (1977) have been made into major action films.

Abraham Rodríguez, from a younger generation, expressed the outrage and frustration of those caught up in the destructive effects of poverty and racism in his collection of short stories, *The Boy Without a Flag: Tales of the South Bronx* (1992), and the novel *Spidertown* (1993). It is a common thread for the Puerto Rican male narratives to highlight the violence and despairing realities of street life in the urban barrios, which often lead to a self-destructive path or to the search for the inner strength and determination to beat the odds.

Contrasting with the male narratives, Puerto Rican women authors have preferred to explore the unequal power relations between men and women and relationships among women family members, especially of different generations. A distinguished pioneer in this genre is Nicholasa Mohr. In her early career, the author had to struggle with mainstream publishers to make them realize that growing up in the urban barrios was not always the self-destructive experience described in most of the published male accounts (see Acosta-Belén 1978). For Mohr, the hardships and discrimination faced by her community are still very central to her work, but her narratives have been overpowered by an impressive tapestry of working-class characters who represented the compassion and human solidarity that also could be found in the urban barrios. Mohr is the author of the novel *Nilda* (1973) and the short story collections *El Bronx Remembered* (1975), *In Nueva York* (1977), and *Rituals of Survival: A Woman's Portfolio* (1985). Many of Mohr's narratives have been critically acclaimed and are often required reading in schools and universities. The author is also a graphic artist and has illustrated some of her stories with drawings and silk screens, especially her novels for children such as *Felita* (1979) and *Going Home* (1986).

Poet and novelist Judith Ortiz Cofer, raised in Paterson, New Jersey, and holding the distinguished title of Franklin Professor at the University of Georgia, has joined other women's voices in their attempts to capture the subordinate roles and experiences of different generations of Puerto Rican women and the tensions between the two cultural worlds they share. After her early collection of poems, *Terms of Survival* (1987), the author, a skillful storyteller, combined poetry and narrative in the volumes *Silent Dancing: Remembrances of a Puerto Rican Childhood* (1990) and *The Latin Deli* (1993). For the most part, Ortiz Cofer's writings have depicted her coming-of-age experiences straddling between the United States and Puerto Rico; she also related many of the stories about life in her Puerto Rican hometown of Hormigueros that were passed along to her by her grandmother, mother, and uncle. Ortiz Cofer's autobiographical novel *The Line of the Sun* (1989) was well received by critics. Another prominent writer in the women's bildungsroman genre is Esmeralda Santiago, author of the autobiographical novel *When I Was Puerto Rican* (1993) and its sequel, *Almost a Woman* (1998). The latter was made into a PBS television film.

The titles of the aforementioned novels suggest their main theme: the recovery of memory and the construction of identity against a backdrop of cultural straddling and cultures in flux. Alternating scenes of life back in Puerto Rico and in the authors' respective US communities, both Ortiz Cofer and Santiago used humor to point out conflicts and contradictions that derived from the clash between cultures and among different generations. Because of a growing interest in the experiences of Puerto Ricans and other US Latinos in these groups' countries of origin, several of these leading authors' best-known works have been translated in recent years from the original English into Spanish.[8]

The Role of Small Latino Presses

It is well known that for a long time mainstream US publishing houses did not see a market for the writings of Puerto Rican or other Latino(a) authors. These publishers, assuming that Latinos were not educated enough to sustain a reading audience, easily conformed to generalized stereotypes and prejudices about an alleged "poverty of culture" within the communities. They also assumed that there would be no interest in the Latino ethnic experience among non-Latino readers, and the prevalent perception was that these writers were not marketable.

These widespread assumptions explain why the publication of works by Puerto Rican, Chicano, and other Latino(a) writers was facilitated initially, not by mainstream publishers, but by small ethnic presses and a few literary and cultural studies journals established by individuals from these groups. These small presses were generally affiliated with the college or university where the individual who initiated the enterprise was employed. Such is the case of the *Revista Chicano–Riqueña* (subsequently the *Americas Review*), founded in 1973 by Puerto Rican literary scholar Nicolás Kanellos while he was a faculty member at Indiana University. A few years later, Kanellos moved to the University of Houston and founded Arte Público Press, first home to a large number of literary works written by Puerto Ricans, Chicanos, Cubans, and Dominicans. Chicano scholar Gary H. Keller initiated the journal the *Bilingual Review/La revista bilingüe* in 1974 while he was a faculty member at York College, CUNY. Keller also founded the Bilingual Press, currently based at Arizona State University, opening another publishing outlet to Latino(a) writers.

In subsequent years, many of the Puerto Rican and other Latino(a) writers first published either by Arte Público or Bilingual Press received increased recognition from critics and literary scholars, and mainstream publishers began to approach them. Sometimes these publishers tried to impose sensationalized versions or formulaic accounts of a particular author's ethnic experiences growing up, versions that bordered on the perpetuation of some of the most common stereotypes. The sobering reality is that it took until the 1990s for many of the major publishing houses to look at US Latino literature in a serious manner and to fully recognize the diversity of nationalities and experiences among Latino groups, the abundance of talent, and the market potential for this literature for both an English- and a Spanish-speaking readership.

A few attempts have been made in Puerto Rico to disseminate the wealth of literary creativity coming out of the diaspora, but most available anthologies have focused primarily on poetry. Works by several of the best-known authors are more frequently available in Spanish now than in the past. The poetry collection *Herejes y mitificadores: Muestra de poesía puertorriqueña en los Estados Unidos* (Heretics and Mythmakers: A Sample of Puerto Rican Poetry in the United States, 1980), was the first to introduce Nuyorican poetry to an island audience. The volume was edited by literary critic Efraín Barradas. Barradas noted that for Nuyorican authors, Puerto Rico represented a mythical fountain of images and symbols in their quest for self-definition. The content of these symbols and images has been accepted, rejected, or modified by the cultural and linguistic contact that Puerto Ricans have had with other ethnic groups and the wider Anglo-American society.

The poetry anthologies *Los paraguas amarillos: Los poetas latinos en Nueva York* (Silén, 1983) and *Papiros de babel* (López-Adorno, 1991) illustrate the presence and coexistence in the United States of Puerto Rican and other Latino(a) authors from different generations writing in English, Spanish, or bilingually. The writings of most of these poets have been a powerful repository of images that affirm a strong sense of *puertorriqueñidad* (Puerto Ricanness) that transcends island borders (see Acosta-Belén 1992). It is a sense of Puerto Rican identity rooted in the notion of being part of a marginalized minority in US society. In fact, many of the authors included in these two collections are read and known on the island, but the writers born or raised in the United States tend to write mostly in English and are still largely absent from the island's literary canon. It should be noted, however, that some publishing houses in the United States, Mexico, Spain, and Puerto Rico are beginning to publish and market Spanish translations of works originally written in English by Latino(a) writers. Interviews have also been a way of entering the inner world of many of these authors, as evidenced by journalist Carmen Hernández's *Puerto Rican Voices in English* (1998). Through her weekly cultural section in the island newspaper *El Nuevo Día*, Hernández has played a leading role in promoting the work of US Puerto Rican writers among island readers.

Performing Culture

The history of Puerto Rican theater in the United States is linked to a long professional and working-class tradition in this genre that dates back to the second half of the nineteenth century and continued to flourish especially in New York City from the 1920s through the 1940s. In *History of Hispanic Theater in the United States*, Nicolás Kanellos noted that New York was an important "model in solidifying diverse Hispanic nationalities on the stage" (1990, xv).

As the largest Latino group in the city, Puerto Ricans made their presence felt on the stage as writers and performers. In his groundbreaking study, Kanellos was able to identify several published and unpublished plays by Puerto Rican and other Latino writers. These plays reflect some of the issues that concerned the various Latin American and Caribbean nationalities during the early stages of settlement and attest to the level of cultural activity taking place in these communities.

There are several plays that stand out in reflecting the social and political concerns of the Puerto Rican community during those years. These include Gonzalo O'Neill's *Pabellón de Borinquen o bajo una sola bandera* (Borinquen Pavillion or Under One Flag, 1929) and *La indiana borinqueña* (The Indigenous Borinquen, 1922). Both plays upheld the proindependence and anti-imperialist ideals of the Puerto Rican Nationalist movement during its burgeoning years. O'Neill's comedy *Moncho Reyes* (1923) provided a satirical view of the Americanization policies promoted by E. Montgomery Reily, the US-appointed governor of Puerto Rico at the time. The name in the title of the play is a Spanish adaptation of his English name, coined by Puerto Ricans to ridicule this North American public official. Another playwright, Frank Martínez, wrote *De Puerto Rico a Nueva York* (From Puerto Rico to New York, 1939), which was performed but never published. According to Kanellos (1990), this work was an important antecedent to René Marqués's *La carreta*.

A popular entertainment form among Puerto Rican and Cuban performers during the 1920s and 1930s was the humorous *teatro bufo–cubano*, which combined elements of vaudeville and African American minstrel shows. Puerto Rican actor, photographer, and playwright Erasmo Vando was known for his contributions to this popular genre and for writing and producing the play *De Puerto Rico al Metropolitano o el Caruso Criollo* (From Puerto Rico to the Metropolitan or the Creole Caruso, 1928).

Many theater productions during the Great Depression years were aimed at consciousness-raising among working-class audiences. The *teatro obrero* (workers' theater), a genre linked to the labor movement, was very popular during the 1920s and 1930s. Community organizations such as the Mutualista Obrera Puertorriqueña (Puerto Rican Mutual Aid Society) regularly sponsored performances by professional companies and also provided space for amateur productions (Kanellos 1990). A play that focused on the exploitation of workers by the capitalist system and the aftereffects of the Great Depression is the earlier-mentioned *Los hipócritas* (1937), by Puerto Rican feminist and labor activist Franca de Armiño.

The Nuevo Círculo Dramático (New Dramatic Circle, 1953–1960) was established in New York by playwright Roberto Rodríguez Suárez, director of the premiere performance of Marqués's *La carreta*. In subsequent decades, the productions of the Puerto Rican Traveling Theater, founded by Miriam Colón in 1967, brought theater to the people of the barrios of New York and offered new opportunities to actors and playwrights. The Traveling Theater was initially a vehicle to introduce the work of island writers to community audiences, but in later years it began to showcase the work of US-born Puerto Rican writers. Colón is considered the *gran dama* (great lady) of Puerto Rican theater in the United States for her efforts in promoting this genre. In addition to her theater activities, she is a very talented performer and has made numerous contributions to film and television.

Under the artistic direction of Rosalba Rolón, the Teatro Pregones, founded in 1980 and located in the Bronx, promotes a mission "to create and perform original musical theater and Latino plays rooted in Puerto Rican cultures in ways that challenge the human experience (www.pregones.org). The company has performed all over the world and provides a stage for young actors, playwrights, producers, directors, and musicians to flourish and be mentored by more experienced professionals.

Poets Miguel Piñero, Pedro Pietri, and Tato Laviera also published several plays, and some new writers have been achieving recognition in the off-Broadway theater circuit. Worthy of mention is playwright José Rivera, author of *Marisol* (1994), a futuristic and apocalyptic dark comedy about urban violence and the breaking down of male and female stereotypes. Rivera's autobiographical play *The House of Ramón Iglesia* (1989) was first produced for television by the Corporation for Public Broadcasting in 1986, before it was published three years later. Rivera won an Obie award in 2000 for the play *References to Salvador Dalí Make Me Hot*. Another US Puerto Rican dramatist is Carmen Rivera, author of *Julia* (1992), a feminist play that challenges traditional women's roles and evokes the poetic rebelliousness of Julia de Burgos. Rivera also won an Obie in 1996 for *La Gringa*.

Theater and film roles for Latino(a) actors have never been abundant. Actors constantly struggle for recognition and most are conscious of the pitfalls of the ethnic typecasting that dominates US entertainment circles. Rodríguez (2000b, 2004) has documented and analyzed many of the stereotypical images and representations of Latinos(as) propagated in the US media and their demeaning effects at the individual and the collective levels. She stated that Latinos in general continued to be "the most underrepresented ethnic group in films and primetime television" despite the unprecedented growth in this population since the latter decades of the twentieth century (2004, 243).

Several Puerto Rican performers have achieved recognition and praise in theater, film, and television. Only a handful were able to have successful careers during times when opportunities for Latino(a) performers were few and limited by typecasting or stereotyping. José Ferrer was the first to receive an Academy Award in 1950 for his leading performance in the film *Cyrano de Bergerac*. Rita Moreno received an Oscar for a supporting role in *West Side Story* (1961). Her versatility in theater and television make her one of the few performers to have also received Tony and Emmy awards. Raúl Juliá had a prominent career in film and the theater, receiving critical acclaim for his many roles and an Academy Award nomination for his leading role in the film *Kiss of the Spider Woman*. In the year 2002 actor Benicio del Toro received an Oscar for his supporting performance in the film *Traffic*. Performer Jennifer López is one of the most popular figures in US entertainment and has a successful career in film and music.

Popular Music

The mythification and yearning for the Puerto Rican homeland expressed in creative literature is also found in some of the most popular songs written by composers and musicians, especially those who at some point in their lives left the island to live in the United States, either for brief periods of time or a longer stay. It is said of Puerto Ricans that they "llevan la música por dentro" (carry the music within them).[9] This popular phrase indicates the importance of this music in the sum of Puerto Rican cultural expression. Classic songs such as Rafael Hernández's "Preciosa" (My Precious Land), Noel Estrada's "En mi Viejo San Juan" (In My Old San Juan), and Bobby Capó's "Soñando con Puerto Rico" (Dreaming of Puerto Rico) are only a few of the best-known examples of the nostalgia, patriotic pride, and love for the homeland expressed by those Puerto Ricans finding themselves on distant shores.

Popular music undoubtedly represents an expressive form that has contributed significantly to propagating Puerto Rican cultural traditions, affirming a national consciousness within the diaspora and generating the cultural vitality that links island and US communities. From typical forms such as the *plena* (a working-class musical expression), the *bomba* (a folk dance of African origin), the *décima* (a peasant musical composition), or the *aguinaldo* (a Christmas carol), to the romantic *bolero* (ballad) or the faster dancing rhythms of salsa, musical expression is a vibrant part of Puerto Rican and the broader Latino cultural and social life in the United States.

Folk music interpreter Manuel "Canario" Jiménez first recorded and popularized his *plenas* in New York. In fact, many of the performers that are part of the island's popular music hall of fame developed their careers outside the island in countries like Cuba, Mexico, or within the Latino communities throughout the United States. Whether they traveled outside the island on a temporary basis or had established residence in the US metropolis, Puerto Rican and other Latino performers often shared the stage of the Teatro Hispano de Nueva York, the Teatro Puerto Rico, the Teatro San José, or the famous Palladium Dance Hall. Harlem's celebrated Apollo Theater also opened its doors to Puerto Rican and other Latino(a) performers.

Music was not only a form of entertainment. The creativity, visibility, and prominence of Puerto Rican performers were important symbols for a community confronted with a constant barrage of negative images in the press, movies, and other media (Glaser 1995; Santiago 1994). The songs and musical styles that emerged from the communities of the diaspora reflected a deep-rooted sense of Puerto Ricanness, and were part of that inexhaustible repertoire of survival strategies that migrants develop in the process of adapting to new and alienating environments.

Included among the best-known early figures in New York's musical circles were the talented performer-composers Rafael Hernández, Pedro Flores, and Bobby Capó. Hernández's Trío Borinquen and Cuarteto Victoria, first performed some of his most memorable compositions in New York. The Puerto Rican homeland was central to Hernández's internationally known songs "Lamento Borincano" (The Peasant's Lament) and "Preciosa," both written in New York. Hernández's sister, Victoria, was a garment industry worker and piano teacher. Her musical inclinations led her to open the music store Almacenes Hernández in 1927, the first major Puerto Rican–owned record store in the city (Glaser 1995).

Singer-composers Bobby Capó, Mirta Silva, and Pedro Ortiz Dávila (Davilita) performed at different times with Rafael Hernández's Cuarteto before they achieved their own individual fame as composers and musical interpreters. Rafael Hernández lived in Mexico for many years and achieved continental fame. In addition to his native Puerto Rico, Capó was well known in New York and Cuba. He also was one of the first performers to host his own television show on a New York network. Silva went on to become one of the most coveted performers in Cuba, and after returning to Puerto Rico, she emerged as one of TV's favorite entertainers with her variety shows, *Una Hora Contigo* (An Hour with You) and *Tira y tápate* (Throw the Rock and Hide Your Hand). While living in New York, Davilita was a featured singer in composer Pedro Flores's New York musical ensembles. Years later, Davilita joined Felipe "La Voz" Rodríguez, and they became one of the most acclaimed duos in New York and Puerto Rico. Raised in New York, singer Daniel Santos also made popular his unique singing style during this period. A fervent Nationalist, Santos also found a less repressive political environment away from the island.

Some of the problems confronted by black Puerto Rican artists, like Hernández, Davilita, and Santos, were caused by the segregationist practices prevalent in US society at the time. Such practices excluded these artists from performing in some of the most prominent whites-only clubs, especially before the 1960s civil rights laws barred segregation. Not only were dark-skinned performers excluded from certain venues, they also were paid less than white or light-skinned Latinos(as) (Glasser 1995).

Musicians such as Noro Morales, Tito Puente, and Tito Rodríguez are among the pioneers of the Big Band and Mambo Kings era of the 1940s and 1950s who along with Cuba's Pérez Prado and Spain's Xavier Cugat entertained audiences in New York's celebrated Palladium Dance Hall. Morales's orchestra, which often alternated on the stage with Glenn Miller's, also performed on Broadway. Born in the United States of Puerto Rican parents, Tito Puente studied at Juilliard and soon became known for his musical experiments in which he combined African American jazz with Latin rhythms. He was known as "el rey del timbal" (the king of the small drums) and of a new genre labeled Latin jazz. Until his death in 2002, Tito Puente was one of the leading percussion artists and orchestra leaders in the United States and the rest of the continent, with a musical career that spanned more than half a century.

Tito Rodríguez and his Mambo Devils were among the first successful Puerto Rican musical groups to entertain US audiences in the late 1940s. Rodríguez came to New York where his brother Johnny Rodríguez and his trio had achieved popularity within the community. In later years, Tito Rodríguez's ventures into the bossa nova beat and his heartfelt style as a singer of romantic *boleros* also gained him fame in Venezuela, Argentina, and other countries.

In the late 1950s and 1960s, a new generation of Puerto Rican performers born or raised in the United States revolutionized the New York Latino musical environment; their popularity extended to the island and other parts of Latin America. New York–born Charlie Palmieri, also a piano student at Juilliard, began to achieve recognition with his Orquesta Siboney in the early 1950s. In 1959, he joined Dominican flautist Johnny Pacheco and founded the Charanga Duboney. Using a combination of the flute, violin, bass, and small drums, they invented the *pachanga* and *charanga* rhythms, which turned into dancing favorites for many US Latino audiences during the early 1960s. Another Puerto Rican *pachanguero*, Joe Quijano, started his own recording label, Cesta, and asked Charlie Palmieri to direct the production of the recordings of the Cesta All Stars, a label that included some of the most popular Latino(a) performers during those years. Charlie Palmieri's brother, Eddie, also contributed to this new musical genre and to the Latin jazz genre. Despite the fact that these performers made an impact on the Latino musical world of the 1950s and 1960s, they were not so successful in "crossing over" into the wider US market and the Billboard charts as were some of the more prominent performers achieving recognition after the 1990s.

Born in Brooklyn of Puerto Rican parents, Ray Barreto was the first *pachanga* performer to "cross over" and make it to the Billboard's list of hits with his recording of the song "El watusi" (Santiago 1994). During the same period, José Calderón, better known by his artistic name of Joe Cuba, also achieved success with his famous Sexteto group for his combination of mambo and North American rhythm and blues to create the late 1960s *bugalú* craze. The *bugalú* was occasionally interpreted in English or bilingually. Ricardo "Richie" Ray, an accomplished US-born Puerto Rican pianist and Juilliard graduate, also started his career with this musical genre. He recruited another US-born Puerto Rican, Bobby Cruz, to become the lead singer in his orchestra, which had an extensive bilingual repertoire and achieved considerable popularity within the Latino communities.

In 1964, Johnny Pacheco created the Fania recording label and opened the doors to many other Latino performers to join the celebrated Fania All Stars, including Puerto Rican performers Bobby Valentín, Willie Colón, and Héctor Lavoe, and Jewish-American saxophonist Larry Harlow. The experimentation and fusion of Afro-Caribbean rhythms with jazz, rock, and rhythm and blues began to be marketed by Fania as the salsa genre, creating an unbreakable musical link between Boricuas on the island and those from the metropolis.[10] Salsa incorporated elements of the most popular Afro-Caribbean musical rhythms— the *son*, mambo, *guaracha*, *pachanga*, *chachachá*, *son montuno*, and rumba. Salsa was a term that reflected most accurately the spirit, vivaciousness, and *sabor* (flavor) of Latino music and a marketing label that unified the diverse musical experiences of the various Caribbean diasporas in the United States.

Unquestionably, the Caribbean rhythms of salsa have penetrated the North American musical mainstream, as demonstrated by the enormous success of many contemporary Latino(a) performers practicing this genre, either in Spanish or bilingually. A new wave of younger and successful salsa interpreters has emerged. A leading salsa singer is Marc Anthony, who also performs ballads and pop rock. Marc Anthony's popularity in the United States has reached levels similar to those achieved by other Puerto Rican pop rock performers such as Ricky Martin and Jennifer López. Hollywood film productions, such as *Salsa* (1998) and *Dance with Me* (1999), the former featuring ex-Menudo Robby "Draco" Rosa, and the latter, Puerto Rican singer Chayanne and the well-known African American performer Vanessa Williams, reflect the growing popularity of salsa and Latino music among US audiences.

Available studies on salsa music (Quintero Rivera 1999; Aparicio 1998) have argued that aside from its entertainment value, this popular genre provides a mirror of social and power relations among various social strata and between the sexes.[11] Cultural definition and affirmation is another important component of this music. Songs such as "Color americano" (American Color), sung by Willie Colón, "Buscando América" (Searching for America), by Panamanian singer Rubén Blades, and "Latinos en Estados Unidos" (Latinos in the United States), by the late Cuban salsa diva Celia Cruz illustrate ways in which interpreters and composers used music as an instrument of social consciousness and as means of reaffirming a panethnic sense of Latino identity that frequently transcended individual nationalities. In "Color americano," a song written by Amílcar Boscán and interpreted by Puerto Rican *salsero* Willie Colón, some of the basic elements of this identity are defined:

> Tengo el honor
> de ser hispano
> llevo el sabor del borincano,
> mi color morenito

ya casi marrón
es orgullo del pueblo
latino señor.
[I have the honor
of being Hispanic
I have the Borincano flavor
my dark-skin color
almost brown
is the pride of the
Latino people, my man.]
(Boscán 1990, Sony International)

Puerto Rican folk music, particularly those compositions reflecting the influence of African rhythms like the *plena* and the *bomba,* have inspired many interpreters. One of the best-known contemporary groups in this genre is Los Pleneros de la 21, a group founded in 1983 by Juan Gutiérrez. Both through their recordings and concerts, this group has revitalized Afro–Puerto Rican traditional music within the diaspora.

Some Puerto Rican folk singers of the genre called *la nueva trova* (the new folk song) became popular during the social and political activist period of the 1960s and 1970s. This music was performed at colleges and universities or at activities sponsored by community organizations. Some performers moved between the island and the United States. One of the most popular is Roy Brown, who recorded the album *Nueva Yol* (a common Spanish colloquial adaptation of the name New York) in 1983. Earlier in his career, Brown had popularized the song "El negrito bonito" (The Beautiful Black Man), a song that captures some of the sadness and perils of a destitute black Puerto Rican migrant worker.

Different forms of popular musical expressions have continued to emerge from the barrios, including rap, hip-hop, and reggaetón.[12] These provide offbeat ways of understanding the cultural, social, and racial interactions among Puerto Ricans and African Americans in the inner city. Flores (2000) argued, "Like other Latino groups, Puerto Ricans are using rap as a vehicle for affirming their history, language, and culture under conditions of rampant discrimination and exclusion" (137). In her study *New York Ricans of the Hip Hop Zone* (2003), Rivera noted that despite the general undermining of Puerto Rican contributions to this genre, this music underscores their African roots and experiences also endured by African Americans in US society. Unquestionably, the participation of Puerto Ricans in these musical forms adds to the many other forms of bilingual creative expression coming out of the urban barrios. Despite their often sexist lyrics and use of foul language, the huge popularity of hip-hop and reggaetón allows their working-class social and political content to reach the US mainstream as much as it does a Latino audience.

The Visual Arts

Puerto Rican visual artists from the island are among the most frequent sojourners and migrants to the United States. Because of the nature of their trade, many of these artists have studied, resided, held exhibitions, or received recognition outside the island. Even many of the artists based in Puerto Rico maintain a continuous exchange with other Puerto Rican artists in the metropolis around some of the same issues of cultural identity and resistance to assimilation found in literary expression.

The struggles and accomplishments of Puerto Rican visual artists during the past half century have reflected some of the same trials and tribulations faced by the earlier masters, in particular their pilgrimages to many parts of the world seeking training or the mentorship of established foreign artists, thus increasing their chances for a successful career. The evocation of the Puerto Rican landscape and traditions and the difficult adaptation to a culturally different and often unwelcoming environment shape the work of most visual artists of the diaspora.

According to Torruella Leval (1998), the activities of Puerto Rican artists in the United States can be placed under three different cycles. The first, beginning in the 1950s, opened the dialogue between artists from the island and the metropolis around cultural issues of self-definition. The second cycle took place during the ethnic revitalization movement of the 1960s and 1970s and focused on social protest and community empowerment. The third one began in the 1980s and linked Puerto Ricans to the cultural debates and struggles of a wider panethnic Latino experience within US society.

Efforts to promote Puerto Rican culture within the United States were part of the mission of the Migration Division (see Chapter 4). The decades prior to the 1950s had witnessed the arrival of a few Puerto Rican artists, but they worked mostly without the benefit of a supportive artistic environment, often in isolation from one another, and their work was, therefore, less known to the community.

A few names stand out when referring to the most notable artists of the pre–World War II migration period. Juan De'Prey, a painter of Puerto Rican and Haitian ancestry, who came to New York from Puerto Rico in 1929, became known for landscapes that illustrate a nostalgia for his native land and his mulatto racial background. De'Prey's style has often been compared to that of Gauguin, particularly his portraits of children (Bloch 1978).

Lorenzo Homar became one of Puerto Rico's artists most acclaimed internationally. Before that, in the early 1930s, he lived in New York and worked as a designer for the famous Cartier house of jewelers. Another island painter, Rafael D. Palacios, arrived in New York in 1938 and developed a prominent career as a book illustrator and cartographer for US publishing houses. Olga

Albizu was another painter achieving some prominence in New York before the 1960s. She exhibited her work at the Organization of American States Gallery and did many designs for RCA record album jackets (Benítez 1988; Acosta-Belén et al. 2000).

Cultural activities within the diaspora were influenced by the cultural and intellectual environment that began to be promoted in Puerto Rico during the 1950s. Reacting to the rapid changes that were occurring on the island during the Operation Bootstrap years, the administration of Governor Luis Muñoz Marín sponsored Operación Serenidad (Operation Serenity). This ambitious cultural endeavor was aimed at maintaining a balance between the overwhelming North American economic and cultural influences on the island and the preservation of Puerto Rico's cultural uniqueness and traditions. Some of the government-sponsored initiatives under Operación Serenidad included incentives in the form of scholarships, travel grants, performances, exhibits, films, and publications that often brought Puerto Ricans from the island to the United States to work on joint creative projects with their fellow artists in the metropolis. Many of these activities were coordinated by the Migration Division in New York, then headed by Joseph Monserrat. This office sponsored the Oller-Campeche Gallery, which allowed many Puerto Rican artists to introduce their work to the community. Puerto Rican fine arts in New York also were fostered by organizations such as the Puerto Rican Institute, directed at the time by Luis Quero Chiesa. The presence in New York of well-known Puerto Rican visual artists Rafael Tufiño and Carlos Osorio during this period also enriched the diaspora's artistic circles (Torruella Leval 1998).

Prior to the ethnic revitalization movement of the civil rights era, it was not easy for Puerto Rican or other Latino(a) artists to make significant incursions into US mainstream artistic circles. This situation began to change when members of the community started to design opportunities for artists to train, create, and exhibit. The founding of Los Amigos de Puerto Rico (Friends of Puerto Rico) in 1953 by artist Amalia Guerrero served those purposes. For more than two decades some of the best-known island artists came to New York to teach or learn at Guerrero's workshop (Torruella Leval 1998).

Nonetheless, it was not until the 1960s and 1970s that Puerto Rican artists born or raised in the United States began to make their mark with works that combined the images, colors, symbols, and traditions of the homeland with some of the sobering realities of urban life. Through murals, sculptures, paintings, silk screens, posters, and photographs, the artistic world of the diaspora began to flourish and to capture what it meant to be Puerto Rican in a bicultural environment. These artists also depicted the many ways in which the Puerto Rican people struggled and endured as part of a disenfranchised US working class.

Although some empty spaces of the urban barrios were often filled with graffiti, many Puerto Rican artists found creative outlets to channel their anger and disaffection or to celebrate and affirm their heritage through different forms of public art. Public art began to bring a mythical Puerto Rico to the many US communities where Puerto Ricans had settled. The reproduction of African and Taino indigenous motifs and folkloric traditions were very popular among these artists. According to Miramar Benítez (1988): "The walls of Puerto Rican business places, particularly those of La Marketa . . . began to blossom with murals painted by folk artists. . . . Artists such as Johnny Vázquez and Millito López painted the rural scenes they had left behind" (78).[13]

Some notable examples of public art include Rafael Ferrer's sculpture *Puerto Rican Sun* (1979), located in the South Bronx. The sculpture brought a tropical flavor to a sterile environment in the form of palm trees holding up a shining sun. Manuel Vega's mural *Playa de amor* (Seaside of Love, 1988) depicted Afro-Puerto Rican dancers celebrating their musical traditions. Nitza Tufiño was hired by New York's Metropolitan Transportation Authority in 1989 to create a monumental ceramic mural at a subway station in Spanish Harlem. The imposing mural *Neo-Borikén* reproduced Taino Indian petroglyphs in bright colors. Marina Gutiérrez, a high school art teacher, tried to capture elements of Puerto Rican social and political oppression in the island and the United States (Torruella Leval 1998). Among her most impressive contributions to public art was her 1996 installation of colorful suspended mobile structures that visually captured images of Julia de Burgos's poetry. This installation is displayed at the atrium of the Julia de Burgos Latino Cultural Center in Manhattan's East Side.

Other artists, such as Pedro Villarini, created paintings that transported the Puerto Rican rural landscape and traditions to the cold and colorless environment of the city. His *El artesano en Nueva York* (The Artisan in New York) is a tribute to the artisan tradition of religious woodcarvings. Capturing different aspects of life in the urban barrios is another important theme, as demonstrated by the works of Ralph Ortiz and his depictions of the violence often experienced by members of these communities (Benítez 1988). Curriculum materials, illustrated anthologies, posters, and the covers of the Comité Noviembre's annual magazine displayed the work of Ernesto Ramos-Nieves, a talented artist who died young. The Comité Noviembre had been established in New York in 1987 to institutionalize the celebration of the month of November as Puerto Rican Heritage Month. The committee was founded by the joint efforts of several community organizations; its annual publication was a way of highlighting the work of Puerto Rican artists and the overall cultural life of the US Puerto Rican community.

An impressive display of the images, traditions, and dilemmas of Puerto Rican barrio life is offered by the works of Juan Sánchez, perhaps the most critically acclaimed artist of the diaspora. Sánchez's powerful paintings and collages fill many public spaces and the covers of numerous books and journals.

Jiménez-Muñoz and Santiago (1995) summarized the essence of Sánchez's body of work:

> Isn't this part of what being Puerto Rican is all about, particularly in the U.S.: being caught between Spanish and English, being the Caribbean/tropical hybrid in Niuyol City's cold wasteland, trying to negotiate between American-ness and Latin American-ness, between "el welfare" and "las 936," crossing "el charco" in "la guagua aérea," etc.? It is no accident that practically all of these are themes which Sánchez has included (explicitly or implicitly) in recent paintings. (22)

One of Sánchez's major works is *Conditions that Exist*. The piece embodies some of the most compelling images and issues of the diaspora. The words Sánchez included on this collage reveal the identity quest that is such an integral part of many US Puerto Rican cultural expressions: "¿Dónde está mi casa? / ¿dónde está mi país? / ¿para dónde vamos?" (Where is my home? / Where is my country? / Where are we going?). Another piece, "A Puerto Rican Prisoner of War and Much More," highlights the active role of the diaspora in the campaigns to free political prisoners.

The few institutions founded to promote artistic endeavors within the Puerto Rican community have been quite successful in achieving their goals. Two of the leading ones are the Museo del Barrio and the Taller Alma Boricua (better known as the Taller Boricua), both established in New York in 1969. Founded in East Harlem by a group of Puerto Rican artists and educators, the museum is now a key cultural and educational resource. In addition to its many rotating exhibits, education programs, and publications, it has a permanent collection. Artists Martha Vega, Rafael Montañez Ortiz (also known as Ralph Ortiz), and Hiram Maristany were among the founders of this prominent institution. The museum's 1973 exhibit, the Art Heritage of Puerto Rico, a joint initiative with the Metropolitan Museum of Art, was a large collective exhibit of a whole gamut of artistic expressions, including Taino *cemíes* (indigenous stone carvings) and other stone and ceramic crafts, *santos* (wooden carvings of religious figures), classical and modern paintings, posters, silk screens, and sculptures. Since then, the museum has sponsored numerous exhibits by Puerto Rican and other Latino(a) artists, and many other cultural activities. Worth mentioning is the 1978–1979 exhibit at the Museo del Barrio, "Bridge Between Islands," aimed at fostering connections between Puerto Rican artists from the island and the diaspora.

The Taller Boricua was founded by Puerto Rican artists Marcos Dimas, Carlos Osorio, Manuel Otero, Armando Soto, Adrián García, and Martín Rubio as a center for community art education in East Harlem. Nevertheless, a large number of the most talented Puerto Rican artists, both from the island and the United States, have spent time working there. The Taller provides a setting for artists to work and exchange ideas; the artwork produced at this

Conditions That Exist (1990), a triptych by Puerto Rican artist Juan Sánchez that underscores some fundamental Puerto Rican identity questions. Over the canvas of a Puerto Rican flag the graffiti-scripted questions appear: ¿Dónda está mi casa? ¿Dónda está mi país? ¿Para dónde vamos? (Where is my home? Where is my country? Where are we going?). Reprinted by permission of the artist.

A Puerto Rican Prisoner of War and Much More (1983), mixed media on canvas, by Puerto Rican artist Juan Sánchez. Highlighting the diaspora's participation in the campaigns to free Puerto Rican political prisoners, the artwork incorporates a picture of a demonstration in front of a federal court building and conveys, according to the artist, "the epic courage of a people in constant struggle for independence." Reprinted by permission of the artist.

workshop often explores the roots of what it means to be Puerto Rican, especially by emphasizing Taino and African symbols and traditions (Torruella Leval 1998). Other Puerto Rican artists, such as Rafael Colón Morales and Diógenes Ballester, have worked at the Taller Boricua and taught art courses at the University at Albany, SUNY, and other US institutions.

New York Puerto Rican writer and artist, Jack Agüeros, a member of Los Amigos de Puerto Rico and a former director of El Museo del Barrio, supported the work of artists through the establishment in the mid-1970s of Galería Caymán in Soho. This gallery later became the Museum of Contemporary Hispanic Art (MOCHA). Other artists also have supported the artistic activity of Latinos(as) in New York in various ways. As a member of the New York State Council for the Arts (1988–1998), James Shine was instrumental in promoting funding for Latino-focused activities. Shine is the owner of an extensive collection of Puerto Rican art posters that he often lends out to schools and universities.

In Philadelphia, the Taller Puertorriqueño, founded in 1974, plays a role similar to New York's Taller Boricua. It is a community-based cultural education organization that houses a cultural awareness program, a gallery, a bookstore, and a museum collection and archives.

Another important institution is Chicago's Juan Antonio Corretjer Puerto Rican Cultural Center (PRCC), which has been instrumental in maintaining the vitality of the Paseo Boricua, considered "the cultural and economic heartbeat" of the city's Puerto Rican community. The Paseo is the site of an impressive architectural display of two steel Puerto Rican flags that run across Division Street, part of a Puerto Rican neighborhood The PRCC supported the development of the Institute of Puerto Rican Art and Culture (IPRAC), an organization that sponsors a wide range of activities in Puerto Rican art and music. Murals by Puerto Rican artists are found on the walls of the PRCC building and surrounding areas. A mural that illustrates the vitality of Puerto Rican nationalism within the diaspora is *Sea of Flags* by Gamaliel Ramírez and Eren Star Padilla. Both artists engaged community youth in the process of painting the mural, commissioned by the PRCC for the Jornada Albizu Campos (Albizu Campos Day) in 2004. The mural is displayed on the front and back covers of the paperback edition of this book. It shows a multitude holding Puerto Rican flags and surrounding Nationalist leader Lolila Lebrón (in the center) holding the revolutionary flag used at the Lares Revolt of 1868. Against the backdrop is one of the two Puerto Rican steel flags that embellish Chicago's Paseo Boricua.

From 1988 to 1996, the Institute of Puerto Rican Affairs, headed by Paquita Vivó, maintained a lively cultural presence in Washington, DC. The institute sponsored art exhibits, concerts, lectures, conferences, and publications. It was associated with the island-based Fundación Puertorriqueña de las Humanidades

214

Sea of Flags (2004) by Gamaliel Ramírez and Eren Star Padilla; mural commissioned by the Puerto Rican Cultural Center (PRCC) in Chicago and reprinted with their permission.

(Puerto Rico Foundation for the Humanities), itself sponsored by the Washington-based National Endowment for the Humanities (NEH).

The arrival of the Internet created room in cyberspace for the dissemination of the work of US Puerto Rican visual artists. This new generation of experimental artists is represented by the work of photographer and visual artist Adal Maldonado. He cofounded with the late Nuyorican writer Pedro Pietri the Web site El Puerto Rican Embassy in 1994, although artist Eduardo Figueroa is responsible for the original concept, which he developed in the Web site El Spirit Republic de Puerto Rico (see www.elpuertoricanembassy.org). Maldonado and Pietri expanded upon the original concept by creating a Puerto Rican "passport," appointing ambassadors of the arts, writing a manifesto, and a "Spanglish" national anthem. El Puerto Rican Embassy is described by its founders as a "sovereign state of mind," an ironic take on Puerto Rico's "unsovereign" political status. Maldonado's collection of photographs, Out of Focus Nuyoricans, which is displayed on this Web site, is described as a collection that "expresses the political and psychological conditions of the Puerto Rican and Nuyorican identity" (www.elpuertoricanembassy.org). It is evident from this Web site that political and cultural issues related to the colonial subordination of Puerto Ricans continue to be important to both island- and US-based Puerto Rican artists.

Increasingly, artists are using the Internet to display and promote their work. Soraida Martínez, the creator of what she calls "Verdadism" or a philosophy of truth, described her style on her Web site as "a form of hard-edge abstraction in which paintings are juxtaposed with social commentaries." Martínez has made the following comments about her painting *Puerto Rican Stereotype: The Way You See Me Without Looking at Me* (1992):

> Throughout my life I have met lots of people that have never experienced meeting or getting to know a Puerto Rican woman. I have had some people admit to me their feelings on what they thought a Puerto Rican woman looked and acted like. "Puerto Rican Stereotype: The Way You See Me Without Looking at Me" is a satirical painting based on the false information given to me by the media and other life experiences. (www.soraida.com/prs.htm)

Of course, New York is not the only art scene for Puerto Ricans. The presence of acclaimed painter Arnaldo Roche Rabell in Chicago, an artist who travels back and forth between the island and the metropolis, like many others, is characteristic of the cultural straddling that is so much a part of the migrant experience and that brings so many different kinds of cultural explorations or "Rican-constructions" around identity issues.[14] In 1984, Roche Rabell was the first Puerto Rican to receive the Lincoln Medal from the governor of Illinois for his artistic contributions to that state. Almost half a century earlier, another Puerto Rican artist, Rufino Silva, had made his mark in Chicago, where he was on the faculty of the famous Art Institute for many years (Benítez 1988).

Chicago-based Puerto Rican artist Bibiana Suárez is a graduate of the Art Institute of Chicago and a faculty member at DePaul University. Artist Juan Sánchez described Suárez's work as "a conflictive plebiscite of the mind" that "illuminates the cultural, social, and political friction of [her] spiritual, human, female, and Puerto Rican state of mind" (Sánchez 1991, 1–2). The artist herself has stated that her work attempted to create "a metaphorical sense of place, . . . not in Puerto Rico, not in Chicago, but my own island" (1).

In Orlando, Florida, artist Obed Gómez has become a leading figure in representing the exuberance of Puerto Rico's folkloric traditions. His colorful paintings have appeared in the cover of the city's Puerto Rican Day Parade brochure and of *Orlando Arts Magazine* (see obedart.com).

For some island Puerto Rican artists, New York and many other US localities are only stops made by the "airbus" that connects the island with the metropolis. Thus, it is difficult to fully understand their body of work without this important dimension. Antonio Martorell is one of those frequent commuters, enriching the life of the US Puerto Rican communities with his impressive mixed-media installations and performances—often combining art, theater, and literary text. He frequently installs exhibits at colleges, galleries, and museums. His exhibition "Blanca Snow in Puerto Rico" (Snow White in Puerto Rico), held at New York's Hostos Community College Art Gallery in 1997, is one of his most impressive contributions to the community's cultural life. Moreover, together with theater director Rosa Luisa Márquez, he has traveled to many US universities to engage students in the process of writing, staging, and acting in performances that rely on the students' own creativity and talent.

Cultural Crossovers

In Puerto Rico, it is often said by those who oppose statehood or independence that, because of its relationship with the United States, the island shares the best of two worlds (Benítez 1998). This statement assumes that the high levels of exposure to the Anglo-American culture and the English language and the population's US citizenship make it easier for some writers and artists to "cross over" into the US market. Indeed there are an increasing number of works by island writers being translated into English. Furthermore, writers such as Rosario Ferré, a native Spanish speaker and well-known author on the island and in other parts of the Spanish-speaking world, are now "crossing over" by writing in English, as illustrated by her novels *The House on the Lagoon* (1995) and *Eccentric Neighborhoods* (1998). Instead of having these novels translated into Spanish, Ferré herself rewrote them later for a Spanish-reading public. Among the 1940s and 1950s literary figures, migrants such as Jesús Colón and Julia de Burgos also published in English, although Spanish was their native language.

A similar statement could be made about US Puerto Rican writers and artists trying to reach out to Spanish-speaking audiences in Puerto Rico and other countries. More frequently than ever before, the literary works of many US Puerto Rican and other Latino(a) authors are being translated into Spanish and distributed and marketed throughout Latin America and Spain. Only a handful of these authors do any creative writing directly in Spanish. This kind of crossover writing is not yet the norm within Latin American or US literature. Nonetheless, it is becoming quite common in the growing field of US Latino literature, confronting both critics and readers with the perennial question of where to place these literary works. Are they part of US or Latin American literature, or are they now unequivocally part of both? There is no doubt that the increasing Latino presence in US society and the transnational dynamics at work in the Americas during the era of globalization are producing new and provocative realities of culture contact and hybridity that challenge old literary canons and models of immigrant assimilation.

Artistic crossovers are also demonstrated by the unprecedented success of bilingual Puerto Rican musical performers Ricky Martin, Marc Anthony, and Jennifer López, along with other Latino(a) singers, such as Gloria Estefan, Cristina Aguilera, Enrique Iglesias, and Shakira. Their ability to sing in Spanish and English and the cultural hybridity reflected in their musical interpretations is more than just an exotic marketing ploy to sell a product to the North American public. It is rather a sign of how the people of Latin America and the Caribbean—Puerto Ricans included—are now "invading the invader," turning the spaces where they migrate into their own, and making their presence felt in the rest of US society. In referring to the Chicano presence in North America, writer Luis Valdez once stated, "We did not come to the United States, the United States came to us" (1990). This statement could also be well applied to Puerto Ricans, since the historic and socioeconomic circumstances of their migration were and still are to a large extent shaped by the conditions created by US interventionist policies and power over their respective countries of origin.

Notes

1. "Autógrafo" (My Autograph) was included in the collection *Mi libro de Cuba* (My Book of Cuba), originally published in Havana in 1893. See Lola Rodríguez de Tió, *Obras completas*, vol. 1 (San Juan: Instituto de Cultura Puertorriqueña, 1968), 317.

2. See the two-part article "La emigración puertorriqueña a E.U.," by Bernardo Vega, in *Liberación*, November 30, 1946, and December 14, 1946.

3. Some of the best sources for the life and writings of Luisa Capetillo include Norma Valle Ferrer, *Luisa Capetillo: Historia de una mujer proscrita* (Río Piedras, PR: Editorial Cultural, 1990), and *Luisa Capetillo* (San Juan, 1975); and Julio Ramos, ed., *Amor y anarquía: Los escritos de Luisa Capetillo* (Río Piedras, PR: Ediciones Huracán, 1992). Also see the chapter "For the Sake of Love: Luisa Capetillo, Anarchy, and Boricua

Literary History," in Lisa Sánchez González, *Boricua Literature* (New York: NYU Press, 2001), 16–41.

4. For an insightful analysis of Pura Belpré's life and work, see Lisa Sánchez González, "A Boricua in the Stacks: An Introduction to the Life and Work of Pura Belpré," in *Boricua Literature: A Literary History of the Puerto Rican Diaspora* (New York: NYU Press, 2001), 71–101.

5. The terms "Neorican" and "Nuyorican" have been frequently used to identify Puerto Ricans born or raised in the United States, although early on they carried some negative connotations. Traditionally, ethnic groups in US society have identified themselves by a hyphenated version of their national origin and the term American (e.g., Mexican-American, Cuban-American). However, historically, US Puerto Ricans have rejected this form of identification. Thus, as of yet, there is not a single generalized rubric that identifies US Puerto Ricans from those on the island. The acceptance of the term "Nuyorican" has been limited to a particular group of writers and artists, although it has been occasionally used to refer to US Puerto Ricans in general, as has the term "Diasporican." The terms "Puerto Rican" and "Boricua" are still the most frequently used terms to identify Puerto Ricans on the island and abroad.

6. See Juan Flores's essay "¡Que assimilated, brother, yo soy asimilao: The Structuring of Puerto Rican Identity in the US," in his *Divided Borders: Essays on Puerto Rican Identity* (Houston: Arte Público Press, 1993), 182–195. The essay was first published in *Journal of Ethnic Studies* 13.3 (1985), 1–16.

7. The word "asimilao" is a Spanish slang form of *asimilado* (assimilated).

8. The Spanish translations of works by US Puerto Rican authors published in recent years include the collection of poetry *Obituario puertorriqueño,* by Pedro Pietri (San Juan: Instituto de Cultura Puertorriqueña, 1977); the novels *Cuando era puertorriqueña* (New York: Vintage, 1994), *El sueño de América* (New York: Vintage, 1997), and *Casi una mujer* (New York: Vintage, 1999), by Esmeralda Santiago; the novel *Por estas calles bravas,* by Piri Thomas (New York: Random House, 1998); the novel *La línea del sol* (Río Piedras: Editorial Universidad de Puerto Rico, 1999); and the collection of poetry and narrative *Bailando en silencio* (Houston: Arte Público Press, 1997), by Judith Ortiz Cofer.

9. In 1999, the theme of the annual musical TV show and videotape sponsored by the Banco Popular de Puerto Rico was *Con la música por dentro* (San Juan: Banco Popular, 1999).

10. This period, known as the Golden Age of salsa music, is recreated in the documentary film *The Golden Age of Salsa Music with Larry Harlow* (New York: Cinema Guild, 1998).

11. A musical competition between *cocolos*—those who favored salsa music—and *rockeros*—those more adept at rock music—was promoted by Puerto Rico's media for many years. This separation in musical tastes paralleled a separation along class and racial lines. The *cocolos, or salseros,* were usually dark-skinned and from the working class. See the documentary film *Cocolos y Rockeros* by Ana María García (San Juan, P.R.: Pandora Films, 1992).

12. The latter is a musical blend of Spanish-language hip-hop, Jamaican reggae, and other Caribbean beats and has been popularized throughout Latin America, North America, and Europe by several Puerto Rican performers like Daddy Yankee, Tego Calderón, Ivy Queen, along with rap trailblazers Vico C and El General. The *reggaetón,* in particular, has turned into one of the most influential musical happenings of recent years.

13. La Marketa is a produce market located in Spanish Harlem, similar to the typical Puerto Rican *plaza del mercado.*

14. The term "Rican-constructions" was coined by artist Juan Sánchez for one of his exhibitions and is also the title of one of his paintings.

8

Overcoming the Colonial Experience: Future Challenges

Y así le digo al villano,
Yo sería borincano
Aunque naciera en la luna.
—*Juan Antonio Corretjer,*
"Boricua en la luna"

Telling the real story of Puerto Rican migration to the United States unavoidably entails dealing with the North American nation's imperialist role on the island and the contradictions and multiple side effects of colonialism on the Puerto Rican people. Throughout this book we have provided only a glimpse of the intricate relationship of domination and subordination between the two entities in order to set the parameters for understanding the historical evolution of this commuter migration. We have portrayed the current status of the Puerto Rican population in the United States, which since the 1970s has continued to grow at an average rate of 41 percent each decade, totaling 138 percent by 2000.

For more than a century Puerto Rico has been repeatedly treated by the United States as not much more than "war booty," a territorial possession experiencing "benign benevolence," (Moynihan 1993), "an imperialism of neglect" (Lewis 1968), "selective inattention," or "oblivious disregard" (Cruz 2000) by the colonial metropolis. Shaped by these experiences, Puerto Rico remains one of the last vestiges of worldwide colonialism, trapped, as a noted scholar succinctly summarized it, "between the forces competing for power under the ruling colonial system and the forces opposing the system" (Maldonado-Denis 1972, 7). The island's daunting political quagmire is magnified by the fact that the Commonwealth and the statehood supporters, who represent around 95 percent of the island's electorate, continue to fiercely battle one another for control of Puerto Rico's local government and for their limited share of political influence over Congress and the US administration, while arrogantly dismissing the proindependence minority that remains the primary locus of colonial resistance.

219

Cultural nationalism, however, has continued to manifest itself quite vigorously among both island and US Puerto Ricans, regardless of their political sympathies or affiliations. In fact, during the decades of the worst political repression exerted by federal and island government agencies primarily against Puerto Rican Nationalists and independence supporters, the continental United States provided Puerto Ricans a less oppressive and threatening space for cultural and political nationalism to grow. Therefore, US Puerto Ricans, whether their first language is Spanish or English, rather than assimilating into US society or turning into a force to promote the annexation of Puerto Rico as another state of the union, continue to promote a separate and distinctive sense of Puerto Ricanness within the diaspora.

Appropriately, the verses of the poem "Boricua en la luna" (Puerto Rican on the moon), which serve as an epigraph to this chapter and were written by one of Puerto Rico's most prominent national poets, Juan Antonio Corretjer, have been popularized on the island as well as in the diaspora in a song interpreted by Roy Brown. The verses imply that no matter where Puerto Ricans happen to find themselves, they are be proud of their national origin. Thus, they capture a generalized resiliency and resistance to the colonizing experience: "This is what I tell the villain / I would be Puerto Rican / Even if I were born on the moon." There could not be a stronger pronouncement about cultural survival. In fact, until recent decades, strong manifestations of nationalistic or patriotic sentiments in Puerto Rico were considered "subversive" and largely left in the hands of independence supporters and the island's intellectual elite. But ironically the Puerto Rican communities in the United States have provided a more fertile ground than the island for the growth of cultural nationalism at a popular level. Expressions of Puerto Rican pride were an integral part of the wider ethnic revitalization movement of the civil rights era, and unquestionably, some of its effects spilled over to the island. Symbols of *la puertorriqueñidad*, such as the many different uses of the Puerto Rican flag, which for a long time were largely the prerogative of Nationalists or independence supporters, have been appropriated in the United States by many Puerto Ricans, regardless of their disparate views on the political status issue, and are now more popular and even more commercialized in Puerto Rico than they used to be a few decades ago.

Old arguments about who is an "authentic" Puerto Rican or about an alleged "pseudoethnicity" among US Puerto Ricans that only tend to complicate Puerto Rico's long-standing fears of Americanization (Seda Bonilla 1977) provoked interesting debates in the past, but in the long run, they fell short in analyzing both the "expressive and instrumental" (Ogbu 1990) aspects behind the claims to a Puerto Rican identity by the generations of Puerto Ricans born or raised in the United States.[1] In other words, the right question to ask would not be who is a Puerto Rican, but what does it mean to be Puerto Rican on the island and in the United States? What are the contextual historical, ethnic, racial, social, and cultural factors that shape different identity constructions of Puerto Ricanness, and what function does identity play for marginalized individuals and groups, such as Puerto Ricans, in their relationship to the wider US society? And last, what are the differences, including generational ones, and similarities in the ways Puerto Ricans from "here and there" negotiate, construct, and assert their respective identities, both in relation to US society and the panethnic US Latino population?

Another interesting question that comes up regarding the Puerto Ricanness of the diaspora relates to whether the people's consciousness of nationality translates into specific political preferences or affiliations regarding Puerto Rico's political status. Unfortunately, there has not been enough research to make reliable generalizations about how US Puerto Ricans would vote on a referendum to determine the political future of Puerto Rico that included the choices of statehood, independence, or an improved Commonwealth. But more important, the issue is far from being a daily concern for the large majority. Although Puerto Rico's colonial condition often filters into the agendas of US Puerto Rican grassroots and professional organizations, political and social movements, and cultural expressions, there are many other pressing issues and priorities confronted by these communities that take precedence over the colonial status issue. After all, even if Puerto Rico were granted its independence, that would not alter the US citizenship status of Puerto Ricans already living in the United States. Nevertheless, one thing remains constant: There is a strong consciousness of nationality among US Puerto Ricans, and the claim to "being Puerto Rican" remains a powerful cohesive force within the communities of the diaspora. To what extent will this force wane as the proportion of US-born Puerto Ricans continues to surpass the population of newcomers is hard to predict and undoubtedly will draw the attention of future researchers.

There is a Kafkaesque quality that permeates party politics in Puerto Rico that has been exacerbated ever since the Populares (PPD) lost the governorship for the first time in 1968 to pro-statehood leader Luis A. Ferré and his then newly created Partido Nuevo Progresista (PNP), after more than two decades of having absolute control of the government. Since then, the gap in subsequent election results between the two major parties began to narrow, establishing a pattern whereby every four years one party's victory over the other is usually determined by a margin of only a few thousand votes. This leaves Puerto Rico hopelessly entangled in acrimonious partisan politics and thus deprived of an effective government. Furthermore, it means that the island's most critical challenges of unemployment and underemployment, elevated poverty and crime rates, inadequate public schools, declining health services, environmental deterioration, inefficient government agencies, and political corruption do not receive the attention they deserve and continue to be among the major problems afflicting Puerto Rican society. It is quite evident that whatever the degree of self-government island Puerto Ricans perceive themselves as having under the current Commonwealth arrangement, it is always subject to the overriding will of US presidential and congressional authority, the military priorities of the Pentagon, and the economic interests of North American corporations. Perhaps among the greatest future challenges is whether Puerto Ricans will be able to envision new alternatives for economic development outside the export-led, US investment–based model, which relies on the North American nation's economic priorities and continues to fuel migration, in order to defend more effectively their national interests and better deploy their own natural and human resources for their own collective benefit.

In the interim, commuter migration between the island and the metropolis remains part of the normal course of events in the lives of the Puerto Rican nation. Migration is not by any means considered a "problem" by the insular government, and only sporadically does the sustained attention of island Puerto Ricans shift noticeably to engage the diaspora in any substantial discussions about the country's future. In this regard, US Puerto Ricans appear to be more willing or committed to engage in debates and find common ground with their island counterparts. A recent issue of mutual concern in which the diaspora played a prominent role was the struggle to end the US Navy's bombing-training exercises on the island of Vieques and relinquish its military control over its territory (see Barreto 2002; Acosta 2002). Many US Puerto Ricans joined island Puerto Ricans in the civil disobedience campaigns that drew both international attention and more than the usual level of interest from the US media and general public. Some prominent US community figures who participated in the many protests endured humiliation and arrests by the military or local police.[2] The death of security guard David Sanes Rodríguez, killed in 2001 by a stray bomb during the Navy's training exercises in Vieques, galvanized an international "Peace for Vieques" movement, which for a few years transcended party lines and was very successful in cutting across existing class, racial, gender, or cultural divisions between "los de aquí y los de allá" (those from here and those from there). The grassroots activism from numerous sectors within and outside Puerto Rican society and the combined efforts of Puerto Ricans and Latinos serving in Congress all contributed to the Navy's final withdrawal from Vieques in 2003.

"El Grito de Vieques" (The Cry of Vieques; Acosta 2002) remains one of the best contemporary examples of the island and the diaspora coming together for a common cause. The Vieques movement set an important precedent for those who believe that Puerto Ricans are "one people, separated by the sea and integrally united by our culture" (Department of Puerto Rican Community Affairs poster). This is not meant to imply that strong disagreements do not persist between those who subscribe to the "divided nation" concept and those who believe that US Puerto Ricans are a national colonial minority and that their nationalistic attachment to their Puerto Rican identity is a necessary symbol that facilitates their survival and future prosperity in US society.[3]

Although no other cause in recent times has brought Puerto Ricans together more than the Peace for Vieques movement, or engaged the support of so many different sectors of Puerto Rican society and the communities of the diaspora, in reality the unity stemming from single-issue movements tends to wane after the main objective is accomplished. This happened after the US Navy's withdrawal from Vieques in 2003, despite the fact that some unresolved issues remain—notably the environmental clean up of several areas of the island heavily affected by decades of bombing during target practices and the high incidence of cancer and other health problems among Vieques's population, which have been linked to the depleted-uranium ammunition used in the live-fire training exercises.

The fact that the conflict over the US Navy's control over Vieques and its explicit disregard for the detrimental effects of the bombing on the population's health and the environment made Puerto Ricans from all political sectors more aware of the limitations of the current Estado Libre Asociado and the powerlessness of their insular government to make decisions to protect their land and their people. It had been a long time since Puerto Ricans had felt such an explicit manifestation of the power and arrogance of the US government and its military establishment toward them. To a large extent, the majority of the island's population before that episode had perceived the North American nation as a generous ally and valued their US citizenship. In many ways, Vieques made it evident that Puerto Ricans were still no more than colonial subjects, and that the costs and consequences of their lack of national sovereignty were not necessarily an ever-present part of the public consciousness.

Another patent demonstration of colonial subordination occurred more recently, on September 23, 2005, when the FBI killed Filiberto Ojeda Ríos, a Puerto Rican leader of the clandestine proindependence group Los Macheteros, also known as the Ejército Popular Boricua (Boricua Popular Army). Ojeda Ríos, in the 1970s a leading member of the Frente Armado de Liberación Nacional (FALN, Armed Forces for National Liberation), had been a fugitive from federal authorities. In 1983, he had been accused of being the mastermind behind a $7.2 million robbery of a Wells Fargo truck in Hartford, Connecticut. A couple of years before the robbery, the FALN had claimed responsibility for a bombing that destroyed eleven military aircraft, with an estimated value of $45 million, at the Muñiz Naval Base in the San Juan metropolitan area. Labeled a terrorist by the FBI, Ojeda Ríos, while on bail awaiting trial for the Wells Fargo robbery, removed his surveillance ankle bracelet and went underground in 1990.[4] He managed to avoid the authorities until the FBI finally tracked him down to a home in the countryside of Puerto Rico's western town of Hormigueros. When the FBI surrounded the building, Ojeda Ríos sent his wife, Elma Beatriz Rosado, out of the house. Shooting started and the residence was assailed by a barrage of over one hundred bullets. The encounter ended when Ojeda Ríos was wounded by an FBI sharpshooter.

What happened in the aftermath of the shooting created a national uproar. While keeping the press at bay and the town of Hormigueros practically under siege, the FBI waited over twenty hours before deciding to enter his home, where Ojeda Ríos had slowly bled to death from the sharpshooter's bullet. An autopsy revealed that he had been alive for many hours after he was shot, but the FBI had refused to call for medical attention and even denied access to the house to a doctor who volunteered to treat him. Authorities alleged that they were fearful of the presence of explosives in Ojeda Ríos's home and thus had to wait for reinforcements to arrive from the United States. No explosives were found.

The circumstances surrounding the killing of Ojeda Ríos led Puerto Rican public officials from all political persuasions to condemn the FBI's behavior and lack of consultation with local authorities. For outraged Puerto Ricans, it did not go unnoticed that the attack against Ojeda Ríos's home occurred on September 23, a date when Puerto Ricans commemorate the Grito de Lares independence revolt of 1868 against the Spaniards, and that this happened despite the fact that the Machetero had been under FBI surveillance for a few days before the actual shooting. The death of Ojeda Ríos has been under investigation by the island's Department of Justice. The incident incited massive protests in front of San Juan's Federal Court and the Capitol Building, with protestors chanting, "FBI fascistas; los verdaderos terroristas" (The FBI are fascists; they are the real terrorists). There was also a demonstration at the Federal Plaza in New York City with extensive coverage in the city's Spanish-language newspaper *El Diario–La Prensa*.[5] Other protests were held in a few cities in New Jersey and in Boston and Chicago. Coverage of the incident by the US mainstream press, however, was minimal even after a declaration from Amnesty International that this case was an example of "an extrajudicial execution." There is no doubt that Ojeda Ríos's name has been added to the long list of martyrs of Puerto Rico's struggle for independence.

Whether one refers to the death of David Sanes Rodríguez, which galvanized the battles against US military presence in Vieques, the killing of Ojeda Ríos, and, in 1987, the killing of university students Arnaldo Darío Rosado and Carlos Soto Arriví at Cerro Maravilla,[6] or the general systematic suppression of the anticolonial struggle by the blacklisting, incarceration, or assassination of proindependence militants, the forces of colonialism have a way of periodically slapping Puerto Ricans in the face, reminding them of the powerless aspects of their bittersweet relationship with the United States.

For the diaspora, the racialization endured in US society is a major factor in the articulation of what are politicized and often contested assertions of individual (being Puerto Rican) and panethnic (being Latino/a) identities. Claims to Puerto Ricanness provide members of the diaspora a shared sense of identity and roots—who they are and where they come from—while empowering them to seek recognition and legitimacy, and to struggle more effectively against the forces of racism and inequality that they collectively confront in US society. These counterhegemonic discourses are expressions of resistance to the dominant racist and marginalizing ideologies that for centuries have eroded the self-esteem and dignity of subordinate groups with limited access to the social and political power structures.

Although the increase of global migration is forcing the dominant industrialized countries, such as the United States, to come to grips with issues of diversity and tolerance, the increased migration also fuels a fundamentally racist anti-immigration backlash, especially against Latinos. The conservative takeover of the US political establishment that began during the Reagan years and has continued more aggressively in the administration of George W. Bush has been reversing some of the most meaningful liberal reforms of the 1960s and 1970s, including Affirmative Action policies, bilingual education for the children of (im)migrants, and many of the social programs and benefits for the poor. Moreover, after September 11, 2001, the spending priorities of the US government shifted to the wars in Afghanistan and Iraq and the fight against global terrorism, often at the expense of critical social and economic domestic agendas, which are now a lower priority.

It is indisputable that the globalization processes of the early twenty-first century intensify the forces that foster international migration, driving migrants of many national origins and from the less-privileged regions of the world to seek their fortunes in highly industrialized metropolitan countries like the United States. Thus, stating that Puerto Rican migration is virtually unstoppable would not be an exaggeration. The specific local factors that impel Puerto Rican migration, most of which, as we have seen, are directly related to the island's colonial condition, confront us with a reality that is not likely to change in the foreseeable future. Puerto Rico's long history of providing US companies on the island and on the continent with a reserve army of workers is still as common a contemporary phenomenon as it was in the early years of the US takeover.

Socioeconomic conditions have been the primary cause of Puerto Rican migration, but the magnitude and patterns of this colonial migration are the result of a subordinate political relationship that impinges upon every aspect of Puerto Rican life. As long as Puerto Rico remains in the shadow of US colonialism and Puerto Ricans are US citizens, the commuter migration between the island and the metropolis will continue in significant numbers. These statements are not meant to minimize the substantial role that Puerto Rico's own insular government has played historically in fostering migration, notably its continued reliance on this exodus as a tool to deal with persistent local problems of poverty and unemployment. In some ways, the insular government has used migration as if it were part of a development program without measuring the full consequences of such a massive displacement of workers.

As we have seen, the US Puerto Rican population will soon surpass the population of Puerto Rico. Perhaps it is this demographic reality, along with the significant continuing growth in the number of US Latinos and the prospects for them in general, and the Puerto Ricans among them, for expanding their political power within US society, that ultimately will make island Puerto Ricans realize the largely untapped economic and political potential of incorporating the diaspora in discussions that concern *all* Puerto Ricans and have a bearing on their future. One of those debates is whether US Puerto Ricans should vote on any referendum regarding the future status of the island. Some leading members of the diaspora argue for their inclusion in these deliberations. Other key issues include the increasing importance of migrant remittances to Puerto Rico's economy and the potential brain drain due to the growing number of professionals moving from Puerto Rico to the United States. These are only a few illustrations of how the current transnational circuit is having an impact on the lives of Puerto Ricans both on the island and in the metropolis.

A few decades ago, a prominent Puerto Rican demographer stated, "An economy which depends on its ability to get rid of its excess population by means of migration cannot be expected to have great stability and finds itself on a very unsound base" (Vázquez Calzada 1979, 235). There is no doubt that the celebrated transformation of the Operation Bootstrap years unraveled at the seams in subsequent decades. This major government initiative showcased Puerto Rico as a model of industrial development, modernization, and democracy, but it also generated the largest population exodus in the island's history. Since the early 1970s all economic indicators began to expose the unstable foundation and volatility of Puerto Rico's economy, thus tarnishing the showcase image of earlier decades (Rivera-Batiz and Santiago 1996, 3).

The underside of the glittering economic picture of the 1950s became apparent because of the following issues: (1) Massive industrialization increased employment in manufacturing, in the public sector, and a few other areas but also brought about the decline of the island's agricultural economy and generated both the largest migration of displaced workers to the United States to date and a continuing pattern of migration. (2) US companies took control of the island's economy, which is still mostly based on production for export, increasing Puerto Rico's dependency on the United States and eventually turning Puerto Rico into the North American nation's poorest regional economy. (3) The significant improvements in health, nutrition, mortality rates, education, per capita income, and overall standard of living of the Operation Bootstrap years were impressive when compared to the standards of other Caribbean and Latin American countries, but not so when compared to the United States. In 2003, Puerto Rico's gross national income per capita was $10,950, a figure not quite half of that of Mississippi, the poorest state of the union (World Bank 2004). (4) Unemployment rates went down from 1950 to 1970 but began to edge up again in the 1970s, ranging from a high of 29 percent in 1990 to 17.75 percent in 2000, the latter figure being twice as high as the rate for US Puerto

Ricans (9.1 percent). (5) The island's poverty rate stood at 53 percent in 2000, an extremely high rate, but a slight decrease from 57.3 percent in 1990. (6) Federal transfers currently represent about one-fourth of Puerto Rico's economy, exacerbating island dependency and leaving Puerto Rico vulnerable to the disposition of the US Congress to maintain the flow of the funds that support most of the island's social programs. (7) There is a generalized social malaise in Puerto Rico that is exacerbated by increases in the overall cost of living and health services, rising crime rates, overcrowded urban and suburban areas, a high incidence of driving fatalities, political corruption, and drug-related problems. (8) The political patronage used by the two main political parties when they are in control of the insular government is another disquieting aspect of Puerto Rican life, since it affects job security for workers from all sectors, especially public sector jobs, which represent a large portion of Puerto Rico's total employment. Moreover, political partisanship quite often influences the efficiency of the services offered by government agencies.

In 1996, Rivera-Batiz and Santiago pointed to the paradoxical nature of Puerto Rico's economic development vis-à-vis its relationship with the United States. They referred to the many different constraints that island government officials and policymakers must face that stem from a combination of global factors, the federal government, and Puerto Rico's integration into the US economy. We concur with their view that one of the most obvious problems is that the needs and priorities of the United States are often at odds with those of Puerto Rico or may work at cross-purposes. In assessing the failures of Operation Bootstrap, Rivera-Batiz and Santiago concluded:

> There is little question that the Puerto Rican government was an effective agent of economic change in Puerto Rico during the early years of Operation Bootstrap. The political consensus and social contract that allowed Operation Bootstrap to proceed were not without their costs and are unlikely to be repeated. And it might be argued that *it was the massive emigration of Puerto Ricans to the United States during the 1950s, more than any governmental policy, that allowed the increased standard of living on the island.* (1996, 163; emphasis added)

The correlation between Puerto Rico's colonial condition and the persistent commuter migration of Puerto Ricans to the United States underscores the transnational character of this process. Moreover, it demonstrates the need for researchers to continue analyzing the many socioeconomic, political, and cultural implications and ramifications of the bidirectional exchanges between the two populations.

Fundamental paradigm shifts have taken place in Puerto Rican migration studies. First, scholars are being more critical of those interpretations of the migrant experience that portrayed working-class migrants as aimless, impoverished, or marginalized masses and that denied agency to a people struggling to make a living in a foreign and often inhospitable environment. Confronting conditions of labor exploitation, along with the class and racial inequalities inherent in a capitalist society, and undergoing the adaptation process faced by most uprooted migrants, Puerto Ricans have striven to improve their individual status and that of their communities, hoping to build a better life in the United States. Second, substantial changes in the socioeconomic status of US Puerto Ricans have been taking place in recent decades, making their future neither engulfed in the uncertainty that characterized the 1970s nor entirely optimistic. Geographic dispersion across the United States and higher rates of educational attainment are proving to be key factors in improving their overall status. Some obvious problems still persist, but progress measured in terms of socioeconomic indicators and social mobility has been evident since the 1980s. Puerto Ricans are moving out of New York, and the city is no longer the place where the majority of them reside. Less than 25 percent of the total US Puerto Rican population was living in New York in 2000, compared to 88 percent in 1940. Although most Puerto Ricans still reside in the Northeast and Midwest states (New York, New Jersey, Connecticut, Pennsylvania, Massachusetts, and Illinois), growing communities are now found in Florida, Texas, and California. Third, there are many differences in the socioeconomic conditions of Puerto Ricans and in the histories of their various US communities. Some of these communities are long established; others are relatively new. Some are still facing serious problems of poverty and unemployment, largely those located in the Northeast; other, more thriving, communities are found in the southern and western regions of the United States. Additional differences in the overall status of Puerto Rican migrants are related to their educational and English-language skills, and to how long they have been living in the United States (see Santiago-Rivera and Santiago 1999).

Documenting the specific formation and evolution of the various US Puerto Rican communities is necessarily an endeavor that calls for the hard work and insights of researchers from many fields. More meaningful comparative research is needed to enhance our understanding of the numerous factors that account for differences and similarities among Puerto Ricans in their diverse geographic locations and contribute to a more nuanced portrait of their multifaceted experience as a commuter nation. More research is also needed about the actual commuter patterns of Puerto Ricans and about the different material reasons and personal motivations that account for this back and forth movement. After all, there is also a significant portion of the diaspora that is permanently settled in the United States, and we expect considerable generational differences in their ties to Puerto Rico.

Regardless of the above-mentioned differences, at the core of the Puerto Rican experience in the United States there is a strong affirmation of cultural identity and a fervent sense of affiliation with Puerto Rico. To a lesser degree, there is also a panethnic identification with the shared experiences and struggles of other US Latinos(as). This latter identification is becoming increasingly important, since Latinos are now the largest minority group in US society and their total population is projected by the census to continue growing at a rapid pace in future decades.

The vitality of Puerto Rican cultural expressions is reflected in literature, music, and the arts, which are finding receptive audiences beyond the confines of the community and receiving growing recognition within the wider US society. Unquestionably, some of the old stereotypes and misconceptions of the past are being eradicated, and Puerto Rican scholars, activists, and other professional and working-class members of the community continue to labor tirelessly to improve the socioeconomic and political status of their compatriots. The invisibility and marginality of the past are gradually waning, and new generations of Puerto Ricans are growing up in the United States with more opportunities to learn about their heritage and develop a consciousness of the issues and obstacles impeding their socioeconomic and political progress. For Puerto Ricans, old assimilation models proved to be elusive; they only bore out the fact that racial discrimination was still a powerful barrier to a full integration into the Anglo-American mainstream. In this context, Puerto Ricans' affirmation of their cultural identity fulfills important social, political, and psychological functions. It is part of a process that empowers them and helps to counteract their experiences of marginality and exclusion within US society.

The emotional, functional, and contextual dimensions of ethnic identity involve both agency and choice by the individuals and groups who define and negotiate these identities. In her "Ode to the Diasporican," poet María Teresa "Mariposa" Hernández refers to being Boricua as a "state of mind," a "state of heart," and a "state of soul," underscoring the passionate ways in which many writers and artists define their Puerto Ricanness—an attribute shared by Puerto Ricans everywhere. Thus, what it means to be Puerto Rican might take different meanings and expressions within the communities of the diaspora when compared to the island, but understanding these differences has the potential for bringing all Puerto Ricans closer together in the process of decolonization, as well as in defining and advancing their respective social and political agendas and in achieving the equal treatment and respect that so far has not been accorded to them by the United States.

Notes

1. Debates about whether or not US Puerto Ricans should be considered "authentic" Puerto Ricans, especially if they did not speak Spanish, have often been fueled by the Hispanophilic tendencies of many island-based intellectuals who have been consistently critical in the past of the Americanization of Puerto Rico, and have feared that the diaspora would only accelerate this process. Ironically, since the 1970s Puerto

Rican cultural nationalism has grown stronger both on the island and the United States, and it is expressed more overtly than it was in the 1950s and 1960s.

2. Among those arrested in civil disobedience demonstrations at the military training ground in Vieques were Puerto Ricans Luis Gutiérrez and Nydia Velázquez, members of Congress, and Roberto Ramírez, member of the New York State Assembly; African American community leader Rev. Al Sharpton; and environmental lawyer Robert F. Kennedy, Jr. Several prominent island political leaders and legislators were also arrested. Representative José Serrano was arrested at a demonstration in front of the White House. US Puerto Rican actor Rosie Pérez was among those arrested in 2000 at a demonstration in front of the United Nations in support of the US Navy's withdrawal from Vieques.

3. For a discussion of various positions on the Puerto Rican national question, see the special issue of *The Rican: Journal of Contemporary Puerto Rican Thought* 2.2 (1974); James Blaut, *The National Question: Decolonizing the Theory of Nationalism* (London: Zed Books, 1987); and Juan Angel Silén, *De la guerrilla cívica a la nación dividida* (Río Piedras, PR: Ediciones Puerto, 1973).

4. For a more detailed account of the Macheteros activities, see Robert Fernández, *The Macheteros: The Wells Fargo Robbery and the Violent Struggle for Puerto Rican Independence* (New York: Prentice Hall, 1987).

5. The September 24, 2005, issue of the New York Spanish-language newspaper *El Diario–La Prensa* provided extensive front-page coverage of the circumstances surrounding Ojeda-Ríos's death.

6. The two proindependence students were ambushed by the police after undercover agent Alejandro González Malavé accompanied them to light a fire to disable a radio transmission tower located at the top of a mountain named Cerro Maravilla. The students were assassinated in cold blood after being captured by the police. This happened under the administration of pro-statehood governor Carlos Romero Barceló (1976–1984). There was a cover-up of the incident that involved the Puerto Rican police and some government officials, but the Judiciary Committee of the Puerto Rican Senate conducted public hearings in 1983 and the details of the crime were revealed to the public. The police had claimed the students had been shot while trying to evade arrest. The taxi driver who had been forced to take the students and the undercover agent to Cerro Maravilla testified that the unarmed students had been killed by the police after being arrested. Soto Arriví was the son of prominent island writer Pedro Juan Soto. For an account of the Cerro Maravilla killings, see Anne Nelson, *Murder Under Two Flags: The US, Puerto Rico, and the Cerro Maravilla Cover-Up* (New York: Ticknor and Fields, 1986); and Manny Suárez, *Two Lynchings on Cerro Maravilla: The Police Murders in Puerto Rico and the Federal Government Cover Up* (San Juan: Instituto de Cultura Puertorriqueña, 2003). The Hollywood film *A Show of Force* (1990), directed by Bruno Barreto, was based on the Cerro Maravilla killings.

Brief Chronology of Puerto Rican History

ca. 2000 B.C. Aboriginal groups from South America settle in the Antilles.

1000 Development of Taino indigenous culture in Puerto Rico

1493 On November 19 Christopher Columbus arrives at the island he called Isla de San Juan Bautista, which the indigenous Taino inhabitants called Boriquén, during his second voyage.

1508 Spanish colonization begins under the command of Juan Ponce de León. He establishes the first settlement, the Villa de Caparra. The administrative center is moved a year later near the island's largest port, named Puerto Rico. Several years later the names of the island and its main port are interchanged: the island becomes known as Puerto Rico and San Juan becomes its capital.

1510 Beginning of the importation of enslaved Africans to Puerto Rico

1511–1513 Major Taino rebellions against the Spaniards

1570 Beginning of the construction of San Felipe del Morro, the island's largest fort, located at the entrance of San Juan Bay

1595 The island is subject to an unsuccessful attack by the British under the command of Sir Francis Drake.

1598 A second British attack takes place under the command of George Clifford, Count of Cumberland. The British take over

231

the city of San Juan and are forced to leave by a dysentery epidemic.

1625   A Dutch fleet, under the command of Balduino Enrico, attacks San Juan. The Dutch take the city of San Juan but are forced to withdraw by Spanish troops. They pillage and burn the city before leaving.

1634–1638 San Juan becomes a walled city.

1765   Visit of Field Marshall Alejandro O'Reilly starts a period of economic reforms. The Spanish colonial government promotes immigration to the island.

1797   A British attack under the command of General Ralph Abercromby keeps the city of San Juan under siege for ten weeks, until they are defeated by Spanish troops and island creoles.

1810   Ramón Power y Giral becomes the first Puerto Rican delegate to represent the island in the Spanish Cortes.

1812   The Cortes of Cádiz in Spain approves the first Spanish Constitution, and some liberal reforms are introduced in Puerto Rico for a brief period.

1815   Spain grants Puerto Rico the Real Cédula de Gracias, which introduces reforms to promote socioeconomic development, the opening of trade, immigration, and some civil liberties.

1821–1848 Numerous rebellions of Puerto Rico's enslaved Africans. One of the largest takes place in 1841.

1849   The *libretas de jornaleros* system of mandatory labor for agricultural workers is introduced.

1865   The Sociedad Republicana de Cuba y Puerto Rico is established in New York by Antillean expatriates.

1867   The Comité Revolucionario de Puerto Rico is founded by Ramón Emeterio Betances and others in New York City. This same year Betances releases his proclamation "Diez Mandamientos de los Hombres Libres."

1868   On September 23, there is an armed revolt in the mountain town of Lares proclaiming Puerto Rico's independence from Spain. This event is known as the Grito de Lares.

1869   Eugenio María de Hostos arrives in New York from Spain and becomes editor of the newspaper *La Revolución*.

1870   Founding of the first political parties in Puerto Rico under the Spanish colonial regime

1873   Africans slavery and the *libretas de jornaleros* system are abolished in Puerto Rico.

1887   The Partido Autonomista Puertorriqueño is founded by Román Baldorioty de Castro.

1889   Typographer Sotero Figueroa leaves the island for New York, where he joins the Antillean separatist movement and starts a printing press.

1891   Arturo Alfonso Schomburg and poet and journalist Francisco Gonzalo "Pachín" Marín arrive in New York and join the Antillean separatist movement. In New York, Marín revives his newspaper *El postillón* a year later as an advocate of Antillean revolution against colonial Spanish rule.

1892   Founding of the Club Borinquen, a separatist group of Puerto Rican male expatriates, the Puerto Rican and Cuban male Club Las Dos Antillas, and the women's separatist group Club Mercedes Varona in New York. Separatist poet Lola Rodríguez de Tió arrives that same year and is a founding member of the latter organization.

1895   Founding of the Sección de Puerto Rico of the Partido Revolucionario Cubano (PRC) in New York

1897   A Charter of Autonomy is granted to Puerto Rico by Spain.

             Founding of the women's separatist club Hermanas de Ríus Rivera in New York.

1898   The February 21 explosion of the US Naval vessel *Maine* at the Port of Havana leads to a declaration of war against Spain by the United States on April 21 and the invasion of Puerto Rico on July 25. The conflict is known as the Spanish-American War, Spanish-Cuban-American War, or the War of 1898.

1899   The Treaty of Paris, putting an end to the Spanish-Cuban-American War, is signed. Spain cedes the territories of Puerto Rico, Cuba, the Philippines, and the Ladrones islands (Guam) to the United States.

Founding of the Federación Libre de los Trabajadores (FLT)

1900   The Foraker Act is enacted by the US Congress to implement a civil government in Puerto Rico.

Founding of the new political parties in Puerto Rico: the Partido Federal and the Partido Republicano

1901   The US colonial government promotes migration of Puerto Rican contract workers to Hawaii.

1904   Founding of the Partido Unión Puertorriqueña (Unionistas), the party of the creole propertied class

1915   Founding of the Partido Socialista (PS), the political arm of the FLT

1916   *Tabaquero* Bernardo Vega migrates to New York.

1917   The Jones Act is enacted by the US Congress granting US citizenship for all Puerto Ricans and restructuring the island's legislature to include a House and a Senate.

1918   Jesús Colón migrates to New York as a stowaway in a ship.

1922   Founding of the Partido Nacionalista Puertorriqueño

1927   The Liga Puertorriqueña e Hispana is founded in New York City by Puerto Rican migrants.

1930   Pedro Albizu Campos takes over the leadership of the Nationalist Party.

1934	Masacre de Río Piedras. Puerto Rican policemen kill four Nationalist students.
1936	Two Nationalists assassinate Colonel Frances Riggs, Puerto Rico's North American Chief of Police. Albizu Campos is arrested and sent to jail for conspiring to overthrow the US government in Puerto Rico.
1937	Masacre de Ponce. Violence erupts when the police interfere with a Nationalist rally in the southern city of Ponce. Nineteen people, mostly Nationalists, die in the incident.
1938	Founding of the Partido Popular Democrático (PPD) by Luis Muñoz Marín
1940	The PPD wins enough votes to make Luis Muñoz Marín head of Puerto Rico's Senate.
1946	Jesús T. Piñeiro is appointed by President Harry Truman as the first Puerto Rican governor since the beginning of the US occupation.
1948	Luis Muñoz Marín becomes the first elected governor of Puerto Rico.
	The Migration Division is established in New York.
1950	Nationalist Revolt begins in the town of Jayuya and extends to other parts of the island. Nationalists perpetrate attacks on La Fortaleza, Governor Muñoz Marín's official residence, and on Washington's Blair House, temporary residence of President Harry Truman. Albizu Campos is arrested and sent back to prison.
1952	Inauguration of the Constitution of the Estado Libre Asociado (ELA), or Commonwealth of Puerto Rico
1954	In Washington, DC, four Puerto Rican Nationalists enter the House of Representatives and open fire, wounding five members of the US Congress.
1959	First Desfile Puertorriqueño in New York, the beginning of the Puerto Rican Day Parade tradition

1961   ASPIRA is founded in New York to promote the education of Puerto Rican youth.

1967   The US Congress authorizes a political status plebiscite that gives an overwhelming victory to Commonwealth supporters.

1968   The PPD loses Puerto Rico's governorship after being in power for twenty years. Luis A. Ferré, an industrialist and one of the leaders of the Partido Estadista Republicano (Pro-Statehood Republican Party, PER), who after having left the PER founded the Partido Nuevo Progresista (New Progressive Party, PNP) in 1967, becomes the first pro-statehood governor of Puerto Rico.

1969   Chapters of the Young Lords Party emerge in Chicago and New York.

1970   Herman Badillo becomes the first US Puerto Rican elected to the House of Representatives.

1972   PPD candidate Rafael Hernández Colón wins the governorship of Puerto Rico.

1973   The Puerto Rican Legal Defense and Education Fund (PRLDEF) is established in New York.

1974   The Centro de Estudios Puertorriqueños is established by Frank Bonilla at the City University of New York. One of the Centro's main activities is the creation of the library and archives to house documents about the migration experience.

1976   PNP candidate Carlos Romero Barceló wins the governorship of Puerto Rico.

1978   Robert García is elected to the House of Representatives and serves until his resignation in 1990.

1980   Carlos Romero Barceló wins reelection by just a few thousand votes. It takes months before the election is finally certified.

1984   PPD candidate Rafael Hernández Colón returns to the governor's post.

1988   Hernández Colón is reelected.

1989	Founding of the Department of Puerto Rican Community Affairs in New York to replace the Migration Division
1990	José Serrano is elected to the House of Representatives and replaces Robert García.
1992	Luis Gutiérrez from Chicago and Nydia Velázquez from New York are elected to the House of Representatives. Velázquez is the first Puerto Rican woman elected to serve in Congress.
	Founding of the Puerto Rican Studies Association (PRSA) as a professional organization that promotes research, teaching, and activism
	PNP candidate Pedro Roselló is elected governor of Puerto Rico.
1993	In his efforts to promote statehood for Puerto Rico, Governor Roselló holds a nonbinding political status referendum won by the Commonwealth supporters.
1996	Roselló is reelected to the governorship.
1999	Security guard David Sanes Rodríguez is killed by a stray bomb during target practice at the US Navy base in the island of Vieques. This is the beginning of a movement to bring peace to the citizens of Vieques and get the Navy out of the island.
2000	The PPD candidate for Puerto Rico's governorship, Sila Calderón, defeats Roselló, becoming the first woman elected to the post.
2003	The US Navy withdraws from Vieques.
2004	The PPD candidate for the governorship, Aníbal Acevedo Vilá, wins by a narrow margin, but the PNP takes control of the House, the Senate, and the position of resident commissioner in Washington, DC.

References

Acosta, Ivonne. 1987. *La mordaza: Puerto Rico, 1948–1957*. Río Piedras, PR: Editorial Edil.

Acosta, Ivonne. 1993. *La palabra como delito: Los discursos por los que condenaron a Pedro Albizu Campos, 1948–1950*. Río Piedras, PR: Editorial Cultural.

Acosta, Ivonne. 2002. *El Grito de Vieques y otros ensayos históricos (1990–1999)*. Río Piedras, PR: Editorial Cultural.

Acosta-Belén, Edna. 1977. "'Spanglish': A Case of Languages in Contact." In Heidi Dulay and Marina K. Burt, eds., *New Directions in Second Language Learning, Teaching, and Bilingual Education*. Washington, DC: TESOL, 151–158.

Acosta-Belén, Edna. 1978. "The Literature of the Puerto Rican Minority in the United States," *Bilingual Review* 5. 1–2, 107–115.

Acosta-Belén, Edna. 1992. "Beyond Island Boundaries: Ethnicity, Gender, and Cultural Revitalization in Nuyorican Literature," *Callaloo* 15.4, 979–998.

Acosta-Belén, Edna. 1993. "The Building of a Community: Puerto Rican Writers and Activists in New York City, 1890s–1960s." In Ramón Gutiérrez and Genaro Padilla, eds., *Recovering the U.S. Hispanic Literary Heritage*. Houston, TX: Arte Público Press, 179–195.

Acosta-Belén, Edna. 1999. "Hemispheric Remappings: Revisiting the Concept of *Nuestra América*." In Liliana R. Goldin, ed., *Identities on the Move: Transnational Processes in North America and the Caribbean Basin*. Austin: University of Texas Press, 81–106.

Acosta-Belén, Edna, and Virginia Sánchez Korrol, eds. 1993. *The Way It Was and Other Writings by Jesús Colón*. Houston, TX: Arte Público Press.

Acosta-Belén, Edna, Marguarita Benítez, José E. Cruz, Yvonne González-Rodríguez, Clara E. Rodríguez, Carlos E. Santiago, Azara Santiago-Rivera, and Barbara R. Sjostrom. 2000. *"Adiós, Borinquen querida": The Puerto Rican Diaspora, Its History, and Contributions*. Albany, NY: CELAC and Comisión 2000.

Acuña, Rodolfo. 1972. *Occupied America: The Chicano's Struggle Toward Liberation*. San Francisco: Canfield Press.

Alegría, Ricardo E. 1997. "An Introduction to Taíno Culture and History." In Fatima Bercht, Estrellita Brodsky, John Alan Farmer, and Dicey Taylor, eds., *Taíno: Pre-Columbian Art and Culture from the Caribbean*. New York: El Museo del Barrio, Monacelli Press.

Algarín, Miguel. 1978. *Mongo Affair*. New York: Nuyorican Press.

Algarín, Miguel, and Miguel Piñero, eds. 1975. *Nuyorican Poetry: An Anthology of Puerto Rican Words and Feelings*. New York: Morrow.

Algarín, Miguel, and Lois Griffith. 1997. *Action: The Nuyorican Poets Cafe Theater Festival*. New York: Simon and Schuster

Algarín, Miguel, and Bob Holman, eds. 1994. *Aloud: Voices from the Nuyorican Poets Cafe*. New York: H. Holt.

Alvárez Nazario, Manuel. 1974. *El elemento afronegroide en el español de Puerto Rico*. San Juan: Instituto de Cultura Puertorriqueña.

Alvárez Nazario, Manuel. 1977. *El influjo indígena en el español de Puerto Rico*. Río Piedras, PR: Editorial Universidad de Puerto Rico.

Anderson, Benedict. 1983. *Imagined Communities*. New York and London: Verso.

Aparicio, Frances. 1986. "*La vida,es un Spanglish disparatero:* Bilingualism in Nuyorican Poetry," In Geneviève Fabré, ed., *European Perspectives on Hispanic Literature of the United States*. Houston, TX: Arte Público Press, 147–160.

Aparicio, Frances. 1988. "*La vida es un Spanglish disparatero:* Bilingualism in Nuyorican Poetry." In Geneviève Fabré, ed., *European Perspectives on Hispanic Literature of the United States*. Houston, TX: Arte Público Press, 147–160.

Aparicio, Frances. 1997. *Listening to Salsa: Latin Popular Music and Puerto Rican Cultures*. Middletown, CT: Wesleyan University Press.

Aponte, Robert. 1990. "Definitions of the Underclass: A Critical Analysis." In Herbert J. Ganz, ed., *Sociology in America*. Newbury Park, CA: Sage, 117–137.

Aponte-Parés, Luis. 1995. "What's Yellow and White and Has Land Around It?" *Centro Bulletin* 7.1, 8–19.

Armiño, Franca de. 1937. *Los hipócritas*. New York: Modernistic Editorial Publishing.

Arroyo, William. 1986. "Lorain, Ohio: The Puerto Rican Experiment: A History Unexplored." In Oral History Task Force, eds., *Extended Roots: From Hawaii to New York*. New York: Centro de Estudios Puertorriqueños, 27–34.

Auletta, Ken. 1982. *The Underclass*. New York: Random House.

Barradas, Efraín, and Rafael Rodríguez, eds. 1980. *Herejes y mitificadores: Muestra de poesía puertorriqueña en Estados Unidos*. Río Piedras, PR: Ediciones Huracán.

Barreto, Amílcar. 2002. *Vieques, the Navy, and Puerto Rican Politics*. Gainsville: University of Florida Press.

Bean, Frank D., and Marta Tienda. *The Hispanic Population of the United States*. New York: Russell Sage Foundation, 1987.

Belpré, Pura. 1932. *Pérez and Martina: A Porto Rican Folk Tale*. New York: F. Warne.

Belpré, Pura. 1946. *The Tiger and the Rabbit, and Other Tales*. Boston: Houghton Mifflin.

Belpré, Pura. 1973. *Once in Puerto Rico*. New York: F. Warne.

Benítez, Marimar. 1988. "The Special Case of Puerto Rico." In Luis R. Cancel, ed., *The Latin American Spirit: Art and Artists in the United States, 1920–1970*. New York: Bronx Museum for the Arts, 72–105.

Benítez-Rojo, Antonio. 1992. *The Repeating Island: The Caribbean and the Postmodern Perspective*. Durham: Duke University Press.

Betances, Samuel. 1972. 1973. "The Prejudice of Having No Prejudice in Puerto Rico," *The Rican*, Part 1, 1.2, 41–54; Part 2, 1.3, 22–37.

Blanco, Tomás. 1948. *El prejuicio racial en Puerto Rico*. San Juan: Biblioteca de Autores Puertorriqueños.

Blauner, Robert. 1972. *Racial Oppression in America*. New York: Harper and Row.

Bloch. Peter. 1978. *Painting and Sculpture of the Puerto Ricans*. New York: Plus Ultra.

Bonilla, Frank. 1974. "Beyond Survival: *Por qué seguiremos siendo puertorriqueños.*" In Adalberto López and James Petras, eds., *Puerto Rico and Puerto Ricans: Studies in History and Society.* New York: John Wiley and Sons, 438–469.

Bonilla, Frank, and Ricardo Campos. 1986. *Industry and Idleness.* New York: Centro de Estudios Puertorriqueños.

Borjas, George J. 1985. "Assimilation, Changes in Cohort Quality and the Earnings of Immigrants," *Journal of Labor Economics,* 3.4, 463–489.

Borjas, George J. 1990. *Friends or Strangers: The Impact of Immigrants on the U.S. Economy.* New York: Basic Books.

Borjas, George, and Marta Tienda, eds. 1985. *Hispanics in the U.S. Economy.* Orlando, FL: Academic Press.

Bosque Pérez, Ramón, and José Javier Colón Morera. 1997. *Las carpetas. Persecución, política y derechos civiles en Puerto Rico.* Río Piedras, PR: CIPDC.

Boucher, Philip P. 1992. *Cannibal Encounters: Europeans and Island Caribs, 1492–1763.* Baltimore: Johns Hopkins University Press.

Burgos, Julia de. 1997. *Song of the Simple Truth: The Complete Poems of Julia de Burgos,* compiled and translated by Jack Agüeros. Willimantic, CT: Curbstone Press.

Cabán, Pedro. 2005. "Puerto Rico Migration Division." In Suzanne Oboler and Deena González, eds., *The Oxford Encyclopedia of Latinos and Latinas in the United States.* London: Oxford University Press, 524–526.

Camacho Souza, Blasé. 1982. *Boricua Hawaiiana: Puerto Ricans of Hawaii, Reflections of the Past and Mirrors of the Future. A Catalog.* Honolulu: Puerto Rican Heritage Society of Hawaii.

Camacho Souza, Blasé. 1986. "Boricuas Hawaiianos." In Oral History Task Force, eds., *Extended Roots: From Hawaii to New York.* New York: Centro de Estudios Puertorriqueños, 7–18.

Carr, Norma. 1989. "The Puerto Ricans of Hawaii, 1900–1958." Unpublished Doctoral Dissertation, University of Hawaii.

Carr, Raymond. 1984. *Puerto Rico: A Colonial Experiment.* New York: Vintage Books.

Carrero, Jaime. 1964. *Jet neorriqueño.* San Germán, PR: Universidad Interamericana.

Casas, Bartolomé de las. 1951. *Historia de las Indias.* 3 vols. Agustín Millares Carlo, ed., Mexico City: Fondo de Cultura Económica.

CEREP (Centro de Estudios de la Realidad Puertorriqueña) and ICP (Instituto de Cultura Puertorriqueña). 1992. *La tercera raíz: Presencia africana en Puerto Rico.* San Juan: CEREP and ICP.

Cervantes-Rodríguez, Margarita, and Amy Lutz. 2003. "Coloniality, Immigration, and the English-Spanish Asymmetry in the United States," *Nepantla* 4.3.

Chardón, Carlos, et al. 1934. *Report of the Puerto Rico Policy Commission.* San Juan: Chardón Report.

Chávez, Linda. 1991. *Out of the Barrio: Toward a New Politics of Hispanic Assimilation.* New York: Basic Books.

Chenault, Lawrence R. 1938. *The Puerto Rican Migrant in New York City.* New York: Russell and Russell.

Chiswick, Barry R. 1978. "The Effect of Americanization on the Earnings of Foreign-Born Men," *Journal of Political Economy,* 86.5, 897–922.

Chiswick, Barry R., and Teresa A. Sullivan. 1995. "The New Immigrants." In Reynolds Farley, ed., *State of the Union: America in the 1990s,* Vol. 2: *Social Trends.* New York: Russell Sage Foundation.

Churchill, Ward, and Jim Vande Wall. 1990. *The COINTELPRO Papers.* Boston: South End.

Cifre de Loubriel, Estela. 1964. *La inmigración a Puerto Rico durante el siglo XIX*. San Juan: Instituto de Cultura Puertorriqueña.

Cifre de Loubriel, Estela. 1975. *La formación del pueblo puertorriqueño: La contribución de los catalanes, baleáricos y valencianos*. San Juan: Instituto de Cultura Puertorriqueña.

Cifre de Loubriel, Estela. 1989. *La formación del pueblo puertorriqueño: La contribución de los gallegos, asturianos y santanderinos*. Río Piedras, PR: Editorial Universidad de Puerto Rico.

Cifre de Loubriel, Estela. 1995. *La formación del pueblo puertorriqueño: La contribución de los isleño-canarios*. San Juan: Centro de Estudios Avanzados de Puerto Rico y el Caribe.

City of New York. 1993. *Puerto Rican New Yorkers in 1990*. New York: Department of City Planning.

Cobas, José and Jorge Duany. 1997. *Cubans in Puerto Rico: Ethnic Economy and Cultural Identity*. Gainesville: University of Florida Press.

Cockcroft, James. 1995. *The Hispanic Struggle for Social Justice*. New York: Franklin Watts.

Colón, Jesús. [1961] 1982. *A Puerto Rican in New York and Other Sketches*. New York: International Publishers.

Colón, Joaquín. 2002. *Pioneros en Nueva York*. Houston, TX: Arte Público Press.

Cruz, José E. 1998. *Identity and Power: Puerto Rican Politics and the Challenge of Ethnicity*. Philadelphia: Temple University Press.

Cruz, José E. 2000. "*Nosotros, puertorriqueños*: Contributions to Politics, Social Movements, and the Armed Forces." In Acosta-Belén et al., "*Adiós, Borinquen querida*," 37–57.

Cruz, José, and Carlos E. Santiago. 2000. "The Changing Socioeconomic and Political Fortunes of Puerto Ricans in New York City, 1964–1990." Unpublished manuscript.

Danziger, Sheldon, and P. Gottschalk. 1993. "Introduction." In Danziger and Gottschalk, *Uneven Tides: Rising Inequality in America*. New York: Russell Sage Foundation.

DeFreitas, Gregory. 1991. *Inequality at Work: Hispanics in the U.S. Labor Force*. New York: Oxford University Press.

Des Verney Sinnette, Eleanor. 1989. *Arthur Alfonso Schomburg: Black Bibliographer and Collector*. Detroit: New York Public Library and Wayne State University Press.

Díaz Valcárcel, Emilio. 1978. *Harlem todos los días*. Río Piedras, PR: Ediciones Huracán.

Diffie, Bailey W., and Justine Whitfield Diffie. 1931. *Puerto Rico: A Broken Pledge*. New York: Vanguard Press.

Duany, Jorge. 2002. *The Puerto Rican Nation on the Move: Identities on the Island and in the United States*. Chapel Hill: University of North Carolina Press.

Duany, Jorge, and Félix Matos-Rodríguez. 2005. "Puerto Ricans in Orlando and Central Florida." Orlando, FL: Orlando Chamber of Commerce.

Duffy Burnett, Christina, and Burke Marshall. 2001. *Foreign in a Domestic Sense: Puerto Rico, American Expansion, and the Constitution*. Durham, NC: Duke University Press.

Espada, Martín. 1982. *The Immigrant Iceboy's Bolero*. Madison, WI: Ghost Pony Press.

Espada, Martín. 1990. *Rebellion Is the Circle of a Lover's Hand*. Willimantic, CT: Curbstone.

Espada, Martín. 1996. *Imagine the Angels of Bread*. New York: W. W. Norton.
Espada, Martín. 1998. *Zapata's Disciple*. Cambridge: South End Press.
Espada, Martín. 2000. *A Mayan Astronomer in Hell's Kitchen*. New York: Norton.
Estades, Rosa. 1980. "Symbolic Unity: The Puerto Rican Day Parade." In Clara Ro-dríguez, Virginia Sánchez Korrol, and José Alers, eds., *Historical Perspectives on Puerto Rican Survival in the U.S.* New York: Puerto Rican Migration Consortium, 97–106.
Esteves, Sandra María. 1984. *Tropical Rain: A Bilingual Downpour*. New York: African Caribbean Poetry Theater.
Falcón, Angelo. 2004. *Atlas of Stateside Puerto Ricans*. Washington, DC: Puerto Rican Federal Affairs Administration.
Falcón, Luis M., and Douglas T. Gurak. 1993. "Dimensions of the Hispanic Underclass in New York City." In Joan Moore and Raquel Rivera, eds., *The Effects of Economic Restructuring on Latino Communities in the United States*. Philadelphia: Temple University Press.
Farley, Reynolds. 1996. *The New American Reality*. New York: Russell Sage Foundation.
Fei, John, and Gustav Ranis. 1964. *Development of the Labor Surplus Economy: Theory and Policy*. Homewood, IL: Irwin Publishers.
Fernández, Ronald. 1987. *Los Macheteros: The Wells Fargo Robbery and the Violent Struggle for Puerto Rican Independence*. New York: Prentice-Hall.
Fernández Méndez, Eugenio. 1972. *Art and Mythology of the Taino Indians of the Greater West Indies*. San Juan: Ediciones El Cemí.
Ferrao, Luis Angel. 1990. *Pedro Albizu Campos y el nacionalismo puertorriqueño*. Río Piedras, PR: Editorial Cultural.
Ferré, Rosario. 1995. *The House on the Lagoon*. New York: Farrar, Straus, and Giroux.
Ferré, Rosario. 1998. *Eccentric Neighborhoods*. New York: Farrar, Straus, and Giroux.
Figueroa, José A. 1978. *Noo Jork*. New York: Plus Ultra.
Figueroa, Sotero. 1892. "La verdad de la historia, I," *Patria*, March 19.
Flores, Juan. [1988] 1993. *Divided Borders: Essays on Puerto Rican Identity*. Houston, TX: Arte Público Press.
Flores, Juan. 2000. *From Bomba to Hip-Hop: Puerto Rican Culture and Latino Identity*. New York: Columbia University Press.
Flores, William V., and Rina Benmayor, eds. 1997. *Latino Cultural Citizenship*. Boston: Beacon Press.
Foner, Eric. 1972. *The Spanish-Cuban-American War and the Birth of U.S. Imperialism*. New York: Monthly Review Press.
Forbes-Lindsay, Charles H. 1906. *America's Insular Possessions*. Philadelphia: J.C. Winston Co.
Friedich, Carl. 1965. Foreword to Charles T. Goodsell, *Administration of a Revolution*. Cambridge: Harvard University Press, vii–ix.
Galvin, Kevin. 1995. "Panel Wants Definition of Poverty Expanded," *Gazette*, May 1.
García Passalacqua, Juan Manuel. 1996. *Los secretos del patriarca*. Río Piedras, PR: Editorial Cultural.
Gautier Mayoral, Carmen, and María del Pilar Argüelles, eds. 1978. *Puerto Rico y la ONU*. Río Piedras, PR: Editorial Edil.
Géigel Polanco, Vicente. 1972. *La farsa del Estado Libre Asociado*. Río Piedras, PR: Editorial Edil.
Glaser, Ruth. 1995. *My Music Is My Flag: Puerto Rican Musicians and Their New York Communities, 1917–1940*. Berkeley: University of California Press.
Glazer, Nathan, and Daniel P. Moynihan. 1963. *Beyond the Melting Pot*. Cambridge, MA: MIT Press.

González, José Luis. 1950. *Paisa*. México: Fondo de Cultura Popular.

González, José Luis. 1973. *En Nueva York y otras desgracias*. México: Siglo XXI.

González, Juan. 2000. *Harvest of Empire: A History of Latinos in America*. New York: Penguin Group.

González-Wippler, Migene. 1973. *Santería: African Magic in Latin America*. New York: Julien Press.

Goodsell, Charles T. 1965. *Administration of a Revolution*. Cambridge, MA: Harvard University Press.

Guzmán, Pablo. 1998. "*La Vida Pura*: A Lord of the Barrio." In Torres and Velázquez, eds., *The Puerto Rican Movement*, 155–172.

Hall, Stuart. 1990. "Cultural Identity and Diaspora." In Jonathan Trutherford, ed., *Identity, Community, Culture, Difference*. London: Lawrence and Wishart, 222–237.

Handlin, Oscar. 1959. *The Newcomers: Negroes and Puerto Ricans in a Changing Metropolis*. Cambridge, MA: Harvard University Press.

Harrington, Michael. 1962. *The Other America: Poverty in the United States*. New York: Macmillan.

Haslip-Viera, Gabriel. 1996. "The Evolution of the Latino Community in New York City: Early Nineteenth Century to the Present." In Haslip-Viera and Baver, eds., *Latinos in New York,* 3–29.

Haslip-Viera, Gabriel. 1999. *Taino Revival: Critical Perspectives on Puerto Rican Identity and Cultural Politics*. New York: Centro de Estudios Puertorriqueños.

Haslip-Viera, Gabriel, and Sherrie L. Baver, eds. 1996. *Latinos in New York*: *Communities in Transition*. Notre Dame, IN: University of Notre Dame Press.

Hernández, Carmen. 1997. *Puerto Rican Voices in English.* Westport, CT: Praeger.

Hernández, María Teresa. 1995. "Ode to the Diaporican." In *Resistance in Paradise*, American Friends Service Committee, 1991, 78.

Hernández Alvarez, José. [1967]. 1976. *Return Migration to Puerto Rico*. Reprint. Westport, CT: Greenwood Press.

Hernández Aquino, Luis. 1969. *Diccionario de voces indígenas de Puerto Rico*. Río Piedras, PR: Editorial Cultural.

Hernández Cruz, Víctor. 1966. *Papo Got His Gun*. New York: Calle Once Publications.

Hernández Cruz, Víctor. 1969. *Snaps*. New York: Random House.

Hernández Cruz, Víctor. 1973. *Mainland*. New York: Random House.

Hernández Cruz, Víctor. 1976. *Tropicalization*. New York: Reed, Cannon and Johnson.

Hernández Cruz, Víctor. 1989. *Rhythm, Content, and Flavor*. Houston, TX: Arte Público Press.

History Task Force, Centro de Estudios Puertorriqueños. 1979. *Labor Migration Under Capitalism: The Puerto Rican Experience*. New York: Monthly Review Press.

History Task Force, Centro de Estudios Puertorriqueños. 1982. *Sources for the Study of Puerto Rican Migration, 1879–1930*. New York: Centro.

Hobsbawm, Eric, and Terence Ranger, eds. 1983. *The Invention of Tradition*. New York: Cambridge University Press.

Horwitz, Julius. 1960. *The Inhabitants*. Cleveland, OH: World Publishing.

Hulme, Peter. 1986. *Colonial Encounters: Europe and the Native Caribbean*. London: Methuen.

Ingalls, Robert P., and Louis Pérez Jr. 2003. *Tampa Cigar Workers*. Gainesville: University Press of Florida.

Jiménez-Muñoz, Gladys, and Kelvin Santiago. 1995. "Re/Defining, Re/Imagining Borders: The Artistic Production of Juan Sánchez," *Latino Review of Books* 1.1, 16–25.

Jiménez Román, Miriam. 1999. "The Indians Are Coming! The Indians Are Coming!: The Taíno and Puerto Rican Identity." In Gabriel Haslip-Viera, ed., *Taíno Revival*. New York: Centro de Estudios Puertorriqueños, 75–108.

Jorgenson, Dale W. 1961. "The Development of a Dual Economy," *Economic Journal* 71, 309–334.

Kanellos, Nicolás. 1990. *A History of Hispanic Theatre in the United States: Origins to 1940*. Austin: University of Texas Press.

Kanellos, Nicolás, ed. 2002. *Herencia: The Anthology of Hispanic Literature in the United States*. New York: Oxford.

Kanellos, Nicolás, and Helvetia Martell. 2000. *Hispanic Periodicals in the United States: Origins to 1960*. Houston, TX: Arte Público Press.

Katz, Michael. 1993. "The Urban 'Underclass' as a Metaphor of Social Transformation." In Michael Katz, ed., *The "Underclass" Debate: Views from History*. Princeton: Princeton University Press.

Keegan, William F. 1992. *The People Who Discovered Columbus*. Gainesville: University Press of Florida.

Koss, Joan Dee. 1965. "Puerto Ricans in Philadelphia: Migration and Accommodation." Doctoral Dissertation.

Labarthe, Pedro Juan. 1931. *Son of Two Nations: The Private Life of a Columbia Student*. New York: Carranza.

Las Casas, Bartolomé de. 1992. *The Devastation of the Indies: A Brief Account*. Baltimore: Johns Hopkins University Press. First Spanish edition 1552.

Laviera, Tato. 1979. *La Carreta Made a U-Turn*. Gary, IN: Arte Público Press.

Laviera, Tato. 1985. *AmeRícan*. Houston: Arte Público Press.

Lemann, Nicholas 1991. "The Other Underclass," *Atlantic Monthly*, December, 96–110.

Levins Morales, Aurora. 1998. *Medicine Stories: History, Culture, and the Politics of Integrity*. Cambridge: South End.

Levins Morales, Aurora. 1998. *Remedios*. Boston: Beacon.

Levins Morales, Aurora, and Rosario Morales. 1986. *Getting Home Alive*. Ithaca, NY: Firebrand Books.

Levy, Frank 1977. "How Big Is the Underclass?" Working Paper 0090-1. Washington, DC: Urban Institute.

Levy, Frank 1995. "Incomes and Income Inequality." In Reynolds Farley, ed., *State of the Union: America in the 1990s*, Vol. 1. New York: Russell Sage Foundation.

Lewis, Gordon K. 1963. *Puerto Rico: Freedom and Power in the Caribbean*. New York: Monthly Review Press.

Lewis, Gordon K. 1968. *The Growth of the Modern West Indies*. New York: Monthly Review Press.

Lewis, Oscar. 1966. *La vida*. New York: Random House.

Lewis, W. Arthur. 1954. "Economic Development with Unlimited Supplies of Labor," *Manchester School* 22, 193–197.

Logan, John. 2002. *Hispanic Populations and Their Residential Patterns in the Metropolis*, May 8 (47 pars.). http://mumford1.dyndns.org/cen2000/HispanicPop/HspReportNew/page1.html.

López, Adalberto. 1974. "The Beginnings of Colonization: Puerto Rico, 1493–1800." In Adalberto López and James Petras, eds., *Puerto Rico and Puerto Ricans: Studies in History and Society*. New York: John Wiley & Sons, 12–41.

López, Adalberto. 1980. "The Puerto Rican Diaspora: A Survey." In Adalberto López, ed., *Puerto Rico and Puerto Ricans: Studies in History and Society*. Rochester, VT: Schenkman Books, 313–343.

Lynn, Laurence, and M. McGeary. 1990. *Inner City Poverty in the United States*. Washington, DC: National Academy Press.

Malaret, Augusto. 1955. *Vocabulario de Puerto Rico*. New York: Las Américas.

Maldonado, Alex W. 1997. *Teodoro Moscoso and Puerto Rico's Operation Bootstrap*. Gainesville: University of Florida Press.

Maldonado-Denis, Manuel. 1972. *Puerto Rico: A Socio-historic Interpretation*. New York: Random House.

Maldonado-Denis, Manuel, ed. 1972. *La conciencia nacional puertorriqueña por Pedro Albizu Campos*. Mexico DF: Siglo XXI.

Marín, Francisco Gonzalo. 2002. "Nueva York por dentro." In *En otra voz*, Nicolás Kanellos, ed. Houston: Arte Público Press, 198–199.

Marqués, René. 1971. *La carreta*. San Juan: Editorial Cultural. First published in 1951–1952.

Massey, Douglas. 1993. "Latinos, Poverty and the Underclass: A New Agenda for Research," *Hispanic Journal of Behavioral Sciences* 15.4, 449–475.

Masud-Piloto, Félix M. 1988. *With Open Arms: The Evolution of Cuban Migration to the U.S., 1959–1995*. New York: Rowman & Littlefield.

Meléndez, Edgardo. 1996. *Puerto Rico en "Patria."* Río Piedras, PR: Editorial Edil.

Meléndez, Edwin. 1993a. "Understanding Latino Poverty," *Sage Race Relations Abstracts* 18:1, 3–43.

Meléndez, Edwin. 1993b. "The Unsettled Relationship between Puerto Rican Poverty and Migration," *Latino Studies Journal,* May.

Meléndez, Edwin. 1993c. "Los que se van, los que regresan: Puerto Rican Migration to and from the United States, 1982–1988," Centro de Estudios Puertorriqueños Political Economy Working Paper Series #1.

Meléndez, Edwin, and Edgardo Meléndez, eds. 1993. *Colonial Dilemma: Critical Perspectives on Contemporary Puerto Rico*. Boston: South End Press.

Meléndez, Edwin, Clara Rodríguez, and Janis Barry Figueroa, eds. 1991. *Hispanics in the Labor Force: Issues and Policies*. New York: Plenum Press.

Méndez, José L. 1997. *Entre el limbo y el consenso: El dilema de Puerto Rico para el próximo siglo*. San Juan: Ediciones Milenio.

Mills, C. Wright, Clarence Senior, and Rose Goldsen. 1950. *The Puerto Rican Journey: New York's Newest Migrants*. New York: Russell & Russell.

Mintz, Sidney. 1974. *Caribbean Transformations*. Chicago: Aldine Publishing.

Mohr, Nicholasa. 1973. *Nilda*. New York: Harper and Row.

Mohr, Nicholasa. 1975. *El Bronx Remembered*. New York: Harper and Row.

Mohr, Nicholasa. 1977. *In Nueva York*. New York: Dial Press.

Mohr, Nicholasa. 1979. *Felita*. New York: Dial Press.

Mohr, Nicholasa. 1985. *Rituals of Survival: A Woman's Portfolio*. Houston: Arte Público Press.

Mohr, Nicholasa. 1986. *Going Home*. New York: Dial Books.

Mohr, Nicholasa. 1989. "Puerto Rican Writers in the U.S., Puerto Rican Writers in Puerto Rico: A Separation Beyond Language." In Asunción Horno-Delgado, Eliana Ortega, Nina M. Scott, and Nancy Saporta Sternbach, eds., *Breaking Boundaries: Latina Writings and Critical Readings*. Amherst: University of Massachusetts Press, 111–116.

Moore, Joan, and Raquel Pinderhughes 1993. *In the Barrios: Latinos and the Underclass Debate*. New York: Russell Sage Foundation.

Morales, Rebecca, and Frank Bonilla. 1993. *Latinos in a Changing U.S. Economy: Comparative Perspectives on Growing Inequality*. Newberry Park: Sage Publications.

Morales-Carrión, Arturo. 1971. *Puerto Rico and the Non-Hispanic Caribbean. A Study in the Decline of Spanish Exclusivism.* Río Piedras, PR: University of Puerto Rico.

Mormino, Gary R., and George E. Pozzetta. 1987. *The Immigrant World of Ybor City.* Urbana: University of Illinois Press.

Moynihan, Daniel P. 1993. *Pandemonium: Ethnicity in International Politics.* New York: Oxford University Press.

NACOPRW (National Conference of Puerto Rican Women). 1977. *Puerto Rican Women in the United States: Organizing for Change.* Washington, DC: NACOPRW.

National Puerto Rican Coalition. 1999. *National Directory of Puerto Rican Elected Officials.* Washington, DC: NPRC.

Negrón de Montilla, Aida. 1971. *Americanization in Puerto Rico and the Public School System.* Río Piedras, PR: Editorial Universitaria.

New York City Department of City Planning. 1993. *Socio-Economic Profiles: A Portrait of New York City's Community Districts from the 1980 and 1990 Censuses.* New York: New York City Department of City Planning.

Noble, David. 2002. *Death of a Nation: American Culture and the End of Exceptionalism.* Minneapolis: University of Minnesota Press.

Novas, Himilce. 1994. *Everything You Need to Know About Latino History.* New York: Penguin Group.

Ogbu, John. 1990. "Minority Status and Literacy in Comparative Perspective." *Daedalus* 119, 141–169.

Ojeda Reyes, Félix. 1992. *Peregrinos de la libertad.* Río Piedras, PR: Instituto de Estudios del Caribe.

Ojeda Reyes, Félix. 2001. *El desterrado de París: Biografía del Doctor Ramón Emeterio Betances (1827–1898).* San Juan: Ediciones Puerto.

O'Neill, Gonzalo. 1922. *La indiana borinqueña.* New York: n.p.

O'Neill, Gonzalo. 1923. *Moncho Reyes.* New York: Spanish-American Printing.

O'Neill, Gonzalo. 1934. *Bajo una sola bandera.* New York: Spanish-American Printing.

Ortiz, Altagracia, ed. 1996. *Puerto Rican Women and Work.* Philadelphia: Temple University Press.

Ortiz Cofer, Judith. 1989. *The Line of the Sun.* Athens, GA: University of Georgia Press.

Ortiz Cofer, Judith. 1990. *Silent Dancing.* Houston: Arte Público Press.

Ortiz Cofer, Judith. 1993. *The Latin Deli.* 1993. Athens, GA: University of Georgia Press.

Padilla, Edwin Karli, ed. 2001. *Lo que el pueblo me dice by Jesús Colón.* Houston, TX: Arte Público Press.

Padilla, Elena. 1958. *Up from Puerto Rico.* New York: Columbia University Press.

Padilla, Félix M. 1985. *Latino Ethnic Consciousness: The Case of Mexican-Americans and Puerto Ricans in Chicago.* Notre Dame, IN: University of Notre Dame Press.

Padilla, Félix M. 1987. *Puerto Rican Chicago.* Notre Dame, IN: University of Notre Dame Press.

Pantoja, Antonia. 2002. *Memoir of a Visionary.* Houston, TX: Arte Público Press.

Pedreira, Antonio. 1934. *Insularismo.* Madrid: Tipografía Artística.

Pedreira, Antonio S. [1941] 1969. *El periodismo en Puerto Rico.* San Juan: Instituto de Cultura Puertorriqueña.

Pérez, Louis A. 1998. *The War of 1898: The United States and Cuba in History and Historiography.* Chapel Hill: University of North Carolina Press.

Picó, Fernando. 1990. *Historia general de Puerto Rico.* Río Piedras, PR: Ediciones Huracán.

Pietri, Pedro. 1973. *Puerto Rican Obituary*. New York: Monthly Review.

Piñero, Miguel. 1975. *Short Eyes*. New York: Hill and Wang.

Piñero, Miguel. 1980. *La Bodega Sold Dreams*. Houston: Arte Público Press.

Portes, Alejandro, and Rubén Rumbaut. 1996. *Immigrant America: A Portrait*. Berkeley: University of California Press.

Poyo, Gerald. 1989. *"With All, and for the Good of All": The Emergence of Popular Nationalism in the Cuban Communities of the United States, 1848–1898*. Durham: Duke University Press.

Presser, H.B. 1980. "Puerto Rico: Recent Trends in Fertility and Sterilization," *Family Planning Perspectives* 12.2, 102–106.

Proctor, Bernadette D., and Joseph Dalaker. 2002. *Poverty in the United States: 2001*. US Census Bureau, Current Population Reports, P60-219. Washington, DC: US Government Printing Office.

Quintero Rivera, Angel. 1976a. *Conflictos de clases sociales en Puerto Rico*. Río Piedras, PR: Ediciones Huracán.

Quintero Rivera, Angel. 1976b. *Worker's Struggle in Puerto Rico*. New York: Monthly Review Press.

Quintero Rivera, Angel. 1980. "Notes on Puerto Rican National Development: Class and Nation in a Colonial Context," *Marxist Perspectives* 9.3, 10–30.

Quintero Rivera, Angel. 1988. *Patricios y plebeyos*. Río Piedras, PR: Ediciones Huracán.

Quintero Rivera, Angel. 1999. *Salsa, sabor y control: Sociología de la música "tropical."* Mexico: Siglo Veintiuno Editores.

Ramírez de Arellano, Arlene, and Conrad Seipp. 1983. *Colonialism, Catholicism, and Contraception: A History of Birth Control in Puerto Rico*. Chapel Hill: University of North Carolina Press.

Rivera, Carmen. 1994. *Julia*. In John V. Ambush, ed. *Nuestro New York: An Anthology of Puerto Rican Plays*. New York: Penguin, 133–178.

Rivera, Carmen. 1996. *La gringa*. Unpublished.

Rivera, Edward. 1982. *Family Installments*. New York: W.W. Murrow.

Rivera, José. 1983. *The House of Ramón Iglesia*. New York: F. French.

Rivera, José. 1994. *Marisol*. New York: Dramatists Play Service.

Rivera, José. 2003. *References to Salvador Dalí Make Me Hot*. New York: Theatre Communications Group.

Rivera, Raquel Z. 2003. *New York Ricans of the Hip Hop Zone*. New York: Palgrave.

Rivera-Batiz, Francisco L. 1991. "The Effects of Literacy on the Earnings of Hispanics in the United States." In Meléndez, Rodríguez, and Barry Figueroa, *Hispanics in the Labor Force*.

Rivera-Batiz, Francisco L. 1992. "Quantitative Literacy and the Likelihood of Employment Among Young Adults," *Journal of Human Resources,* Spring.

Rivera-Batiz, Francisco, and Carlos E. Santiago. 1994. *Puerto Ricans in the United States: A Changing Reality*. Washington, DC: National Puerto Rican Coalition.

Rivera-Batiz, Francisco, and Carlos E. Santiago. 1996. *Island Paradox: Puerto Rico in the 1990s*. New York: Russell Sage Foundation.

Rodríguez, Abraham. 1992. *The Boy Without a Flag: Tales of the South Bronx*. Minneapolis: Milkweed Editions.

Rodríguez, Abraham. 1993. *Spidertown*. New York: Hyperion.

Rodríguez, Clara. 1974. *The Ethnic Queue in the U.S.: The Case of Puerto Ricans*. San Francisco: R and E Research Associates.

Rodríguez, Clara. 1989. *Puerto Ricans: Born in the USA*. Boston: Unwin Hyman.

Rodríguez, Clara. 2000a. *Changing Race.* New York: New York University Press.
Rodríguez, Clara. 2000b. "You've Come a Long Way Boricua! (Re)Viewing Our History in the Media." In Acosta-Belén et al., *"Adiós, Borinquen querida,"* 58–82.
Rodríguez, Clara. 2004. *Heroes, Lovers, and Others: The Story of Latinos in Hollywood.* Washington: Smithsonian.
Rodríguez, Clara, and Edwin Meléndez. 1992. "Puerto Rican Poverty and Labor Markets," *Hispanic Journal of Behavioral Sciences* 14.1, 4–15.
Rodríguez de Tió, Lola. 1968. "A Cuba." In *Obras completas,* Vol. 1. San Juan: Instituto de Cultura Puertorriqueña, 321.
Rodríguez de Tió, Lola. 1968. *Obras completas.* 4 vols. San Juan: Instituto de Cultura Puertorriqueña.
Rogler, Lloyd. 1985. *Puerto Rican Families in New York City.* Maplewood, NJ: Waterfront Press.
Rosaldo, Renato. 1987. *Culture and Truth: The Remaking of Social Analysis.* Boston: Beacon.
Rosario Natal, Carmelo. 1983. *Éxodo puertorriqueño: Las emigraciones al Caribe y Hawaii: 1900–1915.* San Juan, PR: n.p.
Rouse, Irving. 1986. *Migrations in Prehistory.* New Haven: Yale University Press.
Rouse, Irving. 1992. *The Taínos: Rise and Decline of the People Who Greeted Columbus.* New Haven: Yale University Press.
Sánchez, Juan. 1991. "The Metamorphosis/Search for the Island/Self and the Conflictive Plebiscite of the Mind." Catalogue of Exhibition *Bibiana Suárez: In Search of an Island.* Chicago: Sazama Gallery.
Sánchez, Luis Rafael. 1994. *La guagua aérea.* San Juan: Editorial Cultural, 1994.
Sánchez Korrol, Virginia. [1983] 1994. *From Colonia to Community: The History of Puerto Ricans in New York City, 1917–1948.* Westport, CT: Greenwood Press. Reprint, Berkeley: University of California Press.
Sandoval-Sánchez, Alberto. 1992. "La identidad especular del allá y del acá: Nuestra propia imagen puertorriqueña en cuestión," *Centro Bulletin* 4.2, 28–43.
Santiago, Carlos E. 1989. "The Dynamics of Minimum Wage Policy in Economic Development: A Multiple Time Series Approach," *Economic Development and Cultural Change* 38.1, 1–30.
Santiago, Carlos E. 1991. "Wage Policies, Employment, and Puerto Rican Migration." In Meléndez, Rodríguez, and Barry, *Hispanics in the Labor Force,* 225–245.
Santiago, Carlos E. 1992. *Labor in the Puerto Rican Economy: Postwar Development and Stagnation.* New York: Praeger Publishers.
Santiago, Carlos E. 1993. "The Migratory Impact of Minimum Wage Legislation: Puerto Rico, 1970–1987," *International Migration Review* 27.4, 772–795.
Santiago, Esmeralda. 1993. *When I Was Puerto Rican.* Reading, MA: Addison-Wesley.
Santiago, Esmeralda. 1998. *Almost a Woman.* New York: Perseus.
Santiago, Javier. 1994. *Nueva Ola portoricensis.* San Juan: Editorial del Patio.
Santiago-Rivera, Azara L., and Carlos E. Santiago. 1999. "Puerto Rican Transnational Migration and Identity: Impact of English Language Acquisition on Length of Stay in the United States." In Liliana R. Goldin, ed., *Identities on the Move: Transnational Processes in North America and the Caribbean.* Austin: University of Texas Press, 229–244.
Scarano, Francisco. 1981. *Inmigración y clases sociales en el Puerto Rico del siglo XIX.* Río Piedras, PR: Ediciones Huracán.
Scarano, Francisco. 1993. *Puerto Rico: Cinco siglos de historia.* San Juan: McGraw-Hill.

Schmidley, A. Dianne. 2001. *Profile of the Foreign-Born Population in the United States: 2000*. US Census Bureau. Current Population Reports. Series P23-206. Washington, DC: US Government Printing Office.

Seda Bonilla, Eduardo. 1972. *Requiem por una cultura*. Río Piedras, PR: Editorial Edil.

Sen, Amartya K. 1966. "Peasants and Dualism with and without Surplus Labor," *Journal of Political Economy* 64, 425–450.

Siegel, Arthur, Harold Orlans, and Loyal Greer. 1975. *Puerto Ricans in Philadelphia*. New York: Arno Press.

Silén, Iván, ed. 1983. *Los paraguas amarillos: Los poetas latinos en Nueva York*. Hanover, NH: Ediciones del Norte, and Binghamton, NY: Bilingual Press.

Silén, Juan Angel. 1976. *Pedro Albizu Campos*. Río Piedras, PR: Editorial Antillana.

Silén, Juan Angel. 1996. *Nosotros solos: Pedro Albizu Campos y el nacionalismo irlandés*. Río Piedras, PR: Librería Norberto González.

Silva Gotay, Samuel. 1997. *Protestantismo y política en Puerto Rico 1898–1930*. Río Piedras, PR: Editorial de la Universidad de Puerto Rico.

Silvestrini, Blanca G., and María Dolores Luque de Sánchez. 1988. *Historia de Puerto Rico: Trayectoria de un pueblo*. San Juan: Editorial La Biblioteca.

Soto, Pedro Juan. 1956. *Spiks*. México: Los Presentes.

Soto Pedro Juan. 1977. *Ardiente suelo, fría estación*. Río Piedras, PR: Ediciones Huracán. First edition 1962.

Soto Vélez, Clemente. 1979. *La tierra prometida*. San Juan: Instituto de Cultura Puertorriqueña.

Stavans, Ilán. 2003. *Spanglish: The Making of a New American Language*. New York: HarperCollins.

Sued-Badillo, Jalil. 1978. *Las caribes: Realidad o fábula*. Río Piedras, PR: Editorial Antillana.

Sued-Badillo, Jalil. 1979. *La mujer indígena y su sociedad*. Río Piedras, PR: Editorial Antillana.

Sued-Badillo, Jalil, and Angel López Cantos. 1986. *Puerto Rico negro*. Río Piedras, PR: Editorial Cultural.

Thomas, Piri. 1967. *Down These Mean Sstreets*. New York: Knopf.

Thomas, Piri. 1972. *Saviour, Saviour, Hold My Hand*. New York: Doubleday.

Thomas, Piri. 1974. *Seven Long Times*. New York: Praeger.

Tienda, Marta. 1989. "Puerto Ricans and the Underclass Debate," *Annals of the American Academy of Political and Social Science*, January.

Tienda, Marta, and William Díaz. 1987. "Puerto Rican Circular Migration," *New York Times*, August 28.

Tienda, Marta, and L. Jensen. 1988. "Poverty and Minorities: A Quarter-Century Profile of Color and Socioeconomic Disadvantage." In G. Sandefur and Marta Tienda, eds., *Divided Opportunities: Minorities, Poverty and Social Policy*. New York: Plenum Press.

Todd, Roberto H. 1939. *La invasión americana: Cómo surgió la idea de traer la Guerra a Puerto Rico*. San Juan: Cantero Fernández.

Torre, Carlos, Hugo Rodríguez Vecchini, and William Burgos, eds. 1994. *The Commuter Nation: Perpsectives on Puerto Rican Migration*. Río Piedras, PR: University of Puerto Rico Press.

Torres, Andrés. 1995. *Between Melting Pot and Mosaic: African Americans and Puerto Ricans in New York*. Philadelphia: Temple University Press.

Torres, Andrés, and José E. Velázquez, eds. 1998. *The Puerto Rican Movement: Voices of the Diaspora*. Philadelphia: Temple University Press.

Torres, Edwin. 1975. *Carlito's Way*. New York: Saturday Review Press.

Torres, Edwin. 1977. *Q&A*. New York: Dial Press.

Torruella Leval, Susana. 1998. "Los artistas puertorriqueños en los Estados Unidos: Solidaridad, resistencia, identidad." In Hermandad de Artistas Gráficos de Puerto Rico, ed., *Puerto Rico: Arte e identidad*. Río Piedras, PR: Editorial Universidad de Puerto Rico, 371–402.

Tugwell, Rexford G. 1947. *The Stricken Land: The Story of Puerto Rico*. New York: Doubleday.

Turner, Faythe, ed. 1991. *Puerto Rican Writers at Home in the USA*. Seattle, WA: Open Hand Publishing.

Umpierre, Luz María. 1987. *The Margarita Poems*. Bloomington, IN: Third Woman Press.

US Bureau of the Census. 2003. *Annual Social and Economic (ASEC) Supplement, Current Population Survey* (CPS). Washington, DC: Bureau of the Census.

US Commission on Civil Rights. 1976. *Puerto Ricans in the Continental United States: An Uncertain Future*. Washington, DC: The Commission.

US Department of Commerce. 1993. *1990 Census of Population and Housing Public Use Microdata Samples: Technical Documentation*. Washington, DC: Bureau of the Census.

US Department of Labor. 1903. *Report of the Commissioner of Labor on Hawaii, Bulletin of the Department of Labor*, No. 47.

Valdez, Luis. 1990. *Early Works*. Houston: Arte Público Press.

Vázquez Calzada, José L. 1973. "La esterilización femenina en Puerto Rico," *Revista de Ciencias Sociales* 17.3, 281–308.

Vázquez Calzada, José L. 1979. "Demographic Aspects of Migration." In History Task Force, *Labor Migration Under Capitalism*, 223–236.

Vázquez Calzada, José. 1988. *La población de Puerto Rico y su trayectoria histórica*. Río Piedras, PR: Universidad de Puerto Rico, Escuela de Salud Pública.

Vega, Bernardo. 1977. *Memorias de Bernardo Vega: Contribución a la historia de la comunidad puertorriqueña en Nueva York*. Edited by César Andreu Iglesias. Río Piedras, PR: Ediciones Huracán.

Vega, Bernardo. 1984. *Memoirs of Bernado Vega: A Contribution to the History of the Puerto Rican Community in New York*. Edited by César Andreu Iglesias and translated by Juan Flores. New York: Monthly Review.

Vega, Ed. 1985. *The Comeback*. Houston: Arte Público Press.

Vega, Ed. 1987. *Mendoza's Dreams*. 1987. Houston: Arte Público Press.

Vega, Ed. 1991. *Casualty Report*. 1991. Houston: Arte Público Press.

Vega Yunque, Edgardo. 2004. *Lamentable Journey of Omaha Bigelow into the Impenetrable Loisaida Jungle*. New York: Overlook.

Wagenheim, Kal. 1975. *Survey of Puerto Ricans on the U.S. Mainland in the 1970s*. New York: Praeger.

War Department. 1902. Annual Reports of the War Department, *Report of the Military Governor of Porto Rico on Civil Affairs*. Washington: Government Printing Office.

Whalen, Carmen T. 2001. *From Puerto Rico to Philadelphia: Puerto Rican Workers and Postwar Economies*. Philadelphia: Temple University Press.

Wheeler, Major-General Joseph, and José de Olivares. 1899. *Our Islands and Their People as Seen with Camera and Pencil*. New York: N.D. Thompson Publishing.

White, Trumbull. 1901. *Our New Possessions*. Chicago: Henry Publishing.

Wilson, William Julius. 1987. *The Truly Disadvantaged: The Inner City, the Underclass, and Public Policy*. Chicago: University of Chicago Press.

Wilson, William J., and Kathryn M. Neckerman 1986. "Poverty and Family Structure: The Widening Gap Between Evidence and Public Policy Issues." In S. Danziger and D. Weinberg, eds., *Fighting Poverty: What Works and What Doesn't*. Cambridge, MA: Harvard University Press.

Young Lords Party and Michael Abramson. 1971. *Palante: The Young Lords Party*. New York: McGraw-Hill.

Index

status, 144(n7); island vs. diaspora
Puerto Ricans, 167(n4), 184–186;
language barrier leading to declining
socioeconomic status, 129–130;
Nuyorican experience, 192; Puerto Rico
as a crossroads, 27; small Latino
presses, 99; Spanish language press,
170–184; student activists' use of, 152;
Taino symbols influencing modern art,
13
La nueva trova (the new folk song), 206
La Revolución newspaper, 171, 233
"Last hired, first fired" phenomenon, 115,
132
Latin American and Caribbean area studies,
162
Latinismo, 175–176
Latino population, 2, 127–128
Laviera, Tato, 189–190, 201
Leadership, 161
Lebrón, Lolita, 67
Lectores, 181
Lee, Muna, 66, 175
Lee Tapia, Consuelo, 177
Left-wing radicals, 150–151
Levins Morales, Aurora, 194–195
Liberación, 176
Liberal Reformist Party, 23, 73(n19)
Librarians, 184
Libretas de jornaleros system, 232
Liga de Patriotas (League of Patriots),
32
Liga Puertorriqueña de California (Puerto
Rican League of California), 53–54
Liga Puertorriqueña e Hispana (Puerto
Rican and Hispanic League), 56, 234
Lincoln Medal, 215
The Line of the Sun (Ortiz Cofer), 197
Literacy, 50
Literature, 170–184; generational
differences, 188–191; growing up
narratives, 195–198; Nuyorican poetry,
191–193; origins of identity, 10(n9);
poetry, 34, 177–179, 189–195; separatist
movement, 32; small Latino presses,
198–199
Litigation, civil rights, 154–155, 159–160
Living conditions, 52–53, 85–86, 93(fig.)
Lobbying activities, 3
López, Jennifer, 205, 217
López Antonetty, Evelina, 157
Lorain, Ohio, 103; Puerto Rican poverty
rate, 137(table)

Los Angeles, California: public assistance
beneficiary rate, 140(table); Puerto
Rican poverty rate, 137(table)
Los Macheteros (Puerto Rican People's
Army), 154, 223–224
Los Pleneros de la 21, 206
Los Sures, 55
"Love Poem for My People" (Pietri),
190–191
Low-fare flights, 70

USS *Maine*, 35–36, 233–234
Mainland: authenticity of US Puerto Rican
ethnicity, 220–221, 229–230(n1);
community activism linking Puerto Rico
to, 150; counterhegemonic discourses,
224–225; facilitating migrants'
adaptation, 163; increasing racial
stratification, 17; island and mainland
concepts, 25(n9); lack of dialogue with
island Puerto Ricans, 184–185; US
Puerto Rican population exceeding
Puerto Rico's, 83–85
Maldonado, Adal, 215
Malnutrition, 44
Mambo Devils, 204
Mambo Kings, 203–204
Mambo music, 204
Manufacturing sector, 115–116, 124, 129,
143
The Margarita Poems (Umpierre), 195
Marín, Francisco Gonzalo "Pachín,"
33–34, 174, 233
Marín, Wenceslao, 33
Marine Tiger steamship, 69
Marisol (Rivera), 201
Maristany, Hiram, 210
Marital status, poverty rate and, 134–135,
134(table)
Marqués, René, 179–180
Márquez, Rosa Luisa, 216
Martí, José, 32–33, 35, 171–173
Matilla, Alfredo, 161
Martin, Ricky, 205, 217
Martínez, Frank, 200
Martínez, Soraida, 215
Martínez de Figueroa, Inocencia, 34
Martorell, Antonio, 216
Masacre de Ponce, 235
Masacre de Río Piedras, 235
McCarthy, Joseph, 153
Mean household income per capita, 109
Medal of Freedom, 159

About the Book

Though the presence of Puerto Ricans in the United States is longstanding, knowledge about them—their culture, history, socioeconomic status, and contributions—has been decidedly inadequate. Edna Acosta-Belén and Carlos E. Santiago change this status quo, presenting a nuanced portrait of both the community today and the trajectory of its development.

The authors move deftly from Puerto Rico's colonial experience, through a series of waves of migration, to the emergence of the commuter patterns seen today. Not least, they draw on extensive data to dispel widespread myths and stereotypes. Their work is a long overdue corrective to conventional wisdom about the role of the Puerto Rican community within US society.

Edna Acosta-Belén is Distinguished Professor of Latin American, Caribbean, and US Latino Studies at the University at Albany, SUNY, where she is also director of the Center for Latino, Latin American, and Caribbean Studies (CELAC) and a member of the Women's Studies Department. A former president of the Puerto Rican Studies Association (PRSA), Acosta-Belén serves on the editorial boards of the journals *Signs*, *Meridians*, *Centro Journal*, and *Ethnic Explorations* and, with Carlos E. Santiago, is founding coeditor of the *Latino(a) Research Review* and the *New York Latino Research and Resources Network (NYLARNet)*. Her book publications include *The Puerto Rican Woman: Perspectives on Culture, History, and Society; "Adiós, Borinquen querida": The Puerto Rican Diaspora, Its History, and Contributions* (with Carlos E. Santiago et al.); *The Hispanic Experience in the United States* (with Barbara R. Sjostrom); *Researching Women in Latin America and the Caribbean* and *Women in the Latin American Development Process* (both with Christine E. Bose); and *The Way It Was and Other Writings by Jesús Colón* (with Virginia Sánchez Korrol).

Carlos E. Santiago is chancellor of the University of Wisconsin–Milwaukee and professor in the university's Department of Economics. Santiago is a former member of the US Congressional Hispanic Caucus International Relations Advisory Group, as well as a past president of the Puerto Rican Studies Association (PRSA). In 1996 he was named one of the top 100 most influential Hispanic leaders by *Hispanic Business*. His book publications include *"Adiós, Borinquen querida": The Puerto Rican Diaspora, Its History, and Contributions* (with Edna Acosta-Belén et al.); *Island Paradox: Puerto Rico in the 1990s* and *Puerto Ricans in the United States: A Changing Reality* (both with Francisco Rivera-Batiz); *Labor in the Puerto Rican Economy: Postwar Development and Stagnation*; and *Recovery or Relapse in the Global Economy: Comparative Perspectives on Restructuring in Central America* (with Jolyne Melmed-Sanjak and Alvin Magid).